Robert Herbert Story

The Apostolic Ministry in the Scottish Church

The Baird Lecture for 1897

Robert Herbert Story

The Apostolic Ministry in the Scottish Church
The Baird Lecture for 1897

ISBN/EAN: 9783337243029

Printed in Europe, USA, Canada, Australia, Japan

Cover: Foto ©Lupo / pixelio.de

More available books at **www.hansebooks.com**

THE APOSTOLIC MINISTRY

IN THE

SCOTTISH CHURCH

(The Baird Lecture for 1897)

BY

ROBERT HERBERT STORY

D.D. (EDIN.), F.S.A. SCOT.

PROFESSOR OF ECCLESIASTICAL HISTORY IN THE UNIVERSITY
OF GLASGOW
PRINCIPAL CLERK OF THE GENERAL ASSEMBLY; AND
CHAPLAIN TO THE QUEEN

WILLIAM BLACKWOOD AND SONS
EDINBURGH AND LONDON
MDCCCXCVII

These Lectures on the History of the Church of her ancient Kingdom are, by gracious permission, inscribed to Her Most Sacred Majesty, Victoria, Queen and Empress, in the Sixtieth Year of her illustrious and memorable Reign.

PREFATORY NOTE.

My idea, based on the terms of the trust-deed, and the arrangements made for the delivery of the Baird Lectures, is that the founder intended these should be popular rather than academic. I have kept this before me in the treatment of my subject; and I have prepared the lectures for the press in the form in which they were delivered. This will excuse occasional slight repetitions, or explanations, which to the historical reader may appear unnecessary.

To load the page with notes tends to distract the eye and the attention. I have, therefore, except in a few cases where a special reference or quotation was desirable, subjoined to the table of contents a list of books, most of them easily accessible, in which authority for the statements in the text is to be found. For the general ecclesiastical history of the Scottish period under review, the reader may consult the late Principal Cunningham's 'Church History of Scotland,' and the 'Church of Scotland Past and Present' (edited by the present writer), written from the Churchman's point of view; the History by the late Dr Grub, written from the Scots Episcopalian's, and the large work of Dr Bellesheim, in Father Hunter Blair's admirable translation, written from the Roman Catholic's; while for the contemporaneous civil history no authority may be so thoroughly trusted as Dr Hill Burton's.

CONTENTS.

LECTURE I.

PAGE

A Church Catholic and National: The apostolic ministry; its character. Freedom and vigour of primitive Church in its development of office and function. Sacerdotal theory. Bishops and elders: deacons. *Primus inter pares*. Growth of Episcopal idea. Ignatian Episcopacy. Growth of sacramentarianism 1-34

LECTURE II.

Early British Christianity. Valentia. Ninian: at Rome, and Tours. Candida Casa. Martin. Ninian's work. Serf or Servanus. Kentigern: at Glasgow; in Wales. Return to Glasgow. Buried there. Columba: his education and work in Ireland. Reasons for crossing to Western islands. Iona. Method of his mission. Conversion of the northern Picts. His political influence. King Aidan: the dynasty he founded. Results of Columba's ministry   35-70

LECTURE III.

Monastic character of Columban, or Celtic, Church. Eastern origin. S. Antony, in valley of the Nile. Monastic settlements in Southern Gaul. S. Patrick; founder of the Church in Ireland. Numerous, and non-diocesan, bishops. The Columban monasteries and missions. Characteristic features of ritual, doctrine, and government. Christianity in South Britain. Mission of Augustine of Canterbury. Mission of Iona in Northumbria. The Easter question. Conference at Whitby: its results . . 71–112

LECTURE IV.

Indo-Syrian Church. Cuthbert. Lindisfarne. Period of disturbance: disaster at Iona: Danish ravages. Nectan, and the Columban monks. King Kenneth. Dunkeld. Council of Scone. Church acquires national character in united kingdom of Picts and Scots. "Epscop Alban." Characteristics of Celtic clergy and their ministries. Their distinctive ritual. Use of Latin . . . 113–150

LECTURE V.

Advance of Anglo-Saxon influences: decay of Celtic. The Keledei, or Culdees. Malcolm Canmohr and Margaret. Margaret's policy in Church and State. Conferences with Celtic clergy, with intention of reform and union with Rome. Her success: gradual change from Celtic to Roman type of religion and ecclesiasticism. Turgot, Bishop of St Andrews. Assertion of independence of Scottish Church. Introduction of diocesan Episcopacy. David's relation to the Church: dioceses: parishes: teinds: monasteries. Use of Sarum . . . 151–194

LECTURE VI.

The Church Romanised. The Provincial Councils. Their Canons. James V. and the clergy. Clerical degeneracy. Education: sang schools; grammar schools; monastic schools. Want of religious instruction. Approach of reforming ideas and influences. Church's loss of popular respect. The Lords of the Congregation, and the mob.

Outrages: churches and religious houses wrecked. Downfall of the Romish hierarchy and system. Selfishness and rapacity of the nobles 195–229

LECTURE VII.

John Knox: his character; influence; and work. Resumption by the Presbyterate of the functions absorbed by the Episcopate. Return to primitive principles and methods. The General Assembly. Priests accepting the Reformation; and officiating as ministers, or readers. The elder of the Reformed Kirk. Minister and kirk-session. The deacon. The reader. The Superintendent. Mode of appointment of superintendent, minister, deacon, and elder. "The Exercise." Books of Discipline. Recrudescence of Episcopacy: the "Tulchans"; and subsequent Episcopal creations. The Church, throughout, substantially Presbyterian 230–268

LECTURE VIII.

The Reformation in its completeness obstructed by the greed of the nobles; and the intrusion of more or less irregular Prelacy. The clergy hold a difficult position. Patrimony of the Church the prey of the spoiler. Evil effects of the domineering policy of James VI. and Charles I.: and the persecution sanctioned by Charles II. and James VII. Westminster Assembly. "Resolutioners and Protesters." "Aberdeen doctors." Puritanism. Revolution of 1688. Repressive influence of Confession of Faith on theology. Patronage. Moderatism. "Evangelical revival." Reaction towards broader and freer theology. The future before the Church 269–313

APPENDIX.

I. THE TENURE OF THE SCOLLOGS . . 315
II. THE ABERBROTHOCK MANIFESTO . . 317

INDEX . . . 322

AUTHORITIES,

TO WHICH THE READER IS REFERRED.

LECTURE I.

Acts of the Apostles : S. Paul's Epistles to Timothy and Titus : The Apostolic Constitutions : The Didaché : Cypriani Opera (Epistolæ); Neander's Planting of Christianity : The Apostolic Fathers, Clement of Rome, and Ignatius (Lightfoot's edition) : Schaff's Apostolic Christianity, and Ante-Nicene Christianity.

LECTURE II.

Gibbon's Decline and Fall, chap. xxv. : Bede's Ecclesiastical History : Aelred's Vita S. Niniani (Historians of Scotland, vol. v.) Jocelin's Life of S. Kentigern (ditto) : Adamnan's Life of Columba (Bishop Reeves' edition) : Breviarium Aberdonense : Godkin's Religious History of Ireland : Stokes' Celtic Church in Ireland : Montalembert's Monks of the West.

LECTURE III.

Tripartite Life of S. Patrick (Rolls' Series) : Todd's Life of S. Patrick : Montalembert : Stokes : Bede : Reeves' Ecclesiastical Antiquities : Toland's Nazarenus : Acta Sanctorum (S. Antony) :

Authorities.

Neale's History of the Holy Eastern Church (Alexandria): Anderson's Scotland in Early Christian Times: Skene's Celtic Scotland, vol. ii.: Maclachlan's Early Scottish Church. Haddan and Stubbs' Councils and Ecclesiastical Documents, vol. iii.

LECTURE IV.

Skene, as above: Bede, Vita S. Cuthberti: Archbishop Eyre's Life of S. Cuthbert: Warren's Liturgy and Ritual of the Celtic Church: MacGregor's Lee Lecture (Early Scottish Worship): Forbes' Calendar of Scottish Saints: Mackinnon's Culture in Early Scotland: The Book of Deer (Spalding Club, 1869).

LECTURE V.

Reeves' Culdees of the British Islands. Jamieson's Culdees of Iona: Turgot's Life of Margaret: Aelred's Life of David: Scotland in the Middle Ages, by Cosmo Innes: Annals of Scotland, by Dalrymple of Hailes: Origines Parochiales Scotiæ.

LECTURE VI.

Statuta Ecclesiæ Scoticanæ, edited by Joseph Robertson: Spottiswoode's History of the Church of Scotland: History of the Reformation of Religion within the Realm of Scotland, by John Knox: M'Crie's Life of Knox: P. Hume Brown's 'John Knox, a Biography.' Maitland of Lethington and the Scotland of Mary Stuart, by John Skelton, LL.D., C.B.

LECTURE VII.

Fasti Ecclesiæ Scoticanæ: Book of the Universal Kirk: M'Crie's Life of Melville: Calderwood's History of the Kirk of Scotland: First and Second Books of Discipline: Diary of James Melville: Edgar's Old Church Life in Scotland: Keith's Catalogue of Scottish Bishops.

LECTURE VIII.

The Westminster Assembly, by A. F. Mitchell, D.D.: History of the Sufferings of the Church of Scotland, by Wodrow : Burnet's History of His Own Time : Life of Alexander Henderson, by Aiton : Principal Lee's Lectures on the History of the Church of Scotland : Wodrow's Correspondence : Morren's Annals of the Assembly : Autobiography of Dr Carlyle of Inveresk : Lives of the Haldanes : Letters of Thomas Erskine of Linlathen. Hanna's Life of Dr Chalmers. Church of Scotland, Past and Present (Doctrine of the Church, by Rev. Adam Milroy, D.D.)

THE APOSTOLIC MINISTRY IN THE SCOTTISH CHURCH.

LECTURE I.

IN the remarkable "Deed of Trust" by which the late Mr James Baird of Auchmedden devoted half a million of his wealth to the service of the Church of Scotland, it is provided that a certain portion of that munificent gift shall be set aside to found and endow the "Baird Lectureship." The lecturer, appointed by the trustees on this foundation, is to be, in their opinion, "a man of piety, ability, and learning," "approved and reputed sound in all the essentials of Christian truth," as these are understood by them; and he is to deliver "a course of not less than six lectures on any subject of Theology, Christian Evidences, Christian Work, Christian Missions, Church Government, and Church Organisations, or on such subject relative thereto as the trustees shall fix in concert with the lecturer." The responsibility of my appearing here as the possessor of the qualifications specified in Mr Baird's deed rests, I feel, not with me but with the trustees. My part as lecturer is simply to perform the task they have intrusted to me as well as I can. The subject I have chosen for treatment has—perhaps more than any of those with which my reverend and learned predecessors have dealt—relation to several of the topics suggested in the deed. It cannot be considered apart from reference to the Church's theology. Its very roots are bound up with Christian missions and Christian work. The questions of Church government and Church organisation recur at every notable crisis in its history. This is one of its recommendations; but further, in selecting this subject, my choice was not altogether uninfluenced by my recollection of the warm patriotism and zealous churchmanship of the founder of the "Baird Trust," and the conviction that the tribute due by me to his memory could not be more fitly paid than by connecting, as closely as I could, the discharge of the duty assigned to me by his trustees, with an exposition of the nature and history of the ministry of that national branch of the Catholic Church to which he owed his religious training, and of which he was a most loyal and generous member.

I use the term "national branch of the Catholic Church" advisedly, because it, and it alone, properly describes the Church of Scotland. A national Church may lack the note of catholicity, in which case it is but a sect occupying a national position. A branch of the Catholic Church may exist amongst a people without any public sanction or establishment, in which case it lacks the note of nationality.

The Armenian Church, ancient and faithful, and in these days a grievously persecuted Church of martyrs and confessors, is an instance of the one kind, because by its holding to the monophysite doctrine it stands aloof from the orthodox and catholic creed. The various orthodox Churches, Presbyterian and Episcopal, in the United States of America, are an instance of the other, because none of them possesses a historical relation to the nation as a whole, or obtains its legal recognition. In Scotland the Church is at once catholic and national—that is to say, it is orthodox in doctrine, according to the catholic standards of orthodoxy; it is apostolic in its constitution; it has never separated itself from the Catholic Church of Christ, although at the Reformation of the sixteenth century it severed its connection with the corrupt communion which was governed by Rome, and which arrogated to itself the sole right to that noble title; and it has always represented the faith of the great body of the Scottish people, been established by their will, protected by their laws, and acknowledged as the Church of the nation by their Government.

What is the Apostolic Ministry? To that question I reply, A ministry exercised in the spirit and after the example of the first planters of Christianity, and transmitted from them to us in an orderly and recognisable succession. This definition will not satisfy those who maintain that the essential note of an apostolic ministry is to be found, not in its character but in its organisation; and that no ministry deserves the name which is not part and parcel of the threefold order of bishops, priests, and deacons. We in the Scottish Church, with the Reformed Church throughout the world, do not recognise the necessity of this triad. Had it been indispensable to the proper life and functions of the Church, our Lord could hardly have left His followers to discover this for themselves; and He certainly never prescribed it to them. The evangelists, had He done so, would not have forgotten to record it. We do not find it laid down anywhere in the Scriptures. It is not even referred to in any one of the Œcumenical creeds, and is in no sense a part of the true faith of a Christian.

The value and efficacy of a ministry cannot depend on its form and method, so much as on its character and spirit. The letter killeth, the spirit giveth life. The succession, which binds the life of the Church age after age into one unbroken unity, is not that of the members of an ecclesiastical order, but of those who, in virtue of their spiritual oneness with the Father, have been in their day and generation the "friends of God." It is by the members of this sacred guild that the life of the world is preserved from corruption. They are "the salt of the earth"; and they are gathered into the one fellowship, like those that shall enter into the new Jerusalem, from east and west and north and south —out of every region, every rank, every race, every communion of them that believe. These are they who form the "royal priesthood" of the Church of God; and they exercise their priestly function, "not after the law of a carnal commandment, but after the power of an endless life." To their ministry no ordination can admit; from it no excommunication can debar.

While this is so, and while the priestly character of all Christians is a vital principle never to be forgotten, the ministry, in its more exact and technical sense, means the office and service of those members of the Church who have been appointed to preach the Word, to celebrate the sacraments, to administer the discipline, and to conduct the government, of the Christian community. The first Scots' Confession (of 1560) and the Anglican Articles (of 1562) agree in their declaration of the necessity of this ministry to the orderly and healthful life of the Church, and in their definition of its character. It is the ministry of men lawfully called by the congregations to which they minister, and duly appointed in virtue of their proved fitness for the office.[1] This idea of a call to office in the Church, given on the ground of due ability to fill it, and sanctioned by a competent authority, is one that presented itself to the minds of churchmen at the very outset of the apostolic history. The small company of disciples in Jerusalem, after our Lord's

[1] "That sacraments be rightly ministrate, we judge two things are requisite: the one, that they be ministrate by lawful ministers, whom we affirm to be only they that are appointed to the preaching of the Word, into whose mouth God hath put some sermon of exhortation, they being men lawfully chosen thereto by some church."—Scots' Confession of Faith, article 22.

"It is not lawful for any man to take upon him the office of public preaching, or ministering the Sacraments in the Congregation, before he be lawfully called, and sent to execute the same. And those we ought to judge lawfully called and sent, which be chosen and called to this work by men who have public authority given unto them in the Congregation, to call and send Ministers into the Lord's vineyard."—Anglican Articles, article 23.

ascension, decided that the blank in the apostolate, caused by the traitor's death, must be filled up. Two men were chosen as qualified for the vacant place, and after solemn prayer it was agreed that he on whom the lot should fall should be appointed, with the result that Matthias "was numbered with the eleven apostles." A little later, when the first note of discord was heard in the squabbling between the Hellenist Jews and those of Palestine about their widows' share of the common alms, the same idea directed the measures adopted to adjust the difference. The apostles bade "the brethren" to look out from among themselves seven men pious and wise, who could be trusted to administer the charities of the Church. Seven such men were selected; and, again after solemn prayer, they were set apart to the new office of deacon. But it is to be noted that this appointment does not seem to have hampered their freedom of speech or fettered their zeal in witnessing for Christ among the people. Ere long "the wisdom and the spirit by which he spake" so stirred the hatred of the Jewish religionists against Stephen that he was stoned to death. Philip also, as we know, in a short time left Jerusalem to preach the Word in Samaria; and finally, some twenty years after, we find him at Cæsarea, known there not as the deacon, but as "the evangelist." He had not felt himself to be bound to only one function or office in the Church. It is evident that the Christian ministry, in its first developments, was a service full of spiritual liberty and elastic adaptability to the needs and circumstances of the community of disciples, as those developed themselves.

By-and-by we hear at Jerusalem of certain members of the Church, called elders, sitting in council with the apostles, and taking the lead in the congregation. We hear nothing of the time or manner of their election or appointment. The need of them was felt — and they appear. We hear, at Antioch, of others who are called "prophets and teachers," and who also are evidently men of eminent weight and influence; but how they came by these names, or whether these designated an office to which they were chosen, as Matthias or Stephen had been chosen, we are not told. We have some light as to their character—they were men who devoted themselves to the service of God with prayer and fasting; we have none as to the formal steps, if any, in virtue of which they held their high place among their brethren. The realities of the indwelling Spirit, of the inspired and inspiring speech, of the life of self-sacrifice and divine communion, not the formalities of ordination to office, or the niceties of carefully adjusted functions, were the

Elder and Bishop. 9

things of first concern to the founders of the Church, and the writers of the New Testament. Not even S. Paul—founder of many churches as he was—ever condescends to deal with these technical and external matters. He describes minutely the character of a good bishop or overseer; of a good deacon (and even of a good deacon's wife); but he says not a word as to their election, or as to any form or ceremony which was the passport to their duties. He refers to "elders" also, but in terms too indefinite to throw any clear light on the nature or tenure of their office, if in any degree it was not identical with that of bishops. The only title, besides that of apostle, which he applies to himself is preacher[1] and teacher; and his sense of the pre-eminent importance of the preacher's duty is shown by his exhortation to Timothy to make full proof of his ministry by "doing the work of an evangelist."[2] His instructions to Titus[3] leave no doubt that he did not see any difference between an elder and a bishop (the one title indicating the rank, the other the duties, of the functionary);[4] while, in his enumeration of the ministers whom the Lord had given to His Church, he names neither preacher, nor elder, nor bishop, but apostles,

---

[1] 1 Tim. ii. 7 ; 2 Tim. i. 11.   [2] 2 Tim. iv. 5.
[3] Titus i. 5, 7.
[4] Neander, Planting of Christianity, book i. chap. v.

prophets, evangelists, pastors, and teachers.[1] All this tends to prove how little store the great founder of the Gentile churches set by outward ordinance and order, in comparison with inner grace, ability, and character; and how free and flexible in his idea was the constitution of the Church. The names which, as time went on, became subjects of keen controversy and were applied with rigid accuracy, are used in his epistles with what ecclesiastical precisians must regard as a dangerous looseness.

The same laxity is conspicuous in the other apostolic writings. S. Paul uses the terms elder and bishop as interchangeable. He calls Timothy a minister of Jesus Christ and an evangelist, and himself a preacher, a teacher, a minister, an apostle. Philip the "deacon" is also Philip the "evangelist." S. Peter describes himself as an apostle, and an elder, and a bond-servant of Jesus Christ. S. John calls himself simply an elder. S. James and S. Jude call themselves bond-servants.[2] In the Apocalypse the minister is called the angel. Nowhere does any apostle assert a claim to peculiar dignity or rank. Nowhere is the Christian ministry reserved for a

[1] Ephes. iv. 11.
[2] Δοῦλος. The term διάκονος is rendered minister—*i.e.*, ministering servant—in twenty-six out of the thirty times in which it occurs in the New Testament; in the other four it is used in the official sense of deacon.

special class. Within the Church all are brethren; and the names of apostle and prophet, of pastor and teacher, of elder and evangelist, of minister and deacon, mark but the varieties of function within the one brotherhood. "There are diversities of gifts, but the same Spirit. And there are diversities of ministrations, and the same Lord. And there are diversities of workings, but the same God, who worketh all things in all."[1] I ask you to note these characteristics of the ministry in the apostolic times: its variety of function; its freedom in exercise; its unconventional nomenclature; its fulness of the Spirit, the freshness and vigour of its life.

And I must ask you also to note another memorable characteristic—the popular and social, as opposed to the sacerdotal and official, nature of the development of the Church's organisation. We see this in all its early stages. In the appointment of Matthias, and in the election of the deacons, the matter in hand is referred to the judgment of the whole Church. At a later date, when the Church at Antioch consulted the Church at Jerusalem as to the reception of the Gentiles whom Paul and Barnabas had evangelised, "the apostles and elders and brethren assembled with one accord" to consider the question; and the decision come to

[1] 1 Cor. xii. 4-6, R.V.

ran in their name. For the Church is not an order, nor an office, but a society; and the assent of all the members was held to be necessary to give validity to the counsel even of the apostles. The mind of the Church, as a whole, must be expressed freely and fully on questions affecting its welfare and measures regulating its development. That development was not prescribed; it was spontaneous. The institutions of the Church grew to meet the needs of the Church. If the Church be " the body of Christ," and the promise that His Spirit should be with it always holds good, then the Church must be always at liberty to adapt its institutions and functions to the requirements of its members. Its institutions and functions are the garments of a living body, and not the cerements of a mummy. In all the affairs of the Church— doctrinal, liturgical, practical, and disciplinary —this principle is applicable; and, unless it be applied, the life of the Church, at that point or in that department where it is set at naught, loses its healthy freedom and expansive power.

It is the right of the Christian commonwealth as a whole to employ its own spiritual wisdom, its own reasonable choice, in its methods of fulfilling its mission as the witness for the truth of Christ's Gospel—the righteousness of His law, the unity of His body. Freedom of thought and

Unity and Freedom of Spirit. 13

action is the sign of the presence of the Spirit. The Church is a family — a society — living a natural and not a mechanical life (if I may use the term), and, like everything that lives, changing from within in obedience to the movements of the inner life. These movements are ever and anon prompted by changes in the Church's external relations; but they proceed, not under the pressure of outward necessity, but under the influence of the free spirit's judgment of what that necessity requires. Circumstances change; and to meet them the visible life and organisation of the Church change also, — the very freedom which effects the change proving her to be the living Bride of Christ, who yet abides amid all mutations essentially the same, because the inner life through which she is united to her Lord is, like Himself, for ever unchangeable. It is the Church's true wisdom to discern what is permanent and what is temporary, and to believe— and act on the belief—that hers is the spiritual liberty as much as it was the brethren's under Peter and James at Jerusalem, or at Antioch under Barnabas and Paul, which entitles her to alter, to modify, to abolish, to originate—wherever her Christian reason, earnestly bent upon her Master's work and the varying problems of life around her, tells her there is, in any part of her organisation, a system to be remodelled, a redundancy to be pruned down, a deficiency to be made good. "So the whole body fitly joined together and compacted by that which every joint supplieth, according to the effectual working in the measure of every part, maketh increase of the body, unto the edifying of itself in love." The consciousness of this spiritual liberty as the inherent possession of the whole Church, the bond of union and the warrant of life in the Christian family, is one of the most distinct apostolic "notes," which we shall recognise at many a point in the history we are about to trace.

The ministry, as we see it in the Church of the apostles, did not retain its simple apostolic character. Ere long the deacon disappears in his original capacity of the Church's almoner, and reappears as a subordinate, inferior to the elder, and forbidden to exercise the elder's functions. The elder becomes the priest, and the priest ripens into the bishop. The whole idea of the Church undergoes a transmutation, through the revival, in the Christian society, of the superstitions of Paganism and Judaism, and the consequent obscuration of the central truth of the universal priesthood of Christ's disciples.

It is necessary that we should observe and understand the nature of this development, and the revolution it wrought in the constitution of the Church. It was a sacerdotal development.

The Universal Priesthood. 15

By sacerdotal I mean the principle that religion demands the existence of a specially commissioned and consecrated order, without which its functions are invalid and irregular. That there is a basis for the sacerdotal theory, both in Paganism and Judaism, no one can deny; but we deny that there is a basis for it in Christianity as taught by Christ. The sacerdotalism of the Jewish system was, like much else in that system, part and parcel of those "beggarly elements" from which it was the object of Jesus of Nazareth to deliver the religion of the Jew. The Jewish priesthood was one of the "shadows of good things to come," whose substance was Christ. When that which is perfect is come, then that which is in part is done away. A sacrificing priesthood lost all its meaning when the one sacrifice, of which its offerings were but types and adumbrations, had been made, and made once for all—when the material emblem had been superseded by the spiritual reality. The spiritual reality loses all *its* meaning if we maintain that the material emblem, though under a changed form, must still be perpetuated.

The universal priesthood of believers becomes a fiction, if one class or order of believers is recognised as possessing a priesthood of a higher value, not in virtue of a fuller spirituality, but of a formal appointment. The Christian priesthood, if the claims of this class were true, would lapse from its apostolical position: it would no longer be held and exercised by the power of the eternal life, but only, like the pagan or the Levitical, by the "law of a carnal commandment." Once admit the sacerdotal claim — by whomsoever advanced — and you admit that the grace of God ceases to be free, and the fellowship of the Christian Church is not a spiritual communion. The one is limited to a material agency, and the other is fettered by mechanical conditions. You bind yourself to the essentially profane principle that without the formal priesthood you cannot have the Catholic Church, and that outside the Catholic Church there is no salvation, save of that disputable kind which may consort with what are impiously and insolently styled the "uncovenanted mercies of God." Wherever the pretensions of sacerdotalism are accepted, the result is certain. Its full development may be delayed, but it is inevitable. It is the revolt of reason against religion.

No doubt the sacerdotal theory can boast of the support of great minds — of a certain type of greatness, — of a Cyprian in the early Church, of a Newman in these latter days; but it can never be otherwise than repugnant to minds in which the rational and spiritual elements are dominant. To believe that the infinite and eternal God — the

Sacerdotalism. 17

Creator of the universe—the Father of our Lord and Saviour Jesus Christ—is a precise formalist, who insists on being approached and worshipped only along a certain highway of sacerdotal mediation; who has established on the earth, as the visible counterpart of His invisible kingdom, a select communion in which—to take only familiar national examples—Cardinal Beaton and Archbishop Sharp were true members, and Thomas Chalmers and John Tulloch were inadmissible outcasts,—is an outrage on common-sense. It is this fact that makes the modern revival of sacerdotalism of such evil omen. It is a revival of a semi-pagan, semi-Jewish superstition to which the minds of the mass of men will not bow. If religion be presented to them in this guise, they will renounce it. They will either turn to absolute rejection and unbelief, or they will, under the imperious pressure of that spiritual need which superstition and atheism alike fail to satisfy, work out for themselves a greater revolution in the creeds, formulas, and organisation of the Churches, than was effected at the Reformation.

Now the area within which we trace the growth of sacerdotalism most plainly is the eldership. The elder was a name familiar in the Jewish synagogue; and the Christian congregation was, in its beginning, little else than a reproduction of the Jewish synagogue. Indeed S. James uses the very word to designate the Christian assembly.[1] The appointment of elders in the Christian congregations was thus a perfectly natural step in their organisation, and so much a matter of course that in the New Testament we find no explanation of their presence in the Church of Jerusalem; and nothing as regarded their place in the Pauline churches beyond the bare statement that S. Paul "ordained" them wherever he had founded a congregation. The elders in the Jewish economy did not constitute an order or caste. The elder worked at his trade, as did the apostle. There was no demarcation between the secular and the ecclesiastical life.

But the elder had another name. S. Paul enjoins Titus to ordain or appoint elders in every city, and adds, in explanation of the kind of man who should be so appointed, "a *bishop* must be blameless as the steward of God"; and in writing to Timothy he gives Timothy a charge concerning "bishops and deacons," naming these two as the only orders in the Church. He sends for the "elders" of the congregation at Ephesus, and when they come to him he addresses them as the "bishops" or overseers of the flock. All candid interpreters of the apostolic history now admit, with Bishop Lightfoot and Dr Hatch, that

[1] S. James, ii. 2.

the bishop and the elder of the New Testament are one and the same person and office-bearer.

The first indication that meets us of the corporate action of the elders of a church or of neighbouring churches, and their formation into a body discharging a common function, is in S. Paul's first letter to Timothy, where he cautions him not to neglect the gift that was given to him " by prophecy, with the laying on of the hands of the presbytery," or eldership; from which we gather that Timothy's appointment to his office at Ephesus was accompanied by the preaching of the Word, and the imposition of the hands of the elders of the congregation, or possibly of more than one congregation. The statement affords an early glimpse of the united action of the rulers of the Church, and also gives us the first hint of the circumstances in which the episcopate, as a distinct order, took its origin.

In any body of men associated together for any purpose some must take the lead. Even where equality is most sought after and prized, there will be a *primus inter pares*. The most democratic republic has its president; the most Presbyterian presbytery has its moderator. To account for the emergence of the episcopate from the presbyterate, we do not need to invoke any divine command or to invent any apostolic sanction. Neither the one nor the other exists in the

New Testament. The only sanction possessed by Episcopacy is to be found in the universal tendencies of human nature; and it is one sufficiently respectable to satisfy the self-esteem of even the most ambitious prelate of the most sacerdotal communion in Christendom. There is in the New Testament no trace of distinction, either of office or of ordination, between the man who is called "elder" and the man who is called "bishop." How, then, came the distinction, which is now undoubted, to arise? It arose, I believe, through the natural development which, in case of personal or official parity, gradually confers a primacy, in virtue of certain personal qualities or certain official advantages. Such was the personal primacy, among the apostles themselves, accorded to the bold personality of Peter; such was the official primacy accorded to the local eminence of James, as minister of the Mother Church at Jerusalem. Among the elders of a congregation the ablest would come to the front. Among the elders of a city the leading elder of the largest congregation would begin to hold the foremost place.

Dr Hatch,[1] who devoted to the whole question of the presbyterate and the episcopate in the early Church the most recent and most exhaustive investigation, was inclined to make a

[1] Organisation of the Early Christian Churches, Lect. iv.

more radical distinction between the functions of the "presbyter" and those of the "episcopos" than, I think, the facts of the case altogether warrant. He points out, very properly, that in the Jewish economy the elder discharged a double duty. Wherever there was an organised Jewish community — whether in Palestine or among the Gentiles—there existed, along with the synagogue, a local court, which was called the "Synedrion." The synedrion held its meetings in the building used by the synagogue for its religious services; and when the synagogue met for its own special purposes, the elders who formed the local court occupied those "chief seats" which our Lord describes the Pharisees as coveting. The synagogue met on the Sabbath; the synedrion on two other days of the week, for the ordinary purposes of government and administration. And the function of the elders was mainly and peculiarly to govern and administer, not to teach, or to conduct public worship. It is in this relation to the synedrion, rather than in their relation to the synagogue, that Dr Hatch thinks he discovers the origin of the place and function of the elders in the Christian communities which arose within the pale of Judaism. And it is to the office of chairman, or, as we should say, "convener," of this administrative body or court, that he traces the germ of the episcopate.

In all such bodies, especially in large communities, there would be a necessity for a centralised administration, and for, at least, a chairman of the governing body. But I apprehend that this necessity was not so potent a factor in the development of the episcopate as the natural recognition accorded, in all communities whose constitution is as yet unwritten, to those among their members who, by force of character or proof of ability, vindicate a right to the leadership. The office of bishop emerged from the eldership, not so much as a perpetuation of the old system of presidency in the Jewish synedrion, or the Gentile municipal council, as a natural selection of what was fittest for the government of the early churches. What is of importance for us to note is, that it was a mere development; that there is no trace of any divine institution of it, or of any apostolical authority for it; and that while we find the diaconate and the presbyterate fully developed during the age of the apostles, the episcopate, apart from the presbyterate, cannot be traced within that age. It is also to be remembered that, alike in the origination of the diaconate, the presbyterate, and the episcopate, the leading idea was plainly the effective administration of the Church and its works of beneficence and evangelistic enterprises—its organisation and government, in short, and not the assertion of its general unity, or the preservation of purity of doctrine. It is not until the date of the Epistles of Clement that we find the president of the Christian community regarded in the light of the custodian of the rule of faith; and not till a yet later time that the theory grew into general, though not universal, acceptance, that the bishop, no longer regarded as *primus inter pares* and the chairman of the college of presbyters, was to be venerated as the successor of the apostles, the depositary of the supreme power of the Church, and the embodiment of the unity of its doctrine and its discipline, standing out as a member of an order, distinct from and higher than either the diaconate or the presbyterate.

Between the year 70 and the year 120 A.D., darkness broods over the process by which the Church was gradually developing its forms of worship, of government, of discipline, of belief. Up to the beginning of that period the Church was (popularly speaking) Presbyterian. At the close of that period we recognise Episcopacy in a somewhat unpretentious shape and with little dogmatic self-assertion about it, yet recognisable as the healthy and promising infant, whose infancy was in due time to be succeeded by the bloated maturity of the diocesan prelacy of the middle ages. The earliest indication of it is in Justin Martyr's mention of the "president," or presiding elder, who took the lead in the communion service, at his day—about the middle of the second century, or a little before it. This president conducts the service, and pronounces the thanksgiving over the elements, after which the bread and the wine (mixed with water) are distributed to the communicants by the deacons, and a portion is carried to those who are absent. But in Justin's time this presiding elder was simply what the name implied. He had not appropriated the other title, which by-and-by was to signify not merely the performer of a special duty, but the holder of a special rank. This was the Greek title of *episcopos* or overseer, occasionally used in the New Testament, as we have seen, and familiar to Greek-speaking people, as denoting the principal official of the social guilds or fraternities which were common among the Greeks and Romans. It was naturally fitted to the office of president of the Christian congregation, and has stuck to it by the law of survival.

The minister of a Presbyterian congregation is just as much an *episcopos* as any member of the Roman hierarchy, in the original sense of the term. He is the president, the administrator, the representative of the congregation; and the primitive bishop was no more. He is chosen by the congregation, and set apart to his office by his fellow-presbyters, as was the primitive bishop.

Growth of Prelatic Idea. 25

There is no conflict between the Presbyterian minister and the primitive bishop, as to office or order. It is with the later *prelate* that we come into collision, when he asserts his superior rank to the presbyter's, and declares himself to be the only true successor of the apostles. These claims soon began to announce themselves. In the institution of the eldership there was a certain infusion of the aristocratic principle—that is, the principle of the government of the ἄριστοι (the true principle of government, when the real ἄριστοι are set to govern); and, as Neander says, "an aristocratic constitution will ever find it easy, by various gradual changes, to pass into the monarchical." A popular self-governing community, without mature experience of autonomy, is ready to fall in with a gradation of rank and division of administration, which saves itself trouble and seems to guarantee effective management of its affairs. Hence the emergence of the presbyterate —first in the synagogue, then in the Church— from the general congregation. Hence in a great degree the facility with which the episcopate emerged from the presbyterate. Hence the expansion of the claims of the episcopate to apostolic descent and monarchical power—the claim to form an order in itself, invested with prerogative and authority peculiarly its own.

The expansion of these claims was gradual,

but steadily progressive. There is no trace of them in the Didaché, or in Justin, though by their time the sacramental celebration had come, as we have seen, to be conducted by the president of the brethren — the bishop in embryo. Even when we find the triple grade of orders fully recognised, as we do in the Ignatian Epistles (which, whether authentic or spurious, mark a distinct advance in the Episcopal direction), there is no approach to prelatic pretension. The Episcopacy is congregational, not diocesan. "One altar, one bishop," is the maxim. Every fully organised congregation had its bishop—that is to say, had a minister whose place and office were now recognised as above the elder's, and without whom no sacrament could be administered or congregational meeting properly constituted. Even as late as the year 398 the Synod of Carthage enacted, relatively to that rite of ordination which was afterwards held to belong peculiarly to the bishop, that at the ordination of a presbyter all the presbyters, along with the bishop, shall lay their hands on the candidate's head. But all this time the sacerdotal sense of official pre-eminence and the love of that pre-eminence had been taking firmer hold of the Episcopal mind. The distinction between the elder and the bishop, which had, at first and for long, been merely one of degree, became one of kind. The presbyters, though many, came to be regarded as essentially distinct from the bishop, who was one; and who was held to constitute an order in his individuality, as they did in their plurality. He claimed, in fact, to be to the elder and deacon what with us the monarch is to the Lords and Commons—(though with a real power which the constitutional monarch does not possess)—a separate and superior estate of the ecclesiastical realm; while the body of the people—the laity, as they came to be called—stood on a level still lower, and in ecclesiastical opinion wholly subordinate. And yet the bishop of the sub-apostolic age is a functionary of a type essentially different from that of the modern episcopate.

We find the type—in the Ignatian Epistles—very clearly delineated. Ignatius—martyred under Trajan—gives us in these letters the earliest post-apostolic views of the questions about which he writes; and one of these is the government of the Church. But that Ignatian Episcopacy and diocesan Episcopacy, as now known in the Greek or the Roman or the Anglican Church, are one and the same thing, is only maintained by controversialists whose zeal outruns their discretion. It is important to weigh carefully what the first advocate of Episcopacy says of the system, with the view of determining whether Ignatius understood by a bishop a diocesan, or simply a congregational functionary; and I therefore quote his exact words. In a letter to the Church at Smyrna he says: "Let no man do anything connected with the Church without the bishop. Let that be deemed a valid Eucharist which is either by the bishop or by one to whom he has intrusted it. Wherever the bishop shall appear, there let the people also be. . . . It is not lawful without the bishop either to baptise or celebrate a love-feast. . . . He who does anything without the knowledge of the bishop serves the devil."

To the Magnesians he writes: "Neither do ye anything without the knowledge of the bishop and presbyters. Neither endeavour that anything appear reasonable and proper to yourselves apart; but, being come together unto the same place, let there be one prayer, one supplication, one mind, one hope in joy and love undefiled. There is one Jesus Christ. . . . Do ye therefore all run together as unto one temple of God, as to one altar, as to one Jesus Christ."

Again to the Philadelphian Christians: "Take heed to have but one Eucharist. For there is one flesh of our Lord Jesus Christ, and one cup to the unity of His blood; one altar, as there is but one bishop along with the presbyters and deacons."

His brother bishop, Polycarp, he advises thus:

"Address thyself to each man severally as God enables thee. Bear the infirmities of all. . . . Let nothing be done without thee. . . . Let your meetings be held more frequently: inquire after every one by name."

Now, here observe that the Church at Smyrna, at Magnesia, at Philadelphia, has each its own bishop. Ignatius's maxim is a bishop for every altar. Without the bishop there could be no baptism, no love-feast, no congregational assemblage. None but the bishop, or one appointed by him, could administer the Eucharist. It was the duty of the bishop to know every one of his flock by name, to sympathise with each one individually, to have frequent meetings with them, and at the same time to conserve his authority by allowing nothing to be done without him.

It need not be argued that the office which involved all these duties and responsibilities was not—could not be—that of a diocesan bishop. The great number of bishops within a limited area is another proof of the same thing. Palestine, for example, a smaller country than Wales, had some fifty-five bishops.[1] Cyprian was the typical High-Churchman of his time

---

[1] Le Quien, in his map of Palestine (Oriens Christianus : Paris, 1740), marks the sites of at least forty-two bishop's sees, and says there were thirteen besides whose sites could not be identified. Wales has only five bishops.

(middle of the third century) and champion of Episcopal rights; and yet the language he uses in reference to his charge of his church, and his relation to the presbyters and other members, forbids the idea that he was speaking either of a diocesan jurisdiction or an Episcopal authority, in the sense in which these are now understood. The bishop's diocese was his parish; and his authority was shared by the other presbyters, and limited by the constitutional privileges of the congregation or brethren.[1]

[1] A few quotations—many might be made—will bear this out. Cyprian, writing "presbyteris et diaconibus fratribus," speaks of "compresbyteri nostri," and adds: "A primordio episcopatus mei statuerim nihil sine concilio vestro, et sine consensu plebis meæ, privatâ sententiâ gerere."—EPIST. vi. 5.

In regard to ordinations he says: "In ordinationibus clericis, fratres carissimi solemus vos ante consulere et mores ac merita singulorum communi consilio ponderare."—EPIST. xxx. 3. And similarly, in administering discipline, he refers to his acting "cum collegis meis, quibus presentibus, secundum arbitrium quoque vestrum, et omnium nostrum commune consilium," &c.—EPIST. xl. 7.

He apologises to the elders and deacons for ordaining a reader to the eldership in a case of necessity, in their absence: "Nihil a me absentibus vobis novum factum est; sed quod jam pridem communi consilio omnium nostrum cœperat, necessitate urgente promotum est."—EPIST. xxiv.

As the congregation's consent was necessary to the appointment of their bishop, so could they depose him if they deemed it right. Dealing with the cases of two deposed bishops, Martial and Basilides, Cyprian says: "Plebs . . . a peccatore præposito separare debet, nec se ad sacrilegi sacerdotis sacrificii miscere; quando ipsa maxime habet potestatem vel eligendi dignos sacerdotes vel indignos recusandi."

I have enlarged on this office and function more than you may think necessary, because it is in the development of the episcopate we see the widest divergence from the venerable simplicity of the early Church; because with it are connected other developments equally alien from primitive principle and use; and because we find in the Scottish Church, whose ministry is the subject of these lectures, a marked fidelity to the apostolic type in many of its best characteristics.

Among the developments I refer to were the changes in the administration of the sacraments. Instead of the simple plunge into stream or pool, which had admitted the apostolic converts to the fold of Christ, baptism became an elaborate ceremonial. After a course of catechetical instruction, the candidates fasted and prayed, and made a formal renunciation of the devil, his angels, and his works, and a profession of their Christian faith. In addition to this renunciation, they underwent a form of exorcism, by which it was supposed the diabolic power over them was crushed. (This is one of the early traces of that oriental dualism familiar to the Gnostics, and which, in the sphere of demonology, raised the devil to the dignity of a malignant god.) Then followed a triple immersion, with the repetition of the baptismal formula; after which the baptised, wrapped in white garments, were anointed with oil, and the bishop laid his hands on their heads. The priest or the deacon could immerse and anoint, but the bishop alone could bestow the "confirmation," which made the neophyte a full-blown member of the Church.

In the celebration of the Lord's Supper the growth of superstition expelled the natural and Scriptural ideas of social communion and devout remembrance. The priests of paganism had possessed the "mysteries" of the ethnic religions. Christianity must have its mysteries too, in which only the initiated could have a share. As the mystic character of the sacrament was exalted, its celebration was more jealously restricted to sacerdotal functionaries: the words of the institution began to be whispered, as the watchwords of the secret and sacred feast, which was now observed in the early mornings, and preceded by fasting. The communicants no longer received the elements as the disciples had received them from the Lord in the upper chamber, and divided them among themselves. They were first offered to God, with the words, "We give Thee thanks through Him, that Thou hast thought us worthy to stand before Thee, and to sacrifice to Thee"; and after this oblation the bishop partook, then the priests, the deacons, the subdeacons, the readers, the singers, the ascetics, the deaconesses, the virgins, the widows, and the children—in a regular gradation.[1] The wide departure from the sacred memorial, as instituted by our Lord, the change in form, and the infusion of novel doctrinal meaning, need not be pointed out. The sacrament was now a sacrifice, the table an altar, at which the priest, like his Jewish and heathen prototype, had a sacrifice to offer. And this was no less than the body and blood of Christ, present in the sacramental elements, over which the priestly incantation had been pronounced.

All these changes sprang from the sacerdotal root. The system, of which these were parts, in its initiation—in its development—was essentially alien from and repugnant to the spirit of Christianity. "Contemplate," says Bishop Hampden, in his Bampton Lectures on the Scholastic Philosophy, "our Saviour at the last supper, breaking bread and giving thanks and distributing to His disciples; and how great is the transition from the institution itself to the splendid ceremonial of the Latin Church! Hear Him, or His apostles, exhorting to repentance; and can we suppose the casuistical system, to which the name of Penance has been given, to

[1] Apostolic Constitutions, book viii. chaps. xii. and xiii.

be the true sacrifice of the broken and contrite spirit? Or, if we think for a moment of Jesus Christ taking the little children in His arms and blessing them, and declaring that 'of such is the kingdom of God,' and then revert to the minute inquiries as to the state of infants dying unbaptised; do we not seem to have exchanged the love of a brother for the cold charities of strangers to our blood, not knowing the heart of man, and dealing out a stinted measure of tenderness by the standard of abstract theory and the law of logical deduction?"

Could those who first began this system of sacerdotal pretension and sacramental mysticism have foreseen all the sore evils to which it would lead, they might have paused in fear and wonder; but the future lay beyond their ken, and the development went on unchecked. There could be no more attractive study than to trace its progress and its results, as these emerged in the ritual, the government, and the doctrine of the Church. But this lies outside the lines within which I must pursue my special subject. From our view of the ministry of the Church as it existed in the apostolic age, and in its earlier subsequent evolution in the East, we must turn to our own country, and observe the characteristics which marked it, and the conditions under which it developed there.

LECTURE II.

THE time and mode of the introduction of Christianity to Britain are shrouded in obscurity. The first distinct statement about the existence of British Christians is Tertullian's often-quoted mention of places in this island "unreached by the Romans, and yet subdued by Christ," in proof of the wide extension of the Church in his day.[1] The statement is quite consonant with the reasonable probabilities of the case. When Tertullian wrote, the Romans had subdued and occupied Southern Britain for more than a hundred years; and some eager herald of the Cross may have ventured to proclaim the name of Christ in the wilder regions to which the imperial forces had not penetrated. In his Epistle to the Philippians S. Paul speaks of his converts among the prætorian guard and

[1] Tertullian, Adversus Judæos, chap. vii. Tertullian wrote in the latter half of the second or beginning of the third century.

the emperor's household;[1] and it is no extravagant supposition that there were in the army Christian soldiers, through whom some knowledge of the faith might reach friendly natives, and be carried by them to their homes. Roman commerce, also, may have helped the work of evangelisation. A large and active trade in cattle, grain, and metals, followed the Roman occupation, and might bring Christian dealers and merchants to the British shores. A Church of Roman settlers and native converts was formed; and its protomartyr, Alban, suffered in the Diocletian persecution, in the year 286. The tale of his martyrdom is told by Bede[2] with a particularity which suggests carefully preserved local tradition. (And local tradition among a people who have no literature is generally to be trusted. With the spread of education and access of books, the value of the local memory as a receptacle and channel of folk-lore and historical tradition is seriously impaired.) To what extent the new religion introduced into Southern Britain influenced the northern part of the island it is hard to determine. Rome cannot be said to have taken any firm hold of the territory on this side of the Solway until Agricola's invasion in 79 A.D. It

---

[1] Phil. i. 13 and iv. 22, R.V.
[2] Ecclesiastical History of the English Nation, book i. chap. vii.

was he who erected the line of fortified posts, the traces of which, and of the connecting rampart of stone and sod raised forty years later, can still be marked between the Forth and Clyde. The barbarians who lived in the fastnesses to the north of this bulwark were so formidable that in 120 A.D. Hadrian reared another barrier against them, by building his great wall from the Solway to the Tyne. The province lying between these two lines of defence was, though still liable to incursions from its northern neighbours, amenable to the Roman rule and protected by the Roman garrisons. About the year 360, when it had been under the imperial administration for more than 200 years, this region was fiercely invaded by the Scots of Erin. Theodosius, the father of the great emperor, expelled the invaders, cleared and settled the province, and, in honour of his master Valentinian, named it Valentia.

It is in Valentia that we discover the first authentic proofs of a native Christianity. One, at least, of the princes or chiefs living there when the country was overrun by the Scots was a Christian; and if the chief was such, his serfs or clansmen were no doubt Christians also. This chief had a son born about the year 360, whose name was Nynias or Ninian. He was baptised, and brought up as a Christian; but as years advanced, either feeling that he did not see the religion of Christ at its best in Valentia, or knowing that it had reached Britain through Roman agency, he resolved to visit the great city, whose ancient glory was still the pride of the world's dominant empire, and which was the seat of a bishop, of whom the Latin Christians spoke with unwonted reverence. To Rome Ninian accordingly repaired — travelling, no doubt, through Britain and Gaul, and thence by the great Aurelian road, till he reached the Eternal City.

The reluctance shown by some historians to acknowledge his connection with Rome, and the undoubted fact of the Roman commission granted to such a man as Ninian, is somewhat unreasonable. In those days few of the grosser corruptions and errors of the Church of Rome had developed themselves; nor had its claim of universal jurisdiction over the whole Church been seriously advanced. And nothing could be more natural than the interest exhibited by the great Bishop of Rome in the Church of the Roman colonists and military stations in Britain, and in the missionary efforts made by the Romanised and Christianised Britons (of whom Ninian was a type) to evangelise the heathen who lay around the borders of what still were, or had recently been, Roman possessions. It was obviously with the desire of learning " the way of the Lord more perfectly," and of returning to evangelise his native country, that Ninian left it for a time.

After due residence and study at Rome, he was consecrated as bishop in 397, and sent back to Britain. On his way through Gaul he turned aside to the city of Tours, upon the Loire, where S. Martin, now in his eightieth year, was still attracting pilgrims to his monastery by the fame of his sanctity and repute as a worker of miracles. After conference with the aged saint he pursued his journey home, taking with him a band of masons trained by Martin to build in stone—a craft Ninian wished to introduce in Valentia, where the ordinary material was clay, or turf, and wattles. On his return he betook himself to the south-west corner of Galloway, and set his masons to build there the first stone church in Scotland,—the "Candida Casa," or White House, of the monkish chroniclers. While it was a-building he heard of Martin's death, and he dedicated the church to him as its patron saint.

Let us pause for a moment over a name now so familiar to our domestic associations, but of whose history and of the cause of its connection with our own Church most of us are probably ignorant. One day during Julian's campaign in Gaul, when the imperial bounty was being distributed to the troops, a soldier, leaving the ranks, marched straight up to where Julian stood and said, "Cæsar, hitherto I have served *you;* now let me serve *God.* Let him who wishes to fight under your banner take your pay; as for me, I wish henceforth to be Christ's soldier alone. Fighting is no longer lawful for me." Taunted with cowardice, the soldier offered to pass through the enemies' ranks, unarmed, in the name of the Lord Jesus, and with no weapon save the sign of the cross: but he was not put to this trial; nor was he punished for his boldness with the Cæsar, who, inquiring about him, heard that he was brave and dutiful, and much beloved by his comrades, among whom a story was current of his having torn his military cloak into two halves one freezing night, and given one half to a shivering beggar. The youth's name was Martin. Years afterwards he became the famous Bishop of Tours, and was visited by Ninian on his way, as I have just said, homewards from Rome. The saint was adopted as the patron of many Scottish churches besides that of Whitherne; and his festival of Martin's Mass, with the familiar "term" of that date, keeps his name alive in Scotland till this day.

At Whithern—which name, slightly changed, its site still bears—Ninian, following Martin's example, gathered round him a company of religious followers, who lived together according to a monastic rule. He opened schools for the children of the chiefs and notables. He wrote commentaries and meditations on the Scriptures, and *catenæ* of sentences from the Fathers, for the use of his scholars and candidates for the ministry. He travelled not only through Galloway, but through the length and breadth of the whole province of Valentia, preaching the Gospel and appointing pastors. He is even said to have carried his mission beyond the wall which barred the way of the marauding Picts of the north; but of this we have no sure evidence. Bede states in general terms that those whom he calls the "Southern Picts," and describes as dwelling to the south of the "steep and uncouth mountains," were among his converts. If the number and locality of the churches dedicated to him be any indication, we should say that he had been as far north as Elgin and Wick, but was hardly, if at all, known west of the Grampians. There were at least sixty-six churches, chapels, and altars consecrated to his memory: of these the great majority are in the midland counties, but in the western islands only three —one in Sanda, one in Bute, and one at Kilninian in Mull—and only one on the western mainland, at Kildonan in Argyllshire. It is probably fair to conclude that he produced no impression on, and indeed had no access to, the Northern Picts, and that his mission lay mainly among the Britons of the south-west, with possibly occasional visits to the Southern Picts of Angus, Mearns, and Aberdeen. That any religious impression he produced on these Picts was not permanent we may infer from the words of S. Patrick, who, in a letter to the subjects of the Welsh prince Coroticus, or Caradoc, speaks of the "apostate Picts." The Northern Picts had never been Christianised: those of the Southern Picts who were, must have got their Christianity from Ninian. But, in point of fact, the religion which he had been able to plant or foster in Valentia drooped and decayed as the tide of aggressive barbarism swelled and rolled southward on the track of the retreating Romans. It had no hold of the Picts, by which generic term were designated the independent tribes beyond the Forth and Clyde. Of the people of Valentia the Christianised elements were the imperial troops and the public officials with their dependents,—a numerous but always lessening band as the evacuation of the province was carried on, and it was left to its native Britons, who trembled before the rude incursions of the Scots from Erin. Ninian's influence, however, was not confined to the eastern side of the Channel. The repute of his training school at Whithern was well known in Ireland; and though the tradition which says he visited that island is vague, there is no doubt that his establishment had many visitors from Erin, among them Finnian, afterwards the head of the great monastery of Moville, of whom we shall hear more by-and-by.

The date of Ninian's death is uncertain—it was probably in or near the year 432; and for about a century afterwards darkness broods over the face of the land, through which we dimly discern the visionary figures of Palladius, said to have been sent from Rome as a missionary to the Scots, and of S. Serf, the solitary of Culross. According to a tradition preserved in the Breviary of Aberdeen, this old saint was discovered by Palladius, who, finding that his Christianity was not of the Roman type, was moved to instruct him in the true faith as held at Rome, and to ordain him bishop according, says the Breviary, "to the Catholic custom of the Roman Church." This Serf, or Servanus, is an interesting though shadowy personage, as testifying, from the description given of him, to the existence here and there of a British Christian, who had derived his Christianity from a source which differed in rite and usage from the model of contemporary Rome. As Ninian had been trained at Rome, and no doubt brought back with him, as exactly as he could, every detail of ritual and creed in which he had been instructed, it would appear that such solitaries as S. Serf had not come under his teaching, but must have inherited the traditions of an early British Christianity, which was unconscious of the developments that were taking place at the headquarters of ecclesiastical life.

But another interest attaching to S. Serf is his alleged relation to S. Kentigern. The story of Kentigern's youth, as given in the Aberdeen Breviary, is full of incidents that are obviously unhistorical; but local names and traditions impart a certain colour of possibility, if not of probability, to the residence at or near Culross of this old native Christian, with whom Kentigern's name was early associated. That name, indeed, along with the more familiar "Mungo," is said to have been given to the patron saint of Glasgow by the old man; "Kentigern"—*Cean Tighernach*—meaning "lord in chief," and "*Manghu*," Mungo—"darling, or dear friend,"—both significant of his love and admiration for his pupil. For such, according to the legend, Kentigern was. His mother, Thanew, whose name is curiously mixed up with the Arthurian legends, was said to be the daughter of Loth, King of Lothian, whose wife, according to one of the mythical genealogies, was the sister of "the blameless king"—Arthur of the Round Table. Thanew has been canonised, and her name, under a quaint corruption,

S. *Kentigern.* 45

is preserved in the church dedicated to her in this city—popularly called S. Enoch's, but really S. Thanew's Church. Thanew was turned adrift by her father, Loth, the victim of cruel ill-usage and unjust suspicions, and voyaged in a coracle up the Forth to Culross, where S. Serf sheltered her and her child. Kentigern, when he had grown up, weary of quiet Culross, and eager for new scenes and work, travelled westward till he came to where a thick grove marked the site of a burying-ground, said to have been consecrated by Ninian, beside the clear stream of the Molendinar. Here he halted, chose the place for his hut, as such early saints generally did, hard by a well (now enclosed in the crypt of the Cathedral), and began to exercise his gifts in sowing among the rude people the seeds of Christian truth and morality, as he had received these from S. Serf. The fame of his powers spread through all the "regio Cambrensis," by which name rather than that of Valentia the tract of country stretching south of the Forth and Clyde was now known. A British "kingdom" had arisen there early in the sixth century on the ruins of the Roman dominion; and the "king" of it, along with such of his people as were Christian, came to Kentigern and besought him to be their bishop. Jocelin of Furness, in his life of Kentigern, describes this king as reigning over the whole country between the Clyde and the Wall of Hadrian, and speaks of Kentigern's "diocese" as coextensive with the kingdom. But, in point of fact, there was in those days no such thing as a diocese.

What idea the king and his people connected with a bishopric it were hard to tell. Jocelin, writing more than five hundred years after the days of Kentigern, and enlivening his pages with a curious farrago of miraculous incidents, cannot be accepted as a safe guide in matters ecclesiastical. We may conclude, however, that the natives wished Kentigern to remain among them in the definite capacity of their religious head. He made some demur, chiefly on account of his youth and inexperience, but at last he was persuaded, and allowed them—so goes the story—to fetch a bishop from Ireland to consecrate him. This, as stated by Jocelin, is interesting, as testifying to the knowledge, in his time, of an early fraternal intercourse between the Christians of Erin and those of Scotland, and also to the fact of a diversity between their usages and those of the churches that owned the authority of Rome. He apologises for the consecration by one bishop instead of by the canonical three that were necessary on the Continent, by the explanation that the British and Scots being islanders, out of the world, and infested by pagans, were ignorant of

In Wales.

the canons. Kentigern's ministry does not appear to have suffered from this irregularity in his consecration, but to have grown year by year in earnestness, zeal, and exemplary purity and self-denial. Its course, in Jocelin's pages, is studded with miracles of a more or less childish and incredible sort,—such as the causing a stag and a wolf to drag his plough; his finding the ring in the mouth of the salmon, and so on; but there is no mistaking the traces throughout his history of a memorable life of a noble and apostolic type.

After a time Kentigern, in consequence of strained relations with the Strathclyde potentate, migrated to Wales, where beside the river Elwy he founded a large monastery, in which he trained a race of monks and evangelists. Among them the most notable was the young Asaph, who succeeded him in the charge of the monastery, and by whose name the cathedral church of the Welsh diocese is still known. About the year 573, another monarch having gained the sovereignty of Strathclyde and invited Kentigern to return to his kingdom, the saint left his Welsh establishment to Asaph's care, and went back to the north, accompanied by a retinue of six hundred of the brethren and disciples who had gathered round him on the Elwy. He renewed his apostolic labours with undiminished zeal, travelling up and down the country, uprooting idolatry, reclaiming the lapsed, instructing the ignorant, sending his emissaries to preach and plant the cross in regions which he could not reach himself, among the Picts of the Highlands, and even—if Jocelin is to be believed—across the northern seas. But he was not destined to be the Apostle of the Northern Picts. That honour was reserved for COLUMBA—the true founder of the Scottish Church. A visit of Columba to Kentigern is picturesquely related by Jocelin, not without miraculous accompaniments, such as the conversion to stone of the head of a ram feloniously stolen from the bishop's flock and beheaded by certain of Columba's gillies, while the saints were engaged in religious conversation. Had the meeting really taken place, it is hardly credible that Columba's biographer, Adamnan, who wrote within a century of his death, should have wholly omitted all mention of it, as he does. The much later narrative of Jocelin has no corroboration beyond the fact that a *cambo*, or pastoral staff, said to have been given by Columba to Kentigern, was until the fifteenth century preserved as a relic in the Cathedral of Ripon. The story of the ram's head also, though in its miraculous parts evidently mythical, exhibits an acquaintance, on Jocelin's part, with the habits of the western islanders which may have had historical foundation. But the weight of evidence is too slight to

At Glasgow.

make us believe—as we gladly would—that these two great missionaries and benefactors of our race ever saw each other in the flesh. It was not until he had attained a great age that Kentigern ceased from his manifold labours. The day of his death is said to have been a Sunday—the 13th of November—early in the seventh century. He was carried by his monks to his wooden church and buried at the right side of the altar. Beside him, within a year, was laid his friend King Roderick. The saint's tomb became a place of pilgrimage, and cures were believed to be wrought on the diseased who visited it. No church in Scotland is dedicated to him in his proper name of Kentigern; but under the familiar "Mungo," which passed into the popular use and affection, there are at least fifteen dedications north of the Solway, and seven in Cumberland.[1]

"Of Ninian," says the late Principal Shairp, in an exquisite sketch of Kentigern, published several years ago, and now little known—"of Ninian there is no visible memorial save that poor roofless chapel on the bleak promontory; of Columba, only those forlorn walls, bleaching in

---

[1] Yet "Kentigern" appears to have been retained in legal documents, as considered more formally correct. In Crawford's 'History of Renfrewshire' a deed is quoted, granted by the Earl of Montrose in 1560, conveying the lands of Orchil "Kentigerno Graham, filio suo "—"*id est*," says the quoter, "Mungo Graham."

the damp sea-mists and moist Atlantic winds: Kentigern has two lasting monuments, the cathedral built round his grave, and the city built round the cathedral. But for Kentigern and the reverence that gathered round him, no cathedral had ever been there; and but for the cathedral no city. The charters are still extant which show the process by which the city grew in the twelfth century under shadow of the cathedral, 'here a burgess of Haddington taking a house, there the monks of Melrose taking a grant of land; here a toft and a net's fishing in Clyde assigned to the Knights Templar, there a weekly market fixed for Thursday, and "the king's peace" obtained by the bishop for the burgesses, and his protection for their chattels.' And yet, though without doubt the saint is historically the cause of Glasgow, and all the commerce that now rolls through that mighty mart, the link between the ancient saint and the modern Glasgow merchant seems so remote, we so little expect to find the Kentigern of the sixth century develop into the Glasgow merchant of the nineteenth, that we cannot wonder the historical connection should be long since forgotten.

"But no such incongruity arises between the associations of the cathedral and the cell of the saint. The one is the natural outcome of the other. As we stand amid the venerable gloom of that dim crypt, or wander through massive pier

S. Columba. 51

and pillar, arch and arcade, and look here on the grave of Mungo, there on the unlettered stone that hides Edward Irving, do we not feel that the fire which glowed in the Apostle of Strathclyde burned on in the great preacher of our own age, and that we, though living in so changed a world, and looking forth on all things with so different eyes, are yet knit to all the Christian people of those early ages, their spiritual descendants, heirs of the faith in which they lived and died?"

Ninian received his orders at Rome, and exercised his mission as a missionary bishop, in direct communion with the Roman Church. His work was engulfed in the darkness and confusion which rolled over Southern Scotland

> "When the Roman left us, and their law
> Relaxed its hold upon us, and the ways
> Were filled with rapine."

Ninian left but little abiding trace behind him. Kentigern, baptised and instructed by a native British Christian, was "consecrated" by an Irish bishop; and his work both in Strathclyde and in Cambria was more permanent in its results. The south-western region of Scotland never fell wholly back into paganism. The true vine took root in the soil in which Kentigern planted it.

But the real Apostle of the North, the founder of the Scottish Church, was COLUMBA — the

Irish missionary who, crossing from the north of Ireland to the west of Scotland, became the spiritual father of the whole country. Columba, a scion of the great clan of the O'Donnells, was born on the 7th December 521, at Gartan, in Donegal. As far as we can trace the course of his education, he attended in his boyhood and youth the monastic school founded by Finnian or Finnan of Moville, and was there ordained a deacon. He next apprenticed himself—if we may use the term—to the bard Gemman, one of the national guild consisting of the professional chroniclers and poets of Ireland. From him he acquired the literary training which has left its traces in the Latin hymns and the Celtic poems ascribed to his pen. Of the former the most remarkable is that entitled the "Altus" (from the first word of the first line), recently edited, with a prose translation and some scholarly notes, by the Marquess of Bute. On parting from Gemman he betook himself to the most famous Irish seminary of those days—the monastery of Clonard, with its more than two thousand scholars, under the presidency of another Finnian, for Finnian was a common Irish name. In these two great schools—of Moville and Clonard—Columba became acquainted with the monastic system, and the educational curriculum of two illustrious seminaries on the eastern side of the Channel. For Finnian of Moville had studied in the school founded by Ninian at Whitherne; and Finnian of Clonard had been a scholar in that of Menevia, under the Welsh S. David. He was thus all the better fitted in the future to understand the position of the Christian remnant in Valentia, after he had crossed over to the Scottish shore, and the more encouraged to develop in the north of Scotland the free and elastic system of Church life and work, which he knew was already in some degree germane to the soil.

At Clonard Columba remained for several years, and here he was admitted to the priesthood. A story is told about his ordination, which, whether true or false, is ancient, and is thus a testimony to the singular position of the Celtic bishops, and the wide difference between it and that of their Roman brethren. Finnian, the Abbat of Clonard, himself a presbyter, wished to retain Columba beside him as his domestic bishop, and having no bishop on the premises at the time who could ordain, he sent him to the neighbouring monastery of Clonfad, where they had one. Columba went over to Clonfad, and asking for the bishop, was told he was on the farm ploughing. He found him, "like Elisha, at the plough," and imparted his errand, on which the worthy prelate bestowed ordination as desired; but either through misunderstanding or hurry, it was ordination to the priesthood and not to the episcopate. Columba did not seek to have the error rectified; and soon afterwards he left Clonard, and having visited some of the other monasteries and schools, began a course of zealous Church extension, founding establishments of the same kind as well as churches in every district of Ireland. His churches are said to have numbered three hundred.

The greatest of his monasteries were Durrow, Kells, and Derry. One of the favourite occupations in the monasteries was the copying and illuminating of MSS., in which accomplishment the Irish monks attained a skill and delicacy of penmanship and colouring rarely, if ever, excelled in Italy, France, or Germany. Columba himself was a master of this art, and practised it to the day of his death. S. Finnian of Moville was also a famous scribe, and Columba borrowed from him a Latin psalter, of which he took a copy. Finnian regarded this as a violation of copyright, and insisted that Columba should hand over the copy along with the original. On his refusal the case was referred to the King of Meath, one of the Irish monarchs, who, quoting the principle of the Brehon law (the native Celtic code), that "to every cow belongs her calf," decided that to every book belongs its copy, and that Columba's handiwork therefore must be surrendered to Finnian. Columba was furious; and, with true Celtic unreasonableness and passion, he summoned his fellow-clansmen to help him in maintaining his "rights," which, like a patriotic Irishman, he regarded as paramount to all laws or judicial decisions. His priesthood and his monasticism had neither quenched the fiery spirit of the Celtic clansman in his own breast, nor the enthusiasm with which the clan were ready to answer to the call to combat. Columba the monk was still Columba O'Donnell, and the honour of the tribe was not to be insulted in his person. There was a hot and bloody quarrel, which ended in a pitched battle at Cooldrevny, near Sligo, in which the men of Ulster fighting for Columba beat the men of Meath fighting for Finnian, with heavy slaughter. This was the turning-point of Columba's history. The scandal and horror of this feud and bloodshed appear to have sunk into his heart.

On the island of Inismurray, off the coast of Sligo, a small *cœnobium* had been formed—a group of beehive cells with a little church in the middle of the group. Their abbat was Molassius

—to use the Irish phrase—the "soul-friend," or —to use the modern phrase—the confessor of Columba. Thither Columba retired. A synod of the Irish Church excommunicated him as a man of blood and tumults. The natural man would have resented this sentence and defied the Synod; but the natural man had undergone a change. Molassius counselled his friend to withdraw from Erin, to cross over to Pictland, and to prove his penitence for the blood he had shed, and the scandal he had brought on the Christian name, by trying to convert the Northern Picts to Christ. There was sound policy in the counsel. Columba would be safer away from Ireland for a time. There were hosts of monks all over the country who would be ready to follow him across the Channel, if he could but offer them a work to do. Above all, there was a motive, at once Christian and patriotic, that urged a mission to the heathen of the North. In the west of Alban, as it was then called, there was still that remnant of the Christian Britons of Strathclyde who formed Kentigern's flock, and there was also a company of Scots who had crossed from Erin and formed a small colony in the south of Argyll. Both of these had suffered grievously at the hands of the Picts. It was a question whether they could long hold out against fresh incursions.

Arrival in Iona.

Could the Picts be Christianised, the Christian Britons and the Irish Scots would have a chance of peace! Other emigrants might go over and colonise the wasted lands. A Christian community might grow up and restore the civilisation which had dwindled away since the retreat of the Romans. So Columba, humbled by the memory of his violence and warfare unbecoming a Christian and a monk, and transformed in the spirit of his mind, from the mere scribe and scholar and zealous propagator of churches and monasteries into the apostle and pioneer of a new mission to a land as yet almost utterly pagan, and fired with an enthusiasm which drew his Celtic fervour from personal quarrels and trivial feuds into the nobler channels of Christian philanthropy and devotion to the work of Christ—Columba, thus changed, thus animated, travelled from Inismurray to his favourite monastery of Derry, and there embarking, with twelve followers, in one of the coracles—the like of which you may yet see on the west coast of Ireland—crossed over to Oronsay; but finding he could still discern from thence the dark-blue outline of his native island on the horizon, he sailed on to IONA, and landed there on the evening of Whit-Monday 563.

The country now called Scotland was at that

time roughly divided into four principal regions. The kingdom of Strathclyde extended from the northern Roman wall to Cumberland, or farther to the south-west, but did not include Galloway, which was held by a Pictish colony called the "Niduari." On the east of the kingdom of Strathclyde, stretching from the Forth to the Tweed, lay the northernmost part of the kingdom of Bernicia, which extended to the south of the Tweed. North of the Forth and Clyde was Pictland, the country of the Picts. The West Highlands from Cantyre to Lochaber were, in part, occupied by the Scots who had from time to time crossed from Erin. The inhabitants of the Bernician territory were Saxons and Angles, as yet heathen, like the Northern Picts. Those of Strathclyde had retained more or less of the Christianity impressed on that district by Kentigern.

Before Columba's advent, at least one other Irish missionary had tried to shed the light of the Cross on the dark places of the Hebrides. Brendan of Clonfert had founded a church and *cœnobium* in Tiree. His name is still preserved in that of the parish of Kilbrandon and the Sound of Kilbrannan; but his work appears to have been unproductive.

Columba's choice of one of the western islands for his headquarters may have been influenced by the fact of his relationship to Connal, King of Dalriada, by which name the Scotic settlers had called the region of Argyll. Connal subsequently bestowed the island of Hy or Iona on his kinsman. For about two years Columba occupied himself in erecting his buildings, organising his monastic family, bringing the soil of Iona into cultivation, and generally establishing his settlement on a secure basis. His idea— the best of all missionary ideas—was to make his mission the model of a Christian community, industrial and educational as well as evangelistic, where a company of Christian men should present to those who lived around them the picture of what Christian religion and civilisation really meant. The brotherhood was not formed that it might spend its life in a self-centred routine of devotions, meditations, fastings, and penitential exercises; but that it might propagate, by teaching, and still more by example, the morality, the culture, the pure faith of the Christian. The same principle has guided the Moravian Brethren, the most successful of all modern missionaries. It has been adopted by our own missionaries in Eastern Africa,—in this true, though at a late date, to the earliest traditions of our Church as exemplified by its great founder.

At the end of two years the abbat, having by this time acquired a sufficient knowledge of the

Pictish language (a Gaelic dialect), and having gathered under him a family of about two hundred persons, resolved to enter on the definite enterprise which had from the first been in his mind — the conversion of the Northern Picts. He adopted the usual plan, one specially advantageous in dealing with a race which was but little civilised,—he went straight to headquarters and addressed himself to the Pictish king. This was Brude, who kept his Court at Craig Phadrick, close to the eastern outlet of the chain of lochs and glens now penetrated by the Caledonian Canal. Brude was no friend to the Scots of Dalriada, with whom indeed he had already been at war; and when he heard that Columba and his friends were at hand he said, "These men come from our enemies the Scots—they shall not enter here." In this resolution he was encouraged by Broichan, the chief of the Druids, who was with him in his stronghold. But Columba was not to be withstood. According to Adamnan, he had only to advance to the bolted gate and make the sign of the cross, when the bolts flew back, the portal opened, and the awestricken king came forward to meet the great missionary with words of peace.

It is difficult to disentangle the legendary and the actual in Adamnan's narrative; but be the

Visit to Brude.

admixture of the miraculous what it may, it is evident that Columba's mission was rapidly and wholly successful. King Brude took him into his friendship and confidence, and was promptly converted to Christianity. The Abbat of Iona was endowed with that strange force of personal ascendancy which is often the special talent of men of masterful will and strong character; and Brude appears to have been won over by his vigorous individuality, before it was possible for him to understand the Gospel this new teacher came to preach. One of his gifts, which he sometimes used to the wonder of his friends and the terror of his enemies, was a voice of such compass and power that we could hardly credit the feats ascribed to it, did we not know that marvels of the same kind have been, within living memory and on authentic evidence, attributed to the voice of Edward Irving. "The sound of the voice of Columcille," says his Irish Life—"great its sweetness above all other clerics': to the end of 1500 paces, though great the distance, it was distinctly heard." When once the king had accepted the teaching—or perhaps we should rather say had bowed to the influence—of Columba, his people naturally followed his example; and the work of planting Christianity in the Highlands went on apace.

The first and most obvious of the results of his

work was that the reign of heathen violence was arrested. The Scot of Dalriada and the Briton of Strathclyde need no longer dread the lawless neighbour ever ready to carry fire and sword across their borders. The missions of Columba laid the first foundation of intertribal peace throughout Northern Britain, and so paved the way for the consolidation of the Picts, Scots, Britons, and Saxons into one nation. It is not an exaggeration to say that not only the Scottish Church but the Scottish State recognises its founder in Columba. While he was unwearied in his own labours, he possessed and exercised the rare gift of enlisting in his service zealous and capable assistants, who were helpful in his work, and many of whom have left their names in the pious memory of the glens and islands of the north and west. Such were Kainnech or Kenneth, who is commemorated in Inch Kenneth in the Hebrides and the great Abbey of Cambuskenneth on the Forth; Donan, who founded a monastery in the island of Eigg, and gives his name to nine or ten Kildonans; Comgall, who came from Ireland to accompany Columba in his first visit to King Brude, and who held in his own island the high office of abbat of the monastery of Bangor, in County Down, with its 3000 monks; Cormac, "Cormac of the Sea," the most adventurous of all the brotherhood, constantly voyaging among the Hebrides, and as far as the Orkneys and the Shetlands, some say even to Iceland; Drostan, Columba's nephew, and the founder of the Abbey of Deer in Buchan; Machar, who gave his name to the Cathedral of Aberdeen; Mundus, or Mun, who is remembered at Eilean Mun in Lochleven and Kilmun on the Clyde; Blane of Bute, the founder of Dunblane. These, and many more, "true yoke-fellows," willing friends and servants, owned the authority and carried out the plans of Columba—each yielding an implicit obedience to the abbat, but each allowed to exercise, and exercising, the utmost individual freedom of judgment and action in the execution of his mission. Under Columba's sway there was full scope for every individuality to assert itself. This individual liberty, combined with corporate fidelity to an absolute chief, is a striking feature of the Columban system. The personal independence was no less marked than the unity and obedience of the brotherhood as a whole. This characteristic became possible in a community where the uniting bond was not a written rule, nor an authority founded on sacerdotal claim or ecclesiastical tradition, but was devotion to a head chosen and raised to his headship in virtue of his personal qualities, his strong character, his recognised ability to rule. This apostolic characteristic of independence, of free play of individuality, of capacity of generous loyalty to a capable leader, early impressed upon the Scottish Church, is one that, after all its vicissitudes, it still retains—one of the notes of that continuity which links these latter days to the very dawn of its history.

You will have noticed that three, at least, of the places I have mentioned as the sites of Columban churches are not in the Highlands proper, and lie to the east of the Grampian range, which bounded what was strictly the Pictish territory. Deer, Aberdeen, and Cambuskenneth, however, were not solitary instances of the extension of Columba's mission into the east and midlands. On the death of his steady friend King Brude the Pictish throne was secured by Gartnaidh, who was a Southern Pict, living at Abernethy on the Tay. To Abernethy the seat of Pictish sovereignty was transferred, and the erection of a church there is attributed to Columba's influence. The church and monastery of Kilrymont (the Celtic name of St Andrews) are said to have been founded by his disciple Kenneth; and Blane, the son of Aidan, whom Columba selected as King of Dalriada, built, as I have already said, the church of Dunblane. So that not only in the Highlands, but in Buchan, Fife, Perthshire, and Stirlingshire, outside the Highland line, we find clear traces of his Christian work.

King Aidan.

I have alluded to Columba's choice of a king for Dalriada, and said that the State no less than the Church of Scotland may look on him as its founder. His history proves it. He not only converted the Picts from Druidism. He largely controlled the secular affairs, not of Pictland alone but of Dalriada, for which his policy secured the friendly alliance of the Picts. In Dalriada his influence was strong enough to govern the succession to the sovereignty, and to readjust the constitution of the kingdom. The Dalriadan king died. Columba, with a statesman's instinct and a churchman's authority, recognised the incapacity of the legal successor; so he set him aside, and promoted Aidan, a more capable prince, though out of the regular order of succession, as was permissible by the Brehon law. This Aidan was not only chosen, but, according to old tradition, was consecrated by Columba—his consecration being the first instance, in Western Europe, of the religious ceremony of anointment or ordination confirming the secular elevation to the throne. The tradition further bears, that during this ceremony Aidan sat on that "Stone of Destiny" which was afterwards transferred, first to Dunstaffnage, and then to Scone, and is now part of the coronation chair in Westminster Abbey. Be that as it may, there is no doubt that the Dalriadan kingdom, to which Aidan was appointed by Columba, was the real germ of the kingdom of Scotland. While the Pictish monarchy declined, the Dalriadan advanced in arts, in civilisation, in power and importance, until the year 842, when Kenneth Macalpine, a descendant of Aidan, is found ruling over a prosperous realm—to whose ruler the Picts both northern and southern submitted; and he established the Scottish monarchy over a united people. The line of the Celtic kings, of whom Kenneth was the ancestor, continued to reign until a fatal fall from his horse on the cliffs at Kinghorn cut short the life of the last of them, Alexander III., in 1285. The succession then passed over to the dynasties of Bruce and Stuart, which were descended in the female line from the Celtic kings. In the seventeenth century the Stuarts mounted the English throne; and again on the death of Queen Anne the succession came through the female line, and the house of Hanover acquired the sovereignty. It is through that house her present gracious Majesty can trace an unbroken descent from King Aidan of Dalriada and King Kenneth of Scotland, which constitutes her sole hereditary title to the crown of Great Britain and Ireland and the empire of India.

It was to Columba also, we must note in passing, that the Dalriadan kingdom owed the achievement of its independence of the kings of Ireland. His maintenance of a regular intercourse with Ireland, through which he still exercised a practical control over the monasteries he had founded there, was only one instance of that inexhaustible energy and versatility which seemed to combine in his one person the Saxon's dogged capacity for hard work with the spiritual fervour and enthusiasm of the Celt. He was evidently, as has been said of him, "one of the unresting, unhasting men," who find time for all things, and whose capacity of sympathy and of work no single object or set of objects can exhaust. A life so eager, so laborious, so full of sympathy with others and effort for their highest good, was of itself a Christian mission of the noblest sort; but it was a life that made constant demands upon its own vitality. Yet Columba's marvellous vigour, tried as it was by many toils, hardships, and austerities, did not give way till after he had passed his threescore years and ten. He was over forty when he quitted Ireland, and he spent thirty-four years in Iona, dying in 597, in—as we calculate—the seventy-sixth year of his age.

The account of the closing scenes, as given by Adamnan, is one of the most simple, touching, and evidently truthful, narratives to be found in monkish literature. In some slight details there seems to be an introduction of the legendary or miraculous element, but only to a very small extent. It is easy to understand how this should have tinged the affectionate reminiscences of the family of Iona, and transferred itself from the oral tradition of the brethren to the MS. of Adamnan.[1] Early on the morning of Sunday the 9th of June 597 he passed to his well-earned rest and reward,—the noblest type of that Scoto-Celtic race that has played so prominent a part in our national history; the founder of the Scottish Church, and, in a real sense also, the founder of the Scottish nation: for had the Dalriadan kingdom fallen into unworthy hands at the time when Columba named the energetic and able Aidan as its king, and had its delivery from Irish vassalage not been achieved through his persuasion, at the assembly of Drumceatt, one or other of two things would have happened, either of them fatal to Scottish independence and the development of a pacific nationality in which Pict, Scot, Briton, and Saxon should form harmonious elements; —Scotland still feudatory to Ireland would have become a mere appendage to that island; or, divided between hostile tribes of Picts and Scots,

---

[1] It may be found in full detail in Montalembert's 'Monks of the West,' vol. iii., and in the 'Church of Scotland, Past and Present,' vol. i.

it would have fallen a prey to the Saxon aggressors from the east and south. But what Columba did for our country, ecclesiastically and politically, was efficient and permanent, because he had done still more for it, in the sphere of moral reformation and spiritual enlightenment. He had given it a true religion. He had taught the people to believe in Christ, and had shown them the pattern of the Christian life, and so had brought light into their heathen darkness, order into their social chaos, the ideas of peace on earth and goodwill among men into the arena of their senseless and savage feuds. He had revealed to them the beauty of social purity, of personal self-control, of righteous dealing of one with another. He had, in fact, laid the moral foundations of a national character, of an orderly society, alongside of the firm basis of the Christian faith. And so his work endured, and still endures, as all honest work, established and carried out on true principles and in faithful zeal, is sure to do.

Columba passed away, but, though their head was gone, the family of Iona never faltered in their devotion to the great enterprise he had begun. They went about "everywhere preaching the Word," and founding and confirming churches. Iona became year by year a more widely acknowledged centre of a vast educative and missionary organisation, and at the same time, in virtue of its being the scene of Columba's labours, of his rule and death, a shrine of pious pilgrimage, and the home of a far-reaching ecclesiastical authority, owned by scores of dependent monasteries throughout the length and breadth of Alban.

LECTURE III.

IN the church founded by Columba, and which from its birthplace in Iona reached forth and overspread the land, we recognise the parent of the National Church of Scotland. It was the first to take a firm, and, as it proved, a permanent, hold upon the territories which were, by-and-by, consolidated into the Scottish Kingdom. The Scottish Church of to-day is the direct descendant and heir of the Church of the saint and evangelist of Iona. From the first it had distinctive features of its own, which indicated a special character and parentage, and in which it differed from the Churches of the continent of Europe. In particular, it was organised upon a system, and governed on a principle, peculiar to itself, and unrecognised by those Churches in which, by the sixth century, diocesan episcopacy had been fully developed. The organisation was monastic, not congregational; the government was abbatial, not episcopal.

Whence came, or how originated, this difference? To find an answer to this question we must turn to the East, at a date long anterior to Columba's ministry in Iona. The germ of the Columban Church—that in which its differentiating idea originated—is to be found in the monasticism of the valley of the Nile. Of that monasticism S. Antony was the founder. Antony was an Egyptian of noble birth,—his native place Coma, a village close to the boundary between Lower and Upper Egypt, where he was born in or about the year 251. His parents died, and while yet a youth he succeeded to their estate. Not long after, he heard read in the church the words addressed by Christ to the young man, "If thou wilt be perfect, go and sell that thou hast, and give to the poor, and thou shalt have treasure in heaven; and come and follow Me." They wrought on him like magic. He at once resolved to obey them. He divested himself of his property, and sought the society of a solitary near Coma, who instructed him in the ascetic life. These "Eremites" or "Anchorites"—men of the desert, or withdrawers from the world—were scattered up and down the country. After a time, spent in extreme self-mortification, he took up his abode in a remote and deserted castle among the mountains, the door of which he is said not to have opened for twenty years. The fame of his asceticism, and of his conflicts with the evil one, drew visitors from many parts of Egypt, with whom he would converse, though he would neither let them cross his threshold nor see his face. It was not till Diocletian's persecution that he emerged from his retreat, and resolved to found a religious settlement among these mountains, lying between the Nile and the Red Sea, where he chose a spot among the wildest and steepest of them. His abode was a cell hewn out of the rock; and soon the sides of the mountains all around were full of cells and huts; and so vast grew the bands of his disciples that they overflowed from these fastnesses into the deserts on the other side of the river. As the revered head of all these solitaries Antony lived to his 105th year, developing among them the idea of the cœnobite life—that is, the common life—or life of the solitary, no longer in an absolute solitude and renunciation of all commerce with his kind, but forming one of a great community dwelling in adjacent cells or huts, acknowledging the authority of a common master. Later, this idea was merged in that of the monastery, in which the brethren dwelt under one roof.

This further development is traceable not to Antony so much as to Pachomius, who, after Antony's death, brought the monks together in a large establishment and under a definite rule. Pachomius founded his society on the island of Tabennæ in the Upper Nile; and it was joined by 3000 members, who later increased to 7000. The abbat, as we should call him, was over all this great company. The name, from the Syriac *abbas*, meant father, and designated the original idea of his relation to his followers. The Greek title was "Archimandrite," which conveyed the slightly different idea of the chief shepherd of a $μάνδρα$ or fold. But whether its head was called *father* or *shepherd*, the idea of the relation was patriarchal; and the community was regarded as a family or flock, which, however large, was under him as its head. Every cloister or *cœnobium*, however distant from the original and central cell, owned the authority and followed the rule of the abbat. The fame of these great associations of ascetics, withdrawn from the world in order to follow what they believed to be the behests of the higher life, attracted crowds of admirers and devotees from other lands, and especially from Western Europe. Among others Cassian, whose name was known in Southern Gaul, in connection with the semi-Pelagian school of theology there, visited the

Nile and its most celebrated monasteries, and carried back with him an extraordinary account of the marvels he had seen there,—of the 5000 monks on the mountains where S. Antony had lived in his cell; of the 5000 in the desert of Nitria; of the 50,000 who would assemble together to celebrate the Easter Communion; of their meagre diet, of their macerations of "the flesh," of their continual devotions. And Cassian was not a solitary visitor. There were many besides him who returned from Egypt full of the holy ambition of founding pious retreats, similar to those they had seen there, on the islands which stud the western coasts of the Mediterranean. The sea was to these retreats what the Nile or the desert was to their Egyptian prototypes; and the Egyptian model of the monastic life was faithfully reproduced in them.

Intercourse, social, commercial, and intellectual, between Egypt and Gaul was constant, and had been established for ages before the Christian era. The ancestors of those Marseillais, who in the present century have dedicated a monument with the inscription, "Les descendants des Phocéens à Homère," were proud of their connection with the East. Ephesus, Antioch, and Alexandria found their way to Gaul without making Rome a stage on the journey. When Jerome's eulogies of monasticism were resented by Roman society, so angrily that he saw it was best for him to retire to Bethlehem with Paula and Eustochium, the asceticism of the Nile was already winning its way among hundreds of devotees in Liguria and Gallia Narbonensis. The most notable of their communities was that in the isles of Lerins. The visitor to the bright healthhaunt of Cannes, at this day, looks across the blue waters of the Golfe de Jouan to these islands, S. Marguerite and S. Honorat. The former is connected, in all historical imaginations, with the mystery of "the man in the iron mask," and with the escape from prison of Bazaine, the betrayer of Metz; the latter is associated with the name of one of the early disciples of the Egyptian monasticism. From that island the system spread through Western Europe, and became as familiar as the famous definition of the true creed which its great doctor, S. Vincent, dictated from the monastery of S. Honorat.[1] The seven chapels, which may still be seen among the ruins, remind one, like similar groups in Ireland, of the tradition of the seven churches of the Apocalypse, and the Eastern origin of the founders. Here Cassian, if he did not actually teach, was known as a revered teacher in his neighbouring monastery of S. Victor, and as an opponent of the severe dogmas

[1] "Quod semper, quod ubique, quod ab omnibus, creditum sit."

S. Patrick. 77

of Augustine of Hippo. Here too Martin's name was not unfamiliar, for he had lived for a time in the island of Gallinaria, off the Ligurian coast. And hither, with other seekers after light, came Patrick, said to be Martin's sister's son, a youth from Northern Britain.[1]

Patrick's history, like that of most of his notable contemporaries, is obscured by the haze of imaginative tradition that hangs over it, like the morning mist over a distant hillside; but what we can discern through the haze may be reduced to this: Early in the fourth century there was among the Christians of Strathclyde one Potitus, a priest. Clerical celibacy was in those days unknown in Britain; and Potitus had a son called Calpurnius, who held the rank of deacon in the Church and of "decurion" in the Roman civil service. The decurion was a member of the local council, which was appointed under the Roman administration, wherever a population of a few hundreds was assembled in a town or village. Calpurnius, who thus combined in his own person the ecclesiastical office of deacon and the civil office of town councillor, had a son, who in the language of the country was called "Succath" (a name still surviving, almost unchanged, in the estate of Succoth near Glasgow), but who also bore the Latin

[1] Jocelin's Life of Patrick, chap. i.

name Patricius, which implied honourable descent on the part of the bearer. The place where he was born, and where his father was town councillor, was most probably at or near Dunbarton—the only place in the fourth century of great strength, and therefore in all likelihood the only place of considerable population, on the Clyde, and close to the protecting Roman rampart. The addition of the Latin name Patricius to the Celtic Succath suggests that Patrick was the son of a family Celtic by race, but which had adopted the civilisation and the Christianity of the Roman rulers of the island. As Patrick grew up, the West of Scotland was again and again ravaged by the Picts from beyond the wall, and by the Scots from across the channel. In one of the Scots' incursions the country-house of Calpurnius was attacked, and Patrick, then a boy of sixteen, was along with his sister carried off by the marauders. They sold the girl as a slave to a purchaser from Connaught: Patrick himself was kept in bondage in the family of a chieftain on the Antrim coast, and six years elapsed ere he effected his escape. At the end of that time he fled, and got on board a vessel bound for France. His life in France is obscure; but it seems fairly certain he went to Lerins, and studied there the system and mode of life which had been transplanted thither from the

East. In his own "Confession"—preserved in the 'Book of Armagh' in the library of Trinity College, Dublin—he says nothing of having received a commission from Rome to constitute him the missionary of Ireland, though the tradition, repeated by many Roman Catholic historians, is, that he was so commissioned and consecrated as bishop by Pope Cœlestine. There is nothing in what we know of his work in Ireland to suggest that he had received either Roman training or Roman sanction. The idea that he did is scouted by his most erudite biographer, Dr Todd, who does not question the tradition of his having, like Ninian, visited his uncle, S. Martin, at Tours.

It was probably about the year 432 that his mind became so drawn to the island whose inhabitants had torn him from his home and held him in slavery, that he felt impelled to revisit it, and to return good for its evil by proclaiming to it the Gospel of Christ. He accordingly quitted France and landed on the Irish coast, first near Wicklow, and next farther north, at a point which gave him easy access to the region where he had as a youth been held in captivity, and which he now made his base of evangelistic operations. In these his early acquired knowledge of the people, their language, and their customs, stood him in good stead. His own zeal and power were apostolic, and ere long he had shaken the common paganism of Ireland to its foundation. He followed the usual course of Celtic missionaries, in addressing himself to the chiefs. When they yielded to him their people yielded too. Before he died —at a great age, towards the close of the fifth century—he had virtually Christianised Ireland. He had naturalised on Irish soil the monastic system which he had studied abroad. He had founded scores of churches, and had ordained scores of bishops, of the congregational or tribal sort. He had established the primacy of the Irish Church at Armagh, a century and a half before the see of Canterbury was founded by Augustine, and 118 years before Columba landed in Iona. It was in the monastic schools of this Church that Columba was trained: with its system of administration and scheme of doctrine and ritual he was familiar. It was these he carried with him to Scotland; and in accordance with these he organised the Church which he established among the Scots of Argyll and planted amongst the Picts of Northern Alban.[1]

The first and most distinctive feature in the organisation of the Church of Patrick and Columba was the subordination of the bishop and

---

[1] These two peoples, we must understand, were but separate branches of the one great Celtic race.

Bishops in Ireland.

the pre-eminence of the abbat. Not that in Ireland the bishops were few, but that they were ecclesiastically obscure and impotent compared with the abbat. S. Patrick, who was ordained Bishop by Germanus of Auxerre,[1] whom he had visited in Gaul, imparted to others the commission he had himself received, with a free hand. But they were bishops in the apostolic, not in the Roman, sense. S. Bernard complains of the gross irregularities, as he thought them, that, even in his time, prevailed in Ireland, where, he says, "almost every church has its separate bishop." These were the ministers of separate congregations; but besides these there were bishops unattached—who had no congregation and no special see — and some who were the bishops of septs or families, and some who were bishops *honoris causâ*. All this was most offensive to the formalists of Rome. The principle of church government on the Continent was conformity and obedience to Rome. The principle of church government in Ireland was national independence of Rome, and obedience to her own authorities, who were not the bishops, but the abbats. Bishops who presided over a single church, and others who owned no allegiance to

---

[1] This appears the most probable source of his orders. For a succinct statement of the argument in its favour see Stokes's 'Ireland and the Celtic Church,' Lect. iii.

Rome, and who, impelled by the apostolic spirit of evangelism, went "everywhere preaching the Word," were not proper bishops at all, from the papal point of view. Some of these repaired to the Continent in their zeal to evangelise; but they met with but a cold reception from their Continental brethren. The "episcopi vagantes" were formally repudiated, and their right to ordain was denied, by more than one Continental Council.

When Columba had established his monastery in Iona, the authority of the abbat gained a constantly expanding prerogative, while the position of the bishops diminished in importance, and their numbers decreased. As the abbat rose, the bishop sank. He evidently was regarded as having some special duty in connection with the conferring of orders, and a part in celebrating the Eucharist different from that of the ordinary priest; but whatever was implied in the original meaning of an episcopate—a superintendence or overseership—belonged to the abbat, not to him. Where a new centre of Christian life was created —a new mission planted, and a new congregation gathered—the monk was in charge, and over the monk was the abbat, and the abbat only. There might be bishops in the monastery; but if there were, they were under the abbat's rule, and had to obey his bidding. They could ordain, but not without his leave. This power of ordaining had presumably accrued to them, in the West, as well as in the East, because they were *primi inter seniores*. The elders were originally, as we have seen, the leaders of the congregation. As the congregation grew, their duties became more special; and by-and-by they were regarded as in some degree apart from the other brethren — clergy, not laity. From among them the president, who gradually developed into the bishop, was selected (not always, however, as is proved by the cases of Ambrose at Milan, and of Nectarius at Constantinople). Around him, as *primus*, stood the elders from whom he had been chosen. They assisted him in ordaining and in every duty, in which he took the leading part.

A distinct idea, however, controlled the government of the Columban Church. It was the idea of the superiority of personal to official qualification for office. The bishop's claim, where the government was episcopal, was official; the abbat's was personal. The one represented the authority of office; the other the authority of character. This was the stronger, before which the other shrank. The Roman love of exact order and deference to precise law did not attract the Celtic mind and excite the Celtic sympathy. Loyalty to a leader and enthusiasm for a cause did. Besides, in Alban as in Erin, imperial Rome had never mastered the country, and parcelled it out into those territorial divisions, on the lines of which the Church organised itself in subjugated provinces. Among the Scots,[1] says Bishop Reeves, "the spiritual jurisdiction of the bishop was coextensive with the temporal sway of the chieftains,"—in those cases where the bishop was specially connected with the chieftain's family or clan, and not with a particular monastery or church. A diocesan episcopate, or an episcopate independent of the abbat, or rendering fealty to a foreign bishop at Rome or elsewhere, was unknown. And the abbat was a presbyter, not a bishop. Columba was a presbyter; and so was each of his successors.

The monastery of the Irish type differed widely from that of Monte Cassino, and from that of the medieval monkery, as known in this country after the eleventh century. The establishment at Iona had few features in common with the Melrose, Arbroath, or Paisley of later days. The buildings, of wood, or clay, and wattles, consisted of the church, or oratory; the abbat's house; the guest-house; the kitchen; the refectory; the mill and kiln; and the huts of the

---

[1] It is hardly necessary to say that at the time referred to "Scoti" was the name of the inhabitants of Ireland (Scotia or Erin). Later it was confined to those emigrants who crossed over to the west of Scotland.

monks. The abbat's house stood higher than the rest, and somewhat apart from the group; and the whole was enclosed with a "rath" or rampart for protection. The monk was not necessarily a priest; but, whether or not, he had taken the monastic vows, and wore the tonsure, and was the son and servant of the abbat. The community was the abbat's "family." His authority was patriarchal and absolute, not only over the mother monastery, but over all its affiliated communities and churches. The monks were divided into three ranks,—the seniors; the working brethren; and the pupils, who were under instruction. Possession of personal property and marriage were forbidden. Obedience to the abbat must be implicit. Discipline was strict; and enforced, if need be, with the lash. There was daily worship at the canonical hours, to which, on Sundays and saints' days, was added the celebration of the Eucharist.

Like all the rest of Christendom, Columba observed the yearly festivals of the Church connected with the seasons of Christmas, Easter, and Pentecost. But the date on which Easter was kept did not coincide with that on which it was kept at Rome; and the tonsure of the Columbans differed from the Roman tonsure. These two usages, in themselves of comparatively small account, yet, as we shall afterwards see, deemed of great moment at a later date, were the most noticeable of the material marks of the Columban independence of the Church of Rome. As regarded dogma and usage, perhaps the most obvious difference was the absence of any trace of Mariolatry. The real divergence between them consisted not so much in doctrine or observance as in mode of life and government, and the whole tone and character of the clergy. The ecclesiastical type was of an essentially different order. Fasts were frequent, and strictly observed. The dress was a woollen tunic worn under a dark gown or hooded cloak of the same materials; on the feet, sandals. The chief occupations of the older brethren were the performance of divine service, and reading and copying the sacred Scriptures. The middle-aged and active tilled the ground, tended cattle, and looked after the necessary economies of the society.

The doctrines held by the brethren of such an establishment as this were, as far as we can judge, in general accordance with those of the Church at large, as embodied in the Nicene Creed. There is no indication of Arianism having made its way to Iona, or even to Ireland. There is more reason to believe that the ideas of Pelagius, himself a Briton, and venerated at Lerins, found favour among these monks of the West. Adamnan's narrative helps us to apprehend what the Columban doctrines were, as far as shown forth in the Columban ritual. The Lord's Supper was celebrated much like the Roman mass, though with differences to be noticed later. Here, as on the continent of Europe, the primitive idea of the Eucharist had passed away, and instead of the table with the presiding minister and the fraternal communion of the brethren, we have the altar, the priest, and the sacrifice. Columba celebrated mass for the souls of the departed; but evidently not with the idea of thereby mediating with God on their behalf, but by way of showing reverence and loving remembrance, and giving thanks for those whom God had taken to Himself. When Brendan died in Ireland, Columba knew of it by some intuition or revelation, and immediately ordered the mass to be prepared—" for this," said he, " is the birthday of the blessed Brendan." And on another occasion he bade his monks add the name of Columban, who had died the night before, to the names commemorated in the intercessory prayer. In each of these cases his practice differed from any now known either to Catholic or Protestant. The Protestant would refuse to celebrate the Communion in honour of a departed friend, or to insert his name in the prayers; and the Catholic would regard the service as mediatorial.

At this point, as at others, we see in the Columban belief and usage proof of that closer connection with the East than with Rome which is a note of the Celtic Church. In the Latin theology the idea of a purgatorial period after death had taken root—the idea of an intermediate state in which the departed awaited the consummation of their bliss. From this had grown up the cognate idea that their release might be expedited by the efforts of their friends on earth. Hence sacraments and prayers for the dead. But prayers for the dead, offered with this object, differed widely in spirit and meaning from that devout remembrance and giving of thanks which had characterised the purer faith of the early Church, and which inspired the belief and practice of the Celtic monks. Their ideas here are Eastern rather than Latin. So, too, were their ideas about the invocation of the saints, or, as Columba would have put it, prayer to the departed now with the Lord, asking their help and intercession. This was common in the Columban Church; and it appears to us rather the expression of a simple trust in their abiding interest in the welfare of those left behind on earth, and of a conviction of their near though unseen presence, than a practice based on a reasoned system or theory. Is there anything to find fault with in a belief which clings to the idea that death makes but a slight and temporary rupture between the life we live and that within the veil, and which ascribes to those who are no longer beside us some share in our joys and sorrows here? It is a childlike confidence of this sort which we recognise in the Columban invocation of the saints; and here, as at other points, what strikes us in the Columban creed and usage is their openness and tenderness of thought, their sweet and loving if somewhat visionary simplicity, as of a child.

This beautiful simplicity, with its accompanying high strain of holy and self-forgetful life, links the Church of Columba to the very Church of the apostles, more directly perhaps than any quality of its doctrine or its government. In the family of Iona we mark that perfect guilelessness of the religious life — that singleness of heart — that childlike openness and earnestness, which we are accustomed to associate with the primitive Christianity of the apostles and their first followers, as special characteristics of the fresh and beautiful youth of the Church. As has been said of this mark of that spring-time, "All else has been repeated since, but this never. And this makes the religious man's heart turn back with longing to that blessed time when the Lord's service was the highest of all delights, and every act of worship came fresh from the soul. If we compare degrees of devotion, it may perhaps be reckoned something intrinsically nobler to serve God and love Him now when religion is colder than it was, and when we have not the aid of those thrilling and heart-stirring sympathies which blest the early Church. But even if our devotion be sometimes nobler in itself, yet theirs still remains the more beautiful, the more attractive. Ours may have its own place in the sight of God, but theirs remains the irresistible example which kindles all other hearts by its fire."[1] Even in our own dull day the example does not lose its power. The Church still looks back to these ancient times for a renewal of its inspiration. Those of our own era, who have given the heartiest impulses to Christian life, have been men that have proved in their lives that they have drunk deep at the early founts of primitive zeal and love and faith. Those who have done most to impart fresh impetus to Christian devotion to the service of God and man — to raise the standard of Christian character and aim—have not been the theologians and controversialists, the ritualists and sacerdotalists, the philosophers and critics. They have been the great missionaries,—the men like Carey and Patteson, Moffat

[1] Bishop Temple, in 'Essays and Reviews.'

and Livingstone, Damien and Gordon, who showed that the devotion, the service, the stainless loyalty of the Christlike life, as those lived it who had been the first to follow the perfect Example, were their great ambition—who were, though living in this nineteenth century, in a true sense primitive Christians; for to be faithful followers of the primitive Church is not to be, as some aim at being, servile copyists of its practices, but to reproduce its spirit under the new conditions of our modern life.

It is the feeling that Columba and his friends were thus primitive in spirit, were thus near those who had been near the Lord, that endears their memory to us—that makes his name still a power for good after the lapse and the changes of more than 1200 years. They seem to us, certainly, men of clearer insight and directer communion with the Unseen than the controversial and argumentative "Fathers" of the Church, whether Greek or Latin. They do not speculate on the mysteries of the faith: they are content to believe though they cannot prove, and to trust where they cannot comprehend. The world was full of wonder and awe to them. It had secrets that transcended their philosophy, and which they believed were revealed to them that feared that Lord to whom they trusted for all needed revelation.

The Columban brethren were little affected by Patristic tradition or authority. They would not have understood, could they have known, the extreme deference paid by the modern traditionalist to the testimony of the "Fathers." Their own theology was of a more natural type than that of the schools of either Alexandria or Carthage. They lived in a more primitive society; they were in closer communion with free nature; they moved amid an atmosphere fuller of "the freshness of an earlier world," than that of Hellenic philosophy or Latin dogmatism.

After all, were the "Fathers" entitled to the mental subjection which the place accorded to them in the ecclesiastical world seemed to demand? As interpreters of the religion of Jesus of Nazareth, they wanted the personal knowledge of contemporaries which the apostles had enjoyed, on the one hand; and they lacked the calm judgment which results from long historical experience and critical inquiry, on the other. The idea of a purely spiritual religion was yet in a great measure an alien novelty in the world around them. The air they breathed was still heavy with the incense that rose from heathen altars, and the smoke that hung over Jewish burnt-offerings. The manners and customs, on which they looked day by day, were stained with the viciousness of an unbridled

The Fathers. 93

immorality. They were themselves, in many cases, men who bore in their own characters marks which were not those of the Lord Jesus, and whose impress was no sign of their being trustworthy guides in interpreting Holy Writ, or entering into the arcana of spiritual truth: men, for example, such as Origen, whose minds were deeply engrained with oriental mysticism; like Cyril, whose hearts were inflamed with the hot passions and ambitions of a nature yet half savage; like Augustine, all whose thoughts of God and man betrayed the harshness and jealousy of a nature warped, in its inmost fibres, by a youth of heathenish licentiousness. It was not from masters such as these that the Celtic pioneers of the Gospel learned the principles and the doctrine of Christ.

Nor was it from the bigoted precisians of *jure divino* episcopacy that they derived the system on which they administered the government and guided the free activities of their Church. No Church ever laboured in the cause of Christ which gave fuller proof of the effectiveness and validity of its ministry; none could more confidently have appealed to that test of the authenticity of its mission with which our Lord met the questions of John the Baptist's messengers.[1] Can any sane man believe that the presence of a few officials,

[1] Luke vii. 18-23.

unendowed with special gift or power, among the great company of workers and evangelists which formed the monastic family, was the element that consecrated their labour and guaranteed its efficacy? Could Columba, had he been twenty times a bishop, have done one whit more than he did for the spiritual life of the Scots and Picts? Could he have given more convincing proof of the apostolic character of his ministry?

The family of Iona exhibited, in a marked degree, a primitive union of ascetic simplicity and purity with the most active beneficence. Theirs was no "fugitive and cloistered virtue." They lived for others—"for ever roaming with a hungry heart" wherever the cry of human need and spiritual darkness called them. Our own islands offered too strait an outlet for their evangelistic ambition. Two great monks of Ireland led the way across the narrow seas, and carried the cross through Burgundy and Switzerland; but Gallus and Columbanus had a noble following in the first outflow of that stream of Scottish scholars and missionaries who, until a century after the Reformation, connected, by their living intercourse and labours, the religious life of our island with that of the Continental Churches. In Switzerland the people still pray for the Scots and Irish, not knowing why; but we know that the names made their way into their liturgy because they were the first planters of Christianity in the Swiss valleys and the Burgundian plains. "It is touching," says one who has traced the footsteps of some of these early apostles of our Church,[1] "to discover memorials of these our own countrymen and spiritual sires, too long forgotten, among strange people and in the far-off places to which they had betaken themselves in their missionary zeal. I have known no deeper sensation than to find the traces of the Highland hand among the MSS. of Bobbio, and to come upon the Celtic dead in the cathedral of Tarentum."

But it was in Britain, of course, that the influence of Iona was most immediate and powerful,—first, in subduing the Northern Picts, and planting the Church throughout the whole country north of the Tweed; and next, in doing the same work in the regions south of that river—even as far as the borders of the kingdom of Kent. This extension of the Scotic Church had consequences so far-reaching, and so closely bound up with the future of the Christian religion both in Scotland and England, that we must attend to its character and results ere we pass on to the more special examination of the development of the Columban system, and its final decadence in the North.

[1] Bishop Ewing, Memoir, p. 430.

The early Roman Christianity of Southern Britain was all but extinguished, when the Saxons and Angles swarmed across the North Sea and attacked the timid natives, left defenceless by their Roman masters. England was paganised: Thor and Woden were worshipped where the Cross had stood. Weak bands of Christian fugitives found safety in the fastnesses of Wales and Cornwall. At last, in the autumn of 597—the year of Columba's death—a mission, conducted by Augustine, a Roman abbat, was despatched by Gregory the Great to win back Britain to the faith of Christ. The King of Kent, on whose shores the missionaries landed, received them kindly, and allowed them to establish themselves and build a church at Canterbury. Ere long he, with a multitude of his people, was baptised.

From Kent the message of the Cross was borne into the neighbouring kingdom of Essex, and ultimately penetrated to Northumbria, the northernmost of the Saxon kingdoms. A daughter of Ethelbert married Edwin, the Northumbrian king, and was accompanied to her new home by the bishop Paulinus, who founded and filled the see of York. It was at the council called by Edwin to hear the bishop's exposition of his faith that an aged thane contributed to the debate a short and touching apologue, which, often as it has been quoted, is too beautiful and characteristic to be passed by. "When, O King! you and your ministers and warriors are seated at table in the winter, and the fire burns brightly on the hearth, perchance a sparrow, chased by the wind and snow, enters at one door of the hall and escapes by the other. Whilst it is within, it enjoys the warmth and light, but immediately vanishes from your sight, returning from one winter to another. So does this life of ours appear for a little while; but of what went before or what is to follow we know nothing. If, therefore, the new religion offers us here any certain knowledge, it deserves that we should follow it." "Suchlike discourses," says the Venerable Bede, "the other elders and king's counsellors, by divine inspiration, advanced;" and the result was that Northumbria too became, in name at least, one of the kingdoms of the Lord and of His Christ. But the triumph of the Gospel was short-lived. In October 633 Edwin went out to battle against Cædwalla, King of the Britons, and Penda, King of Mercia, the latter the fiercest and most powerful of the heathen Saxons. Edwin was slain, and his widow with her children, along with Paulinus, fled to her father's kingdom of Kent. The nascent Christianity of Northumbria disappeared, and the tide of evangelisation rolled backwards to the south.

During the seventeen years of Edwin's reign his nephew Oswald, who was the rightful heir of the Northumbrian dynasty, had lived in exile among the Scots. He resolved now to strike a blow for the recovery of his rights. With a small but chosen band he encountered, near Hexham, the hosts of the Britons who had overrun Northumbria, and utterly defeated them. Their leader fell; and they, quitting all their positions, fled westward, till they had placed the Severn, like a moat, between them and the possibility of pursuit. Northumbria welcomed Oswald to its throne; and the realm, consolidated under his sway, became the head of the whole Heptarchy.

During his Scottish exile Oswald had been admitted to the Church by the monks of Iona; and on the eve of his decisive battle the great Columba had appeared to him in a vision, and promised him the victory. It was not unnatural that, seeking ministers of the Word who should anew plant the Church in Northumbria, he should appeal to those who were his own spiritual fathers, the successors of the great Abbat of Iona. The appeal was heard, and the Celtic Church prepared itself to occupy the new field thus opened to its missionary enterprise. But "the first effort of their zeal," says Montalembert, "was not fortunate. Their first representative seems to have been animated by that spirit of pedantic rigour, by that stubborn and intolerant austerity, which have often shown themselves in the national character of the Scots, along with Christian devotion and self-denial, and which culminated in the too-celebrated Puritans."

His name was Corman; and after a futile attempt to gain an influence over the Angles, he returned to Iona to report his failure. As he recounted to the assembled fraternity his experiences and disappointment, a voice from among them exclaimed, "Brother, the fault was yours. You exacted from the barbarians more than their weakness could bear. You should first have stooped to their ignorance, and then have raised their minds to the divine maxims of the Gospel." The voice was Aidan's. His brethren recognised in him the man for the emergency. He was at once despatched to the south along with a company of assistant monks. With a touching remembrance of his island-home in the Hebrides, he established his dwelling, his church, his monastic discipline and order, on the Isle of Lindisfarne, which, under his apostolic ministry, became the Iona of the Anglo-Saxons.

From this centre the evangelical fervour of the Celtic bishop and his monks, aided by the influential zeal of the king, carried the doctrines and rites of Christianity far and wide over the north of England. But Oswald was soon cut off. The terrible old pagan, Penda, again waged war against Northumbria; and on the 5th of August 642 Oswald fell in battle, crying as he fell, "Deus, miserere animabus." Disaster, divided succession, war, and confusion followed; but still the Cross made way.

Aidan too died; but a new bishop from Iona replaced him, Finan; and again on his death, after a ten years' episcopate, that nursery of apostles sent forth Colman to fill his vacant place. By this time Oswy, the brother of Oswald, was on the throne; and the kingdoms of Northumbria, of Essex, and of Mercia had been evangelised by the Celtic monks of the Columban order. The Roman mission, which had won Kent, had since that first conquest been comparatively ineffective. The Celtic mission, of which Iona was the birthplace, Lindisfarne the headquarters, and Aidan the leading spirit, had for years been the really active and aggressive Christian influence in almost every region of England, except Kent and the distant south and west.

The time of Roman revival and renewed organisation had now, however, arrived, and the man who was to rule the movement had appeared. He was a young Northumbrian noble of the name of Wilfrid. When yet in his teens he had chosen the monastic life, and had entered Aidan's monastery at Lindisfarne. While learning there the discipline and the rites of the Church, according to the usages of the Columban brotherhood, it dawned upon him that there was an older centre of ecclesiastical authority than Iona, and that in some respects the traditions of Rome differed from those which Columba had brought with him from Ireland. He quitted Lindisfarne and made his way to the Eternal City, where he acquired a full knowledge of the usages from which the Celtic Church diverged, obtained the blessing of the Pope, and returned to England, bearing in the Roman tonsure, which he had adopted, the visible badge of his conviction of the just supremacy of the Papal See. Alchfrid, son of Oswy, had in the year 658 been associated with his father in the government of his kingdom. On hearing of Wilfrid's return from abroad, he sent for him. Oswy had been instructed by the Scottish monks; but his mother, Eanfleda, daughter of Edwin, had been trained by Paulinus the Roman, and the young prince, as was to be expected, was more inclined to the religious observances and beliefs of his mother than to those of his sire. He lent a willing ear to Wilfrid's teaching, and turning the Celtic monks out of the monastery which he had founded at Ripon, he installed his tutor in their room. In this place of power

Wilfrid began openly and eagerly to urge the rules of Rome and to preach the duty of Catholic uniformity.

The conflict between Rome and Iona, Ripon and Lindisfarne, soon became general and violent, and at last, at the summons of King Oswy, the representatives of the two great parties came to Whitby to fight it out. The question of the tonsure was not mooted, though it had stirred keen enough feeling. The tonsure had originated with the first cœnobites of the East, who had shaved their heads in token, according to oriental custom, of humiliation and affliction. When monasticism spread, and monks came to fill the highest offices in the Church, the practice of shaving the head continued, though its origin was lost sight of; and as clerical garb and usage acquired individuality, the tonsure became one of the marks of the sacerdotal order. But the oriental "clean shave" was not observed in the West. The priests of Rome shaved only the crown of the head; those of the Celtic Church shaved the forehead in a wide circle from ear to ear. The Romans said their practice came down to them from Simon Peter, and that the practice of the Celts had come down from Simon Magus. But bitter and personal as was the feeling upon this knotty point, the attention of the conference was concentrated upon the more urgent difficulty of the Easter celebration, and it seems to have been understood that the decision upon it would rule that upon any other matter in dispute.

The early Eastern Christians used to celebrate Easter on the day of the Hebrew Passover, which was held on the 14th of the first Jewish month. The Western Churches celebrated it on the Sunday following the day of the Passover. The Council of Nice decided in favour of this usage; and those who, in spite of the decision, still adhered to the 14th were considered heretical, and went by the name of "Quartodecimans," or *Fourteenthers*. It was not upon this point, however, that the dispute at Whitby turned. The Celts were not Quartodecimans. They simply were, like the Russians at the present day, wedded to the "Old Style," and prejudiced against the New. The New Style had been adopted by the Roman Church about the middle of the sixth century, at a time when the Christians of Britain were almost wholly cut off, through their local and domestic troubles, from intercourse with the Churches of the Continent. Isolated communities, whether ecclesiastical or social, become bound to their own forms and traditions; and when intercourse began to be renewed, the Celts were not disposed to give in to what they considered a Roman novelty.

It had been determined by the Council of Nice that the astronomers of Alexandria should make the necessary computation for fixing the date on which in each year the Easter festival should occur, and should intimate the result to the Roman Pontiff, who in turn should notify it to the remoter Churches. This plan, however, did not work well. The Romans sometimes questioned the accuracy of the Egyptian calculations, and departed from them; and it was not until after nearly two hundred years of divergency and dispute that the uniform method of reckoning was adopted which is still in force, and which restricts the paschal celebration to the interval between the 22d of March and the 25th of April. To this method the Celts did not conform; and as a consequence their Easter from time to time fell on another day than that on which the Roman churches were celebrating it. They also refused to begin their Lenten fast on Ash Wednesday, according to the Roman usage, and deferred it till the Monday of the following week, thus abbreviating the proper period of forty days. A variety in practice is often felt to be more intolerable than a divergence in doctrine, and King Oswy no doubt was irritated and annoyed when, in the midst of the festivity and gladness of his Celtic Easter, he saw his queen with all her court still practising the austerities of her Roman Lent. Personal feelings, family unity, social order, as well as religious prejudice, were all involved in this Easter question. It was determined that a council should be summoned to decide it. The council met at Streaneschalch, now Whitby, in 663, and within the monastery which had been founded there five years before by Hilda, a daughter of the royal family of Deira, who had taken the vows of a nun, and who was now Abbess of Streaneschalch, which soon became frequented and famous under her rule.

According to a common Celtic usage the monastery afforded religious shelter to both monk and nun, dwelling in houses adjacent yet apart, but owning the one common authority of the abbess. King Oswy of Northumbria proposed to hold under Hilda's roof this conference, which, he hoped, might adjust the differences between the rules and usages of Rome and those of Iona. Hilda acquiesced; and the king arrived at Whitby to preside in the assembly, accompanied by Alchfrid his son, followed by Bishop Colman from Lindisfarne, and a great company of the Celtic clergy: while the Roman party were led by Agilbert, formerly Bishop of Wessex, but now the friend and companion of Alchfrid; by the young Wilfrid, and by two aged priests, in one of whom the spectators recognised James the deacon, who alone of all the Christian clergy had stood fast by his post at York, when Paulinus the bishop and all the rest fled southward before the heathen Penda, who had slain King Edwin and embroiled his kingdom, some thirty years before.

King Oswy presided in the conference. In those days there were no troublesome theories of Church and State. The Church strove to imbue the whole people with Christian faith and order, and accepted without scruple whatever help in this work "the secular arm" could bring. So Oswy "took the chair" as of right, and called on his bishop, Colman, to open the debate. Cedd, bishop of the East Saxons, was to act as interpreter for the Celts, who did not understand Latin or the Anglo-Saxon tongue; and Wilfrid was to speak on behalf of the Anglo-Saxons, as Bishop Agilbert possessed their language but indifferently. "We all," said Oswy, "serve one God, and should observe one rule of life; and as we all expect one kingdom of heaven, we ought not to differ in the celebration of the Divine mysteries, but rather to inquire which is the truest tradition, that we all may follow it." The debate then proceeded between Colman and Wilfrid; the one founding his argument on the personal usage of his predecessors, and the peculiar tradition of the Celtic Church, derived, as he maintained, from S. John; the other on the Catholic practice of all other Churches, and the authority of S. Peter, the prince of the apostles, and of S. Paul, the Apostle of the Gentiles. The argument was not on either side very logical or cogent; but on Colman's it scarcely moved from the austere and tenacious assertion of the obligation of the example of S. John and the holy abbat Columba. In the true spirit of ecclesiastical conservatism and Celtic clansmanship, his key-note was, "We cannot change the customs of our fathers." "Can we admit," he demanded, "that our most venerable father Columba and his successors, men beloved of God, have acted contrary to the Divine Word?" "Beloved of God, I doubt not," replied Wilfrid, "and serving Him in their rustic simplicity, with pious hearts; and because knowing no better, sinning not in keeping Easter on a wrong day. But as little do I doubt that if a Catholic calculator had come to them, they would have followed his admonitions as readily as they are known to have kept those commandments of God, which they believed to have come to them from Him. But you, who now know the decrees of the Apostolic See—nay, of the Catholic Church—sin inasmuch as you refuse to obey." "And as to Columba, holy as he was," said Wilfrid, perhaps unwittingly clinching the argument, "is he to be preferred to the most blessed prince of the apostles, to whom our Lord said, 'Thou art Peter; and upon this rock I will build my Church, and the gates of hell shall not prevail against it'; and 'To thee I will give the keys of the kingdom of heaven'?" "Colman," said Oswy, turning to the Celtic bishop, "is it true that these words were spoken to Peter by our Lord?" "It is true, O king!" confessed Colman. "Can you show any such power given to your Columba?" was the next question. "No," said Colman. "Do you both agree then," pursued Oswy, "that these words were addressed specially to Peter, and that the keys of heaven were given to him by our Lord?" "We do," was the answer of both. "Then," said the king, "I too say he is the doorkeeper, whom I will in nowise contradict, but in all things, so far as I know and am able, will obey; lest when I come to the door of the heavenly kingdom, there should be none to open it for me, he being my adversary who is proved to have the keys."

"The whole assembly," says Bede, "assented to the royal decision." The clergy and the laity, nobles and commoners, with uplifted hands accepted and confirmed the sentence.

The Celtic Easter was doomed. On this quaint notion of King Oswy's, suggested by the most unspiritual interpretation of our Lord's language, hinged the future of the British Church. The great wave of Celtic influence, which, rolling down from Iona to Lindisfarne, and swelled by another current spreading outward from Bangor on the Dee, had wellnigh submerged all England, was stemmed at Whitby. It was long ere it wholly receded; but the retrocession began here. Cedd conformed to the Roman order, and returned to his bishopric at London; but Colman, true to the traditions of Columba, and too proud to change, quitted Lindisfarne for ever, and taking with him the bones of Aidan, went back disconsolate and defeated to Iona. With him the Celtic independence and individuality that had broadly stamped the religion of England with its own character retired towards the North, henceforth destined to recede ever farther and farther before the Anglo-Roman advance, until every vestige of the early Scottish peculiarities had vanished, and Iona had become but a memory and a name.[1]

While Colman shrank away into obscurity,

[1] "The independence of the Celtic missionary is a patent fact. . . . The missionaries owed allegiance not to the Bishop of Rome, but to the Presbyter-Abbat of Iona. There is no evidence that they sought or accepted any authoritative directions from the Roman mission in the south of England. Their usages were different in many respects from the usages of Rome. When these came under discussion, and it was a question between allegiance to Iona and allegiance to Rome, they unhesitatingly chose the former."—Bishop Lightfoot's Leaders of the Northern Church: 1. The Celtic Mission.

Wilfrid withdrew from the conference to enter on a conspicuous but stormy career of forty years, in which he was to be the champion of the Papal See, and through many apostolic labours, ecclesiastical strifes, civil discords, and personal vicissitudes, to extend and consolidate the Anglo-Saxon Church under the broad uniformity and discipline of Rome. "England owed it to him," says Montalembert, in the eulogy he has pronounced on one whom he evidently held in highest honour among his heroes of the Church, "that she was not only Christian, but Catholic, Apostolic, and Roman. No other Anglo-Saxon exercised a more decisive and more sovereign influence on the destinies of his race."

Among the forces that have moulded Anglo-Saxon life and character, S. Wilfrid claims a foremost place. The ruins of the Norman abbey which occupy the site of Hilda's monastery, and crown the cliff above the gay and busy town of Whitby, form one of the most noteworthy landmarks in the history of England.

This Roman victory had nothing to do with any question of the Orders of the Celtic Church. The purity and validity of these were never questioned by the Anglo-Roman party. Bede, who was a keen Romanist, though he notes with disapproval the subjection of the Celtic bishops to the abbats, suggests no doubt of the character

Celtic Orders.

and efficiency of the monastic ministry. He relates how Oswald sent for a bishop "to the elders of the Scots," that he might instruct the Northumbrians[1] in the faith. He never questions the propriety of Oswald's doing so, or the right of the Scots' elders to comply. He knew that Iona did not own the jurisdiction of Rome, but he did not regard this as invalidating Iona's power to organise a mission to Northumbria. Rome's claim to be the sole fountain of ecclesiastical prerogative and evangelistic grace had not yet been formulated with the arrogance which marks it at the present day.[2]

[1] The kingdom of Northumbria contained two provinces,—Deira, stretching from the Humber to the Tees; and Bernicia, stretching from the Tees to the Forth.

[2] "All the priests of Iona together with the abbats could ordain no bishop whatsoever. The consecration of every bishop must be by another bishop; and the bulls of consecration can alone be issued by the Holy Roman See, which is the centre of apostolic unity, power, and jurisdiction."—The Monks of Iona, by J. Stewart M'Corry, D.D., p. 103.

"The Catholic faith teaches that the Roman Pontiff is in possession of *direct* and *immediate* ordinary jurisdiction over every baptised person. His jurisdiction over every Christian, man and woman, is *ordinary*, to use an ecclesiastical phrase—that is to say, jurisdiction belongs to him in virtue of his office, and he has power to delegate his jurisdiction. In other words, every Catholic lives in subjection to two bishops. He is directly subject to the local prelate within whose diocese he has his dwelling. He is also as directly subject to the episcopal jurisdiction of that universal Bishop—*cujus diocesis est orbis terrarum*—whose diocese is the world, or, in other words, is world-wide."—Humphreys' Recollections of Scotch Episcopalianism (a curious autobiographic history of a passage to Rome).

No incident in the history of our Church recalls more vividly the first missionary enterprises of Antioch and Jerusalem than the despatch of Corman from Iona, at Oswald's desire—his return and report of his failure—the council of the brotherhood—the criticism of Aidan, and its result in his own undertaking the unsuccessful work. As we study the picture, we seem to be again in the assembly of the apostles and elders, marking their cordial conference, their wise counsel, their readiness to go forth on the Church's errand at the brethren's wish. The college of elders in Iona is recognised as the sole depositary and source of the authority bestowed on Corman, on Aidan, on Finan, on Colman — on all those apostolic emissaries who, Bede tells us, were appointed and sent out from "the island which is called Hii." Imbued as he was with Roman prejudice—regretting as he did the "ordo inusitatus" which regulated their government—Bede could not deny that the monks of Iona, by whomsoever or according to whatsoever rite ordained or consecrated, exercised an episcopate which no one could gainsay. At no time did the ministry of the Scots bear the stamp of more unquestioned apostolicity than in those days of unworldly devotion and communion with the unseen, of intense missionary earnestness, of free individual action, and close fraternal union under their patriarchal head.

LECTURE IV.

THE Cross had penetrated where the legions had never trod, in other regions than Britain. In the extreme East, as in the farthest West, a Church existed which had not bowed the knee to the Roman bishop. And there we find the same conditions as at home,—a clergy ignorant of papal claims and of episcopal pretensions— a Christian communion free from errors which were part and parcel of the system of the Latin Church. When, in the end of the fifteenth century, the Portuguese, having rounded the Cape of Storms, made their way to India, they found on the coast of Malabar a settlement of Christians, whose hundred churches had, for thirteen centuries, been ruled by a regular succession of bishops who looked to the Patriarch of Antioch as their head. They refused to acknowledge the Pope, though harried and persecuted by the invaders because of their refusal. They knew nothing of the invocation of saints; of Purgatory; of seven sacraments. They held there were only two sacraments, and only two orders—those of priest and of deacon, for their bishop differed from the priest not in order but in function only.[1] Their isolation from the imperial influence had secured them from the aggression of the ecclesiastical power, which had served itself heir to the traditions of the empire. The existence of the Syrian Church on the shores of the Indian Ocean helps us to understand the causes which differentiated the Scotic Church, in Erin and Alban, from Churches which were subject to the dominion of Rome. But as the Portuguese Inquisition, which followed like a vulture in the wake of Vasco da Gama's ships, crushed the ancient independence and defaced the historic features of the Indo-Syrian community, so the Anglo-Roman policy of proselytism and spirit of aggression gradually depressed the vigour, and changed the character, of the Scotic Church. Yet the depression and the change were gradual, nor were they in any case accelerated by persecution.

The last of the great Celtic missionaries, who spent their lives in planting the Scotic Church, was the first to set the example of conformity to the

---

[1] Buchanan's Christian Researches in Asia, 9th ed., p. 106 *et seqq*.

new usages. Cuthbert, who, as a shepherd lad on the Lammermoors, was moved by a strong and sudden religious impulse to adopt the monastic life, under Boisil, Prior of Melrose, had, at Melrose and Lindisfarne, won universal veneration by the singular sanctity of his life and his untiring devotion to the work of an evangelist. No toilsomeness of road, no perils of mountain or flood, no stress of summer's heat or winter's cold, availed to check the ardour of his apostolic energy. Along with this active self-devotion he exhibited a singular revival, in his own person, of the extremest asceticism of which the Egyptian Antony had been the type. Quitting Lindisfarne, where he was prior, he withdrew after a time to the isle of Farne on the coast near Bamborough, as in his earlier years he had withdrawn to a "desert" in the North. Here he spent some eight years in the strictest solitude, only admitting to his cell those who came to seek, in urgent need, ghostly counsel or comfort. Tales were told of his strange powers of prayer, of insight, of self-denial, of the ingenious austerities—such as reciting the whole Psalter while he stood neck-deep in icy water—with which he mortified the flesh. He was persuaded to accept a new bishopric, erected at Hexham for the province of Bernicia; but he could not bring himself to say farewell to his beloved island, and returned to it after only two years' unwilling tenure of his episcopal office. Soon afterwards, in March 687, he passed away, in his little oratory in the isle of Farne, with his last words exhorting the monks who had come to watch by him, to "preserve always peace among themselves and divine charity"—to practise hospitality and think humbly of themselves; but, oddly enough, adding to these charges a warning to have nothing to do with those who "erred from the Catholic unity, either by keeping the wrong Easter or by a perverse life." It is strange that a man so holy and wise should have come to regard a matter of ceremonial observance of such moment, as to be named with his latest breath along with his fatherly counsels of peace, charity, and well-doing.

Owing to the civil conditions of the region in which he chiefly laboured, and which annexed that region to the Northumbrian monarchy, his name has not been so intimately identified with the history of the Church of Scotland as the names of his three predecessors—Ninian, Kentigern, and the great Columba; but it well deserves to be classed with theirs as the name of a true saint and apostle, and to be held in reverent remembrance as a symbol of exalted piety, pure self-devotion, and self-sacrificing labour in the Lord.

Cuthbert marks the transition from the old order to the new. Beginning his career as a

Columban monk, he closed it as a bishop in full communion with the Romanised Church, of which Canterbury was the metropolitan see. But the wisdom, devotion, and charity of his life are enough to prove that his conformity was dictated by no selfish ambition or easy-going indifference, but by a sincere conviction of what was best for the peace and progress of the Church to whose ministry he had dedicated himself. How widely he was known, and how affectionately remembered, is attested by the dedication to him of at least twenty-three churches, mainly in the region between the Forth and the Tyne, the chief of which is that which bears his name under the Castle Rock of Edinburgh; but there is also Kirkcudbright (Kirkcuthbert) in Galloway, another at Weem in Perthshire, and one as far north as Wick.

The death of Cuthbert was followed by a period in which the civil and the ecclesiastical history of our country is but obscurely traceable. Constant warfare between Picts, Scots, and Angles, and invasions and ravages of Danes and Norwegians, fill up the confused picture, until we reach the one vital fact (amid all the turmoil) of the union of the Scots of Dalriada and the Pictish tribes, under the sceptre of Kenneth Macalpine, in 844. We have no clear light as to the causes out of which this union sprang, beyond the facts that Kenneth was the representative of the royal house of Dalriada, while his mother was of Pictish descent, and he thus combined the claims of both branches of the Celtic race. Further, the Danish incursions, from which Scots and Picts alike suffered, served to draw both into a common league for mutual defence; and the transference of the Columban primacy from the Scotic Iona to the Pictish Dunkeld formed a bond of ecclesiastical union. As we know, the Pictish territory had been evangelised from Iona; but in the year 717, Nectan, the King of the Picts, influenced by the arguments of certain Anglic or Roman emissaries, placed his kingdom under the guardianship of S. Peter, and drove all the Columban monks and missionaries out of it. Many of these retreated to Ireland; others to Iona, where they helped to strengthen what might be called the "national party." The conflict between the Columban and the Roman tradition and usage had penetrated to the sacred island; and even in Columba's monastery some were found to favour the innovations of Whitby. Even there the general tendency was towards the adoption of what was now represented to be Catholic, as opposed to local or national, custom. In 767 the succession of abbats of the family of Columba—his "coarbs," as they were called—came to an end: in the first years of the ninth century the monastery was burnt; the whole community, with the exception of the abbat, was slaughtered by the Danes; and the relics of the great founder were removed, for better security, to Ireland. It was some time after this downfall of the ancient settlement that Kenneth, King of the Picts, moved either by reverence for the memory of Columba, to whom his people had owed their faith, or in pursuance of the policy of union which gained for him the sole monarchy, built a church at Dunkeld, in which he enshrined a part of the Columban relics that had been recovered from Ireland; and this church, in virtue of its possession of these, became the mother, or metropolitan, church of his dominions. The primacy of the monasteries in Ireland, which owed allegiance to Columba and his successors, had already, during the Danish inroads, been transferred to the Irish abbat of Kells. The primacy of the monasteries in Scotland was now vested in the abbat of Dunkeld.

Kenneth desired to reverse the policy of Nectan (who had striven to create a religious division between Pict and Scot by the expulsion of the Scotic clergy, and the erection of a bishopric at his royal town of Abernethy on the Tay), and to restore the Columbans to their old position in his extended and united kingdom. At the same time the Romanising policy of Nectan had so far left its mark upon the ecclesiastical organisation, that we now find for the first time the episcopal office formally associated with that of the Columban abbat. The Abbat of Dunkeld bore the title which Nectan had given his bishop at Abernethy, and was the Bishop of FORTRENN—the name of the kingdom of the Southern Picts. The title and office were significant of the impending change, which was to strip the abbacy of its old prerogative and prestige, and finally to transfer the ecclesiastical primacy from the abbat to the bishop—the title and the revenues of the abbat being ultimately transferred to a lay holder. The primacy, however, still retained so much of its Celtic character that it was national and not territorial. Its seat was a movable one; and the primate was not the bishop of a diocese, but of a people. The seat was, towards the close of the ninth century, again removed to Abernethy, and early in the tenth to St Andrews, from which it was never afterwards shifted.

But at none of these seats did the bishop bear a diocesan title. His diocese, in fact, was coextensive with the realm. At Dunkeld and Abernethy he was the Bishop of Fortrenn; at St Andrews he was the Bishop of Alban, which was now the name given to the whole region lying between the Forth and the Spey, and which formed the real nucleus and centre of that kingdom of Scotland to which Edgar of England by-and-by ceded the Lothians, and with which the Britons of Galloway and of Cumbria, of whom Kentigern had been the apostle, became incorporated in the end of the tenth century.

It is in the beginning of that century that we have the first record of what we may call a "mixed council" of the Scottish Church and nation.[1] It was in the reign of Constantine the king, and the episcopate of Kellach the bishop, and probably in the year 906. The place was Scone, a place held in deep veneration by the Scots. The assemblage which met there in 906 is the first symbol of that union of Church and State which has lasted in this country ever since. There had before that been alliance between the two, and endowment of the Church with the benefactions of the monarch; but here for the first time we find the official representatives of both meeting in solemn council, in the presence of the people, and along with them entering into common engagements and covenants, civil and religious. The record of the council is brief, but it shows us thus much. It tells us that Constantine the king and Kellach

[1] A "mixed council" was the name for one in which both the civil and the ecclesiastical authorities were represented and took part.

the bishop swore, together with the Scots, on the "Mount of Belief," beside the royal city of Scone, to keep "the laws and customs of the faith, and the rights of the churches and the Gospels." What was involved in either branch of this engagement we have no means of exactly determining. What were the particular laws and customs of the faith, and rights of the churches and the Gospels, does not appear. But obviously there was a covenant made between king, bishop, and people, to maintain, in their respective places and relations, the purity of the faith and worship of the Church on the one hand, and its rights as an evangelical corporation on the other. The object and the method are alike significant, and are specially interesting as giving us an early example of that tenacity of religious conviction, of that firm hold of corporate rights, and of that resolution to defend these, and to compel each member of the body politic to do his duty by them, which have distinguished the Scottish people in much later periods of their history, and most notably in their conflicts with ecclesiastical and monarchical misrule, in the sixteenth and seventeenth centuries.

Here also for the first time we find the Church assuming a distinctively national character, not merely in sentiment and mode of government, but in extent and comprehensiveness of jurisdic-

Idea of a National Church. 123

tion. Hitherto we have seen it marked by those Celtic traits which Columba brought from Ireland, and imprinted on the Church he founded in the Western Isles. We have noted its abbatial government; its sparse, undiocesan episcopate; its special points of usage in which it differed from Rome. And all these have stamped on it a certain signet of Celtic nationality; but never till now have we seen the Church, not any longer as the Church of a set of separate or loosely connected clans, but as the Church of a united kingdom of Scots and Picts, represented—as one corporation—by one high official, and through this representative entering, like a co-ordinate power, into formal covenant with the head of the State, and with the people under his sceptre. It is a distinct step towards the realisation of the idea of a NATIONAL CHURCH.

We shall presently see a great change accomplished in the constitution and character of this Church : let us, ere we reach the period of vicissitude, try to obtain as distinct a view as we can of the old order, the old ministry, the old life with its usages, its worship, its Celtic romance and enthusiasm.[1]

[1] For the particulars which follow in this lecture I am largely indebted, not only to the published works of the Rev. Duncan MacGregor, minister of Inverallochy, but to much valuable information imparted in his correspondence with myself, for which I take this public opportunity of thanking him.

We have not found that in Scotland there was the same multiplicity of bishops as in Ireland, and in the early sub-apostolic Churches. If the bishops were still numerous, though some were devoted evangelists, they were not conspicuous as rulers of churches. Their special distinction was the possession of that right of ordination which the original presbyterate had come to intrust to one of its senior members, selected mainly with a view to the orderly continuance of the apostolic commission; but this right of ordination they exercised in strict subjection, as I have already said, to the authority of the abbat, the head of the ecclesiastical community. The abbat was the choice of the brethren, according to the primitive usage; and although his power was absolute, it is evident, as in the case of the mission of Aidan to Northumbria, that after the example of Jerusalem and Antioch, the action of the Church, in all important crises, was resolved upon in the council of the elders, or general fraternity. As the Church extended itself throughout the land, the missionary monk, settling down amongst his converts, became, at one point after another, the head and centre of a new community, whose bond of union was their acceptance of the Christian faith. Thus in district after district, in glen and island and strath, the Church was founded, and the nucleus of a future parish formed.

But the evangelist-monk and the bishop-monk were not the only representatives of the Christian ministry, under the primacy of the abbat. There were, as in apostolic times, diversities of ministration; and these were founded not on the mechanical idea of the restriction of grace and spiritual influence to a threefold order, secured by a carnal succession professing to trace its origin to the apostles, but on a rarely exalted conception of the essential character of the Christian ministry. That ministry, according to the Celtic idea of it, was the reproduction on earth of the living energy of the Church's head in heaven. Christ on high, through His Spirit, raised up men who were His witnesses in the lower world. He that would be a true minister of the Gospel must be filled with the Spirit, must understand the apostles' doctrine, must follow their way of life. The Celt believed the minister should live by the work of his own hands, because the apostle did so. Having food and raiment, he was to be therewith content, like those whose leader told them to provide no purse nor wallet for their journeys; and like them he was to travel on foot, and preach the Gospel as he went. He was to own no property, like the great Master who had not where to lay His head; and he was to fast and pray, and withdraw into lonely places, after the same divine exemplar. By all available means he was to wean himself from the world, and to conform to the model of the life which was "the light of men." The aspirant to the ministry had, above every other preparation, to inure himself to a mode of living whose root was hidden in Christ,—to subdue the flesh, and to come into conscious relation to a life which, in its essence and its principles, was supermundane. He who could not or would not do this, was not apostolical. He who achieved it, approved of His Master, received from Him a gift of divine knowledge and of supernatural grace, in some degree corresponding to the measure of his triumph over human weakness and concern in the things that perish in the using. Those who endured the trial and gained the victory of the agonistic life, gained too a victory over the minds of men, which invested their persons and their office with a sanctity no formal consecration could impart. "Their mysterious times of seclusion, their constantly praying to an invisible Being, their total lack of interest in mundane things, their habits of silence except to speak in God's name, struck the people with awe, and even fear, and produced an ideal of a minister in the Scottish mind which is far from having yet evaporated."[1]

---

[1] The Celtic Inheritance of the Scottish Church, by the Rev. D. MacGregor, in "The Scottish Church Society Conferences"; 2d series, vol. ii.

"Who lives by rule then keeps good company," says George Herbert; but this high life was not prescribed in any mere rule of the Columban brotherhood: it was the product of the noble and unworldly ideal of the apostolic character and career, which inspired their founder and his brethren. The ministries which occupied those who held this ideal before them were various.

There was the ministry of the DISEARTACH—the man of the desert,[1] who, after the fashion of the Egyptian eremite, withdrew from the world to exercise himself in spiritual communion with God and conflict with evil; not to win for himself the name of saint, but to gather those around him whom he might teach and influence for good. If a man thus devoted himself, even in the most secluded spot, it was believed God would honour him, by making his gifts so well known that disciples would rally to his call and learn the secrets of the higher life.

Another of these ministers, and friends of God, was the SOSCELAIGHTE, or gospeller. He was an itinerant evangelist. He who dwelt in the desert was regarded as in a peculiar sense the imitator of Christ; but the wayfaring preacher was rather the imitator of the apostles, who did not wait till hearers were attracted by the bruit of their powers, but

[1] Hence Dysart among Scottish place-names.

went everywhere preaching the Word. So he witnessed for Christ wherever he could make his voice heard, devising no provision for his wants, but trusting to the hospitality of those whose hearts God opened to show him kindness. We find these two types of ministry occasionally combined in a single individual: as in two notable cases — those of Comgall and of Cuthbert. Comgall was a student monk for many years; then he became a "diseartach," retiring from the world for uninterrupted devotion, as the necessary means of attaining great spiritual power. After this he emerged from the desert and went about as an itinerant preacher; and finally he was the founder and president of a great monastic seminary, the Irish Bangor. So with the holy Cuthbert. He is said to have spent ten years in a desert in Strathtay, before he itinerated through Lothian, Cumbria, and Galloway; and when a bishop he reverted, in the end, to the hermit life, as we have seen, in the isle of Farne. Columba was the most conspicuous example of the itinerant. In the 'Book of Deer,' says Mr MacGregor, there is a glimpse of his mode of operations, which I take as an illustration. "He came to the Forest of Buchan, laboured, crushed resistance, planted his church and seminary at Deer, left his nephew and others in charge, and then passed away to some other place." Such was the method of the wandering evangelists—to convert the heathen, plant a church among them, provide for the maintenance of its services, and then go on to install the faith and the ministry elsewhere,—travelling, in the strength of the Lord, through savage fastnesses and among savage tribes—in perils oft from the wolf and wild boar, from the roving cateran, from the swamp and the torrent and the stormy sea. Nor were they content with merely planting the church and leaving it in another's charge. They would, like S. Paul, return time after time to visit and confirm the disciples, and to revive their spiritual life by renewed instruction and united acts of worship.

Again, there was the CLEIRICH MAINISTRICH, or the monastic clergy—*i.e.*, those who formed the permanent staff of the monastery, and remained at its headquarters. These men, according to their several gifts, had their respective functions assigned to them. Some acted as the pastors of the monastic community; some conducted the education of the sons of the nobles, the chiefs, and the people of the vicinity; some prepared students who aspired to the ministry; some were intrusted with the fitting out and direction of missionary expeditions; some gave themselves assiduously to special offices of devotion. Among the various functions discharged by these monastic clergy, in the monastery itself, were those of the preceptor or preacher; the chaplain; the mass-priest; the chancellor; and the scribe, a man of much importance. Among the teachers of the candidates for the ministry were the expounders of "the three fifties"— *i.e.*, the Psalter; the "man of lore," who taught "the ten books of science"; and the "disciple," who taught "the twelve books of science"; the historian; the lecturer, whose province was grammar, with orthography, criticism, arithmetic, and astronomy; the "doctor of the Canon," who lectured on the New Testament; the "lector," who gave instruction in the classical languages.

The highest degree in this educational institute (for such, in one aspect, the great monastery was) was that of the DRUIMELI, which implied "perfect knowledge of all wisdom, from the smallest book called the 'Ten Words,' to the greatest book called 'Cuilmen'"—the meaning of which, alas! is, according to Mr MacGregor, unknown. Who shall unravel its more than Delphic mystery? Among the Druimeli the chiefest rank was that of the OLLAMH,—a word which, with a gratifying appreciation of the value of modern academic

The Celtic Ministry.

distinctions, is now applied to a Doctor of Laws, and even to a Doctor of Divinity.

There was yet another grade of clergy—the SECULARS, or "priests of the order of the laity." Their special work lay apart from the monasteries, and was to minister to the chiefs and their clans; and they were subject to the chiefs, and apparently under very slight, if any, ecclesiastical supervision.

Last of all, and not properly of the clergy, there were the SCOLLOGS, or crofters,[1] who rendered services in the choir as equivalent to their rent.[2] They existed at Kirkcudbright as late as the twelfth century, and at North Berwick even later.

These functions of the ministry appertained to the priesthood. The one source of the priesthood was Christ, the Head of the Church. What may be meant by it is quite uncertain; but of several Irish saints it is recorded that they were ordained by Christ Himself. I should suppose the idea was that they had some such direct conviction of an immediate and personal call, superseding the necessity of any formal ordination, as that which changed S. Paul from the persecutor to the apostle. A priesthood so full of spiritual freshness and freedom, so rich in variety of function and in buoyant vigour of

---

[1] See 'Celtic Scotland,' vol. ii. pp. 446-448 and notes.
[2] See The Tenure of the Scollogs—Appendix I.

development, neither could nor would trace its principle and inspiration to any lesser source than that which had given to the primitive Church every gift needed for the perfecting of the saints, for the work of the ministry, for the edifying of the body of Christ. Through what outward arrangements appointment to these functions was regulated does not appear with any distinctness. In Ireland the numerous (undiocesan) bishops ordained to the diaconate and the priesthood. That they frequently discharged the same function in Scotland is evident, but that they did so uniformly and always is not clear. That they did not, is argued with considerable force in Dr Jamieson's erudite and elaborate work on the Culdees.[1] That they in any way controlled the assignation to, or the selection of, special offices for special men, is never suggested; nor can careful scrutiny detect in the Celtic literature of the Church any recognition of the necessity of apostolical succession, in the Roman sense.

Yet where in Christendom could a Church be found, bearing more plainly in its character and constitution the stamp of apostolicity, bringing forth richer fruits of the Spirit, recalling more brightly in its force, its freedom, its

[1] An Historical Account of the Ancient Culdees of Iona. By John Jamieson, D.D., F.R.S. Edinburgh, 1811.

versatility, its devotion, the era of the apostles? In the annals of what branch of the Holy Catholic Church shall you read names more worthy to be enrolled along with those of "the glorious company of the apostles, the goodly fellowship of the prophets, and the noble army of martyrs," than the names of Columba, Kentigern, and Cuthbert; of Donan, massacred with fifty companions before their altar by the heathen Picts; of Kessog, who, after evangelising the Lennox, went over seas in his irrepressible desire to win souls for Christ, and was slain in a foreign land; of Maelrubha, whose labours far and wide in north-western Scotland, from Ardnamurchan to Applecross, left so deep an impress on the people's memory, that even years after the Reformation they came to worship at his shrine; of Odran, the hermit of the Isle of May, slaughtered, with the disciples who had gathered around his cell, by the fierce Danes; of Mun, who left his followers the Rule: "Always preserve a pure heart burning with love to God. Be in life and discourse what worldlings expect religious men to be. Never speak except for necessity or utility. Do nothing but what you are willing God and all men should see. Love one another, and drive instantly from your mind whatever is calculated to rend mutual and fraternal charity"? What better proof of a divine commission, and of a consecrated ministry, could be given than was given by these men, and others of like spirit and power, whose names are now forgotten, or survive only in dim tradition, or as marking the crumbling ruin where ages ago they worshipped God, and taught some wild clan—long since broken and scattered—to love God and their brethren, and to forego their evil ways for those of peace, righteousness, and purity?

Wherever there was a congregation, whether in the monastic community, or in the church founded by the itinerant evangelist, or in any other way, there was a canon of worship, the original manuscripts of which no longer exist. Still there are materials, in the remnants of the Celtic religious literature, from which the diligent investigator can deduce a general idea, at least, of the principles and details of the divine offices of the Church of our fathers, in its pristine days. The latest, and a full, exposition of these principles and details is to be found in the "Lee Lecture" for 1895 by the Rev. Duncan MacGregor, which every churchman interested—as all ought to be—in the history of the Church should carefully study. At the root of the Church's worship, says this author, lay "the sublime conception of the Church herself as the living temple of the living God, with its various courts in heaven and on earth—the mystical body of Christ with its divine Head and its variously gifted members—the vast whole shining with heavenly grace, glowing with the presence of the Holy Ghost, pulsating with supernatural life, and armed with thaumaturgic powers."

The common worship of the members of this Church was rendered after two distinct types— the "Celebrad" (*celebratio*) and the "Oiffrenn" (*offerendum*). The first consisted mainly in psalmody, with prayers and lessons of Scripture,—the constant reading of the Scriptures being a marked feature of the education, and the worship, of the early Scottish Church. The second was the eucharist or mystic offering, always kept apart from the other, and consisted essentially of the supreme thank-offering and act of communion, with appropriate prayers, lessons, and anthems.

The Celebrad was a daily service offered at morning and evening, when all were expected to attend; and also at midnight and the third, sixth, and ninth hours, when attendance was of course impossible to many. But the presence of a congregation was not considered a necessary condition of the performance of the sacred offices. "On all occasions the body and soul of celebration was the singing of psalms. To render the work at once easy and more effective, the choir, or, what was often the same thing, the congregation, was invariably divided into two half choirs. These, arranged in lines on either side of the church, stood facing each other. The chief singers of each choir formed the front ranks, and the presiding presbyter at the altar appeared as standing between the two choirs. Each choir sang the successive verses alternately—a custom alluded to in a verse of Cuchuimne's hymn where the Church's praise is said to alternate—

> 'Bis per chorum hinc et inde';

and the purpose of this custom is stated—

> 'Ut vox pulset omnem aurem
> Per laudem vicariam.'

The antiphons, on the other hand, were sung by both choirs combined. The canonical posture during psalmody was standing, but when many psalms were sung the rule was to stand at one psalm and sit at the next, and so on alternately. The Prose Rule of the Culdees gives the reason —because continual standing tends to weariness, but continual sitting tends to sleep." On weekdays the worshippers knelt in prayer, but on Sundays, in obedience to the Canon of the Nicene Council, they stood erect with bowed head.

The Bible, and especially the Gospel, was emphatically to the Columbans the rule of faith,

The Celebrad. 137

Their reverence for, and implicit obedience to, the Word of God in the Gospel, which was sometimes called the "co-arb or vicar of Christ," was inherited by them from their forerunner S. Patrick. This saint would close an argument with a Scriptural quotation, adding in the same words and in the same unquestioning sense in which Luther employed them in the Marburg Conference, "God hath spoken." But the Psalter was the portion of holy Scripture most constantly used and most affectionately valued alike by clergy and laity. "Their enthusiastic but beautiful idea was to set their lives to music, so that all the actions of the members of the church should be, as it were, the rhythmic movements of a great oratorio. The moment they awoke the Song of the Lord began. Long before daylight they were in church, replenishing the fire in their hearts with coals from the altar of God. When they worked in the fields, they made the rocks and valleys ring with their sacred melodies. When they journeyed, the unutterable joy of their hearts burst into David's triumphant strains."[1]

This extraordinary delight in the exercise of psalmody and the prominence of music in the Celtic services were, no doubt, the origin of the "sang schools" established by the Church after it was Romanised; and possibly also of the deep-

[1] Lee Lecture, p. 21.

rooted prejudice, which still lingers in the Highlands, against the singing of what the Highlander calls "human hymns." Yet a dislike of hymns was no feature of this early Church. Subordinate to the Psalms they were freely used; and the "Altus" is only one specimen of many which Columba himself composed for public worship. The service also included what may be called Responsories—apparently a kind of short anthem, of a few verses of a psalm or passage of Scripture, in which one of the verses recurred as a refrain. The Lord's Prayer, the Trisagion, the Gloria in Excelsis, and the Amen, were sung by all the people. The Lessons of Scripture were read at the principal services, the first from the Old and the second from the New Testament on weekdays; the first from the Epistles and the second from the Gospels on Sundays. The version from which these lessons were read would appear to have been one which, judging from the Scriptural quotations found in early Gaelic literature, can be identified neither with the "Vetus Itala" nor the Vulgate, but which must have been in current use throughout the native British churches.

In their liberal use of the Bible, as in the congregational psalmody, and also in the free introduction of extempore prayer, the Celtic ritual stood quite apart from the Roman. Although there were prayers and collects proper to the day and hour—most of them addressed to Christ Himself, the risen and exalted Lord—the worship was not confined to these forms. The utmost reverence of demeanour was rigidly observed. "Yawning, sleeping, smiling, and all offensive sounds, especially during prayer, were severely punished. In a church founded by Finan the Leper, the apostle of Deeside, any one who became drowsy was ducked in the waters of the neighbouring lake, because Finan said his church was built for prayer, not for sleep."[1] Somnolency was all the more inexcusable, because the lively variety of the worship, the brevity of the several acts, and the interspersion of singing, praying, and reading, were calculated to keep up a constantly invigorated attention. One of the principal prayers was the Intercession, in which it is noteworthy that in no known example is there a prayer for the Pope, or for the dead in such terms as to imply belief in the doctrine of Purgatory. A sign of the absence of the Mariolatry common in the Roman Church is that the Ave Maria has no place in the Celtic ritual, except as the Antiphon to the Magnificat.[2]

In the early Scottish Church, as in all the apostolic Churches, the Eucharist was the highest religious solemnity. It was commonly called the *Oiffrenn* or Offering, but also the Spiritual or

[1] Lee Lecture, p. 27.   [2] Ibid., p. 33.

Mystic Sacrifice, the Holy Oblation, or the Mass. It was usually celebrated every Sunday, but in great churches daily, and followed the ordinary Celebrad of the third hour. The ideas of oblation and of communion appear to have been combined in it. The word sacrifice was equally applied to that offering of the elements which was made to God, and that which was received by the communicant. The sacrament was administered in both kinds; the bread was unleavened. There is no suggestion in the liturgical language, or in the mode of administration, of any belief in a corporeal presence, or a miraculous transubstantiation. The officiating clergy and their assistants entered the church processionally, bringing in the sacred vessels, the elements, and the books, with grave ceremonial. The holy table, or altar, as it was called, covered with a white linen cloth, stood at the east end of the church, and the priest beside it.[1] The liturgy of the Oiffrenn began with the Confession and a prayer for par-

---

[1] "The position of the celebrant was before the altar (*ante altare*) —that is to say, facing the altar, and with his back to the congregation." So says Warren, p. 3, and I own this was my own impression; but I am shaken in it by Mr MacGregor's assertion that "the eastern side of the altar was reckoned its front, and there the priest stood during the service." He adduces reasons for this conclusion stronger than Mr Warren's for the opposite. If Mr MacGregor is right, then the Celtic celebrant and the Bishop of Rome were at this point in accordance. In S. Peter's the Pope celebrates standing behind the altar and looking down the nave.

don and peace, followed by the Introit from the choir, while the elements were arranged on the altar. After this the priest recited the preface and collect proper to the day and the "Commemoration." Then followed the epistle; an anthem; the "Half-Uncovering," or lifting of the outer of two veils which had been laid over the elements on the altar; the Gospel, read by the deacon; and the offertory; and on special occasions a sermon from one of the priests, which concluded with a prayer, "conceived" (to use a phrase familiar at a much more recent date) by the preacher. Next came the singing of the Nicene Creed. During the offertory the deacon removed the inner veil ("the Full-Uncovering") from the elements, and after sundry other observances the Immolation or Action Prayer was repeated, amid the deepest stillness and display of profound reverence on the part of the congregation. The details at this point are so singular that I must quote them in full from Mr MacGregor's narrative.

The Immolation, which was preceded by the Sursum Corda, "consisted," he says, "of three great parts and acts — viz., 1, the *Actio gratiarum* or Thanksgiving; 2, the Consecration; 3, the Great Oblation. It was invested with awful solemnity, and all present were bound to concentrate upon it all their attention, and to take part in it with the most profound reverence. Especially at the words of institution, every person present was obliged to preserve deathlike stillness under heavy penalties, so as not to disturb the priest, for it was reckoned essential to his office to recite these words with his mind wholly fixed upon God. If he stammered, or altered even unintentionally the traditional arrangements of the sacred words, his punishment was for the first offence fifty lashes, for the second a hundred, and for the third imprisonment on bread and water for a certain period. Our forefathers were stern men, and for carelessness or presumption on the part of a clergyman their first remedy was the lash. Opposite the sacred words on the margin of the Service-Book there was written, in bold characters, the ominous word PERIL; hence the formula was often called the Perilous Prayer (*Oratio Periculosa*). If the Church's regulations, however, were observed, as they probably always were, the Immolation, united as it was supposed to be with the most exalted worship of the angelic armies and the whole Church in heaven and earth, flowed forcefully on like the roll of a mighty anthem, swelling and swelling till it reached its climax in the Great Oblation."[1]

The service proceeded, in a combination of

[1] Lee Lecture, p. 49.

The Act of Communion.

prayer, versicles, anthem, words and acts of adoration, full of devout symbolism (as when after a brief paraphrase of our Lord's command, "This do in remembrance of Me," the people bowed the knee while the priest "took three steps backwards, bowed thrice in token of sorrow for the sins of mankind, and then, by three steps forward, returned to his place at the altar"), till, lifting the paten and chalice, the priest in "the Great Oblation" offered the elements to God the Father, with an appropriate prayer. Then followed the Fraction, with much symbolic detail; the Collect, and the Pater Noster, sung by the people, without the doxology and Amen; the Sacramental Benediction, and finally the Act of Communion. The celebrant himself first partook in both kinds; and next administered to the other clergy, while a hymn beginning, "Come, ye saints, receive the body of Christ, and drink the blood by which ye have been redeemed," was sung, during which the rest of the communicants drew near to the altar, where, standing, they received the bread from the priest, or the bishop if he was present, and the cup from the deacon —to whom the charge of the cup was specially assigned. When all had received, the celebrant delivered a brief exhortation and a short prayer of thanksgiving, and then dismissed the congregation with the words, "Mass is ended: depart in peace."[1]

The sermon, which accompanied the eucharistic service, or which, on occasion, formed by itself the body of a non-eucharistic service, was sometimes read, sometimes delivered without notes. The Gaelic preacher, like Origen, was not content to extract a onefold lesson from his text. He was expected to expound its literal, its spiritual, and its moral, meaning; and the value of the discourse depended on the skill and unction with which it was treated under the second of these heads.[2] It is evident that the Columban preachers—like their Gaelic successors in modern times—dealt much in warnings and appeals, addressed to the excitable temperaments and warm imaginations of their hearers. "Some preachers first enlarged in terrifying accents on the necessity of repentance, and then encouraged their hearers by the promises of God. Some, giving scope to their perfervid imaginations, enlarged the sayings of Scripture into vivid pictures of the judgment, the glories of heaven, and the terrors of hell. Subjected to these floods of fiery eloquence, even the stolid and haughty Picts often wept and

---

[1] All these particulars are to be found in the Gaelic Tract published, with a translation, in the 'Transactions of the Aberdeen Ecclesiological Society' for 1896.

[2] Lee Lecture, p. 45.

wailed aloud, and beat their breasts, and sang for joy."[1]

We have not sufficient information to warrant a description of the mode of administering the sacrament of baptism; or an exact estimate of the extent to which the doctrine of baptismal regeneration had affected the Scottish theology. The administration so differed from the Roman rite that it was not only regarded as irregular, but of doubtful validity, by Theodore, the Roman Archbishop of Canterbury towards the end of the seventh century. The Stowe Missal (the earliest surviving missal of the Irish Church) contains an " Ordo Babtismi," which, presumably, is at least akin to the type generally adopted among the Scots not only of Erin but of Alban. It is obviously appropriate for use only in the case of adult baptism, which no doubt was generally that of a convert from paganism, and may not have been employed in other circumstances. It includes an office for the admission of the catechumen and his post-baptismal communion, as well as for baptism proper. The whole is marked with an admixture of more or less superstitious or unreasonably symbolical matter, as in the prayer for the consecration of

---

[1] Celtic Inheritance, &c., p. 40. I demur to the epithet "stolid"; and the alleged effects of the preaching contradict the idea that it is applicable here.

the water and the salt; for the expulsion of the demons (like the exorcism, a relic of the pestilent dualism of the East); the anointing of sundry parts of the body with oil; the signing with the cross not only on the forehead, but on the right hand; the feet-washing, &c. The phrase "the water of regeneration," and the prayer that, "renewed of water and the Holy Spirit," the baptised, having put off the old man, may put on the new, no doubt suggest the doctrine of baptismal regeneration, but in a sense not objectionable when applied to the baptism of an adult; and the impressive elaboration of the whole service may have been carefully designed to intensify the sentiments of awe and solemn responsibility with which the catechumen presented himself for his formal reception into the Church. Throughout it gives evidence of being drawn from other than Roman sources. And in this connection we may note that no trace exists proving the use of incense in the Celtic ritual; and that although confession was practised, it was not made in private, nor required as a necessary preparative for the Communion.[1]

The question inevitably suggests itself, In what language were these services conducted? This, no

---

[1] The *anamchara* or soul-friend—the relation in which Molassius of Inismurray stood to Columba ere he crossed to Iona—was, in point of fact, the "confessor."

Use of Latin Tongue. 147

doubt, was mainly Latin. "Whatever may have been done by 'seculars,'" Mr MacGregor writes, "in monasteries most of the services were in Latin. This does not mean that they believed in saying their services in a dead language. Latin at that time was very much alive. It was a vernacular, as much as English is in Scotland to-day. It was the vernacular of North Italy, France, Spain, and North Africa; and it was the recognised language of South Britain. It was a spoken, living, fireside language. Whoever did not understand it was really uncivilised. . . . No mortal man would have thought of writing or using a mass in Punic, or Celtic, or Belgic, or Aquitanian, or Allemanian, or Frisian, or Saxon. No man *thought* in these languages regarding religion. Of course the Scots adopted Latin as the religious language. They said mass in it, and sang the Psalms in it. They talked of religion in it. It was taught and used in the schools, &c., not as an ancient tongue, but as a then modern language. It was found very convenient to have a common language, for while there were many different languages in the British Isles, each had its very various dialects. Even now the Gaelic of Cork is scarcely intelligible in the north of Ireland; and although almost the same orthography is used, is altogether a foreign language in Sutherland.

The very reason why so many Irish Picts came as missionaries to Scotland (more correctly Pictland) was doubtless to be found in the linguistic difficulty, for the Irish Dalriadic or Pictish Gaelic was practically the same as the Albanian. . . . Such institutions as Columba's were attended by a heterogeneous mass of men speaking mutually. unintelligible tongues, but all more or less accustomed from infancy to speak the Latin language." My correspondent goes on to point out that the existence of numerous Gaelic hymns, of prayers adapted to public worship, and of several litanies — such as that of Aireran the Wise in the eighth century—proves that in the services of the Church "the vernacular was mixed with Latin in a way not known to Continentals of that period. . . . The plan followed was to use the Latin prayers, psalms, &c., and to teach their meaning to the people, that they might understand them, while they freely and readily added vernacular hymns." This use of the mother tongue of the people in their religious offices, in conjunction with the canonical Latin, wise and rational as it was, may probably have been one of the "barbarous rites" which incurred the disapproval of Queen Margaret, whose enthusiasm for "Catholic" uniformity warped her judgment as to what was best for the edification of the people, and for enabling them to offer to God an intelligent as well as a devout worship.

From the sketch I have given you will gain some idea of the character of the worship of our forefathers, ere the ancient Scottish Church succumbed to the influence of Rome. Of their doctrinal convictions, as formulated in a theological system, we have little means of judging, as I have already indicated. Their most distinctive characteristic was their familiar knowledge of their Bible, and their intense deference to holy Scripture, as the supreme standard of authority in all that concerned the Christian faith. The bent of their divines was practical rather than dogmatic. Of their discipline, except in the indications of its unwarrantable severity and repulsive harshness in visiting any dereliction in ritual, we have no distinct report. But of their worship we can form a picture on which the mental eye can rest. Its offices, in their congregational character; their abundance of purely Scriptural material; their musical richness in psalmody, rhythmical canticles, and responses; their tone of fervent adoration; their imaginative symbolism; their pervading reverence, and rejoicing belief in the presence with the Church of her living Head; their rubrical precision, yet their freedom of prayer and exhortation, offer an example of a high type of Christian culture and profound devotional sentiment, but little contaminated by sacerdotal superstition or speculative error, and of singular adaptability to the spiritual needs and the religious genius of the race among whom the Church was planted by Columba, and nurtured by his successors. How far our worship has fallen below that high standard, in the lapse of centuries and amid the disastrous vicissitudes of its later developments, I do not need to point out. But it is something for the churchmen of our day that they have so goodly a standard to look back to, that, amid the bareness of our ritual and the dulness of our devotions, they may endeavour to regain its principles, and to revive some, at least, of the old Church's manifold modes of service and varieties of ministry.

LECTURE V.

THE Church of Columba was destined, ere three centuries had seen the summer's sun shine on his island sanctuary and heard the winter's storm howl above his tomb, to lose those unique characteristics whose outlines we have traced. The Roman influence, with its external uniformities, its prelacy, its cold disregard of national individuality, was destined, following up its success at Whitby, to advance northward from its Anglican headquarters, and to gain a mastery, first in the regions where Kentigern's evangelisation had laid the foundations of the Church; in Lothian and the south-east, where Cuthbert had lived and laboured; and later, throughout the whole of Alban. That influence, essentially the same under its successive manifestations, from these early days down to the "Oxford movement" of the nineteenth century, has always reached our country from the south of the Tweed. On its first invasion, it found elements of weakness in the Scottish Church which lent themselves to its triumph. The monastic system, under which the Church had developed that high ideal of which I have spoken, was unable to adapt itself effectively to the changes that began to affect the civil and social condition of the people. It lacked the coherence and the power that come from unity.

It is during the period in which this defect becomes most noticeable, that we mark the frequent recurrence of a name which has been the subject of much antiquarian interest, and the theme of much learned debate—"the Culdees." It has afforded a kind of battle-ground for the discussion of prolonged arguments as to whether Presbytery or Episcopacy was the original form of Scottish Church government. The dispute loses its interest when we discover that neither of them, as we understand them now, had anything to do with that government. The Columban Church knew nothing of diocesan bishops on the one hand, or of kirk-sessions and presbyteries on the other; and the Culdees throw no light whatever on the question of the relative merits of Presbytery and Episcopacy, or of their relation to the Scottish Church. As to the signification of the name itself there is a controversy, I suppose still surviving — for such

The Culdees. 153

controversies tend to become interminable — as to whether it means *servus Dei* or *cultor Dei*. In the English and Irish records we find the latter idea predominate; the word used in these being *colideus*, from *colo* and *Deus*, and reproducing the classic phrase, as we know it, for example, in Horace's "parcus deorum cultor et infrequens." Hector Boece and George Buchanan in their histories followed this example, shortening the word into *Culdeus*, whence the common form Culdee. But in the old Scottish records it wears a different garb: it is there "*keledeus*"—the *kele* representing not the Latin *colo*, but the Celtic *kelei*, a servant, and meaning therefore not *cultor Dei*, a worshipper of God, but *servus Dei*, a servant of God; or, as some render the phrase, a spouse of God. This seems the preferable etymology, not only because it is reasonable to suppose that a name familiar to a Celtic people, and popularly designating persons well known among them, is more likely to be derived from a Gaelic than from a Latin etymon; but because the word conveys, more exactly than its classical counterpart, the idea which suggested its use. *Cultor Dei* was a general term which might be applied to any worshipper of God; but *servus Dei* had a specific meaning which was only appropriated to a certain class of worshippers. That class was composed of those who followed the anchorite life.

The caves of the Scottish "deserts" and the beehive cells, the remains of which may still be seen in Eilean Naomh and other Hebridean isles, bear witness to the long survival, in the West, of the mode of religious life which had travelled thither from the East. They are the memorials of the same idea that animated the oriental hermits, and peopled with these devotees the Nitrian solitudes and the Vale of Meteora. Such was the exaggerated value attributed to this species of religious seclusion and self-discipline, that in the heyday of the monastic enthusiasm "*servire Deo*" meant to forsake the world and enter the cell or the cloister. Thus the Pictish Chronicle, wishing to state the fact that in his latter days King Constantine withdrew from public life and joined a fraternity of Culdees, says, "In senectute decrepitus baculum cepit, et *Domino servivit*." The statement "servivit Domino" was equivalent to saying (at that date) that he became a Culdee. It was the highest — the ideal — form of service of God. The earliest instances in which we find the name employed in Scotland are in Jocelin's Life of Kentigern, where the term Keledei is used to describe a religious society of men (altogether, observe, unconnected with Iona) living together, each in his separate cell, under a common superior. There was, he says (though the fact

The Culdees. 155

is doubtful), such a society at Glasgow in Kentigern's time.

Such societies were not peculiar to the Celtic Church, whether in Ireland or Scotland. They were more or less known in Ireland, in Southern Britain, and throughout the continent of Europe. On the Continent, however, their position differed from that of the societies in Ireland and Scotland. In the system of the Roman Church monasticism — whatever its special type — was an organisation within the Church, but in subordination to a hierarchy of secular clergy — *i.e.*, of clergy who were not necessarily monks, and who derived their authority from an ecclesiastical and not a monastic source. In Ireland and Scotland monasticism was not a mere feature of the Church, or an institution within it. The Church was wholly monastic, and governed on monastic principles. There was thus the stronger tendency, on the part of any religious body, to draw together in a kind of monastic association, as did the Culdees, who were what we may call mere voluntaries or independents, clerics under no monastic vow or rule, and yielding no allegiance to Iona or any other recognised authority. It was inevitable, therefore, in these circumstances, that as Roman influence grew, and the rule of an episcopal hierarchy began to be urged as the only canonical government of the Church, the most zealous efforts on the part of the ecclesiastical authorities, who looked to Rome as their metropolis, should be directed to the reduction of the solitaries and cœnobites to canonical conformity. A rule, or canon, of this conformity was first elaborated by Chrodigang, Bishop of Metz, in 747, who founded the institution of what were called "secular canons," or clergymen, who, though not monks, should observe a rule which might bring their lives into a closer uniformity with each other, and a more orderly agreement with one model than hitherto. The hermits and cœnobites of Ireland — who, like their Scottish brethren, it must be remembered, were not necessarily monks of any regular order, although adopting a monastic mode of life — accepted the rules of Chrodigang, or others of a similar character, early in the ninth century; and about the same time, or a little later, these were introduced into Scotland, and were, presumably, adopted by many, if not most, of the Culdees. We find Wyntoun, the Prior of Lochleven, designating the Keledei by the name of "secular canons," indicating thereby that, though not monks of a regular order, they had adopted the canons of Chrodigang.

We may conclude, therefore, that the title Culdee, which originally and strictly described the hermit, or solitary, who resorted to the desert, or its nearest equivalent the lonely island or remote glen, to live there the ascetic life, was applied also later to the cœnobite, who associated himself with others in their effort to live out of and above the world, and continued to be so applied after these cœnobites had been brought so far into line with the secular priesthood as to accept the secular canons, and had in fact become what we should call, popularly, *Clergymen.* In later days the name was used with considerable latitude, as applicable alike to the solitary or the cœnobite; to the regular or the secular; but, however employed, it seems always to have had some reference to the hereditary connection or tradition of the person whom it designated, marking him as one who had a sympathy with the distinctive Columban methods and usages, as differentiated from those of Rome,—with the Celtic race and type, as opposed to the Saxon and Norman.

The existence of these Culdees in organised societies of their own, and their expressly religious or clerical character, were, after the expulsion of the Columban monks from Pictland, taken advantage of by the founders of churches in order to provide ministers for the necessary services. Mylne, a canon of Dunkeld, in his Lives of the Bishops of Dunkeld, states that King Constantine, the founder, placed in that church religious men who were popularly called Keledei, otherwise Colidei; and these, he intimates, conducted the services of the church. He also mentions that, like the priests of the Oriental Church, they were married men — another point which emphasises the practical divergence between the Celtic Church and the Church of Rome; for though celibacy was not absolutely imposed upon the clergy till the second Lateran Council in 1139, it was regarded in the Roman Church as an all but essential element in its discipline and order. The old Celtic idea and practice were much less rigorous; and the many Scottish patronymics, which attest a clerical or Culdee descent, bear no stigma of illegitimacy. Indeed, had any disgrace been associated with these names, they would never have been assumed. Thus we have M'Nab, the son of the abbat; M'Briar, the son of the prior; M'Taggart, the son of the priest; M'Kellar, the son of the superior; M'Vicar, the son of the vicar; M'Pherson, the son of the parson; M'Anaspie, the son of the bishop; M'Clery, the son of the clerk; and, more suggestive than any of an origin in Culdee times, M'Gilchrist, the son of the "ghillie" of Christ.

This fact of the married life of the Culdees, however, marks the distinct difference between them and the early members of the Columban orders, among whom celibacy was the rule. But the Culdee, although a Celt and traditionally attached to the usages of Iona, and bearing a name which had at first signified a specially ascetic and undomestic life, had not preserved the asceticism in its original force and purity. Nor was there for the Culdees any one great centre and authoritative Scottish standard of monasticism, to which they could refer or submit themselves, even had they wished. Iona had been despoiled and its community broken up. Dunkeld had never gained the same spiritual ascendancy that had belonged to the seat of the first great abbat. The supremacy which Columba had exercised was now little more than a tradition. In a country almost wholly Christianised there was not the old call for heroic missionary enterprise; and there was no one great spiritual leader, to gather round him a monastic family and to evoke the enthusiasm of his followers. The marriage of the clergy (for, as I have said, we may call the Culdees by that name) had, in one respect, a disintegrating effect on the discipline and on the endowments of the Church. It tended to create a set of hereditary clerics who, for convenience' sake or motives of family advantage, rather than in virtue of personal qualifications, handed on their incumbencies from father to son, and assumed office without "spiritual collation," and at the institution of a lay patron. It tended equally to the alienation of ecclesiastical property, as the hands of the family at large could not always be kept off the possessions, which ought to have descended with the title or cure.

The state of St Andrews in S. Margaret's day will serve as an example of what was common throughout the Culdee churches. The old endowments of the monastery founded there by King Angus were in lay hands. The "oblations of the altar," as the offerings and dues of the Church were called, were divided among several persons, of whom one was the "Epscop Alban," Bishop of Alban; some were married officials, apparently laymen; and the services of the church, such as they were, were performed by a prior and twelve canons cleric, or Culdees, who held their benefices by hereditary right, or "carnal succession," as the phrase went. The religious persons, who at first had formed in their association a priestly or clerical caste, with a profession of superior unworldliness and piety, had degenerated to a caste of another sort—of persons who seem to have traded on their religious character, in order to support their families. The degeneracy was the natural result of lack of strict control and absence of central authority, and of the obligation to regular and continuous duty. It was a natural result in a Celtic community.

The Celtic Church was stamped with the Celtic character, which is full of noble daring, of visionary fervour, of capacity for personal devotion and self-sacrifice; but is rarely equal to sustained exertion—prone in solitude and ease to lapse into indolence and content—requiring the stimulus of rivalry with others, or the pressure of a master's will, to rouse it to systematic labour. The Celt, left to himself, is apt to become indifferent to progress, and lives rather in the memory of the past than in the activities of the present. If he is deprived of his leader—be the leader his priest or his chief—his strength and energy are sapped. The Celtic race is possessed more strongly, perhaps, than any other, by what we may call the patriarchal instinct. If you would sway a Celt, you must appeal to him through his chief, or leader. Him he will follow when he will follow none else. He will go with the family or the clan whither it goes: he will obey the word of the head of the family or the clan, whatever it command him. The monastic system appealed to this instinct. The monastery—like that of Clonard in Ireland, or of S. David in Wales, or of Iona—was the home of a great religious family, at the head of which stood the abbat. They came and went at his command: now he led them forth in person to some strath or island, specially dangerous or desolate, as when Columba made his way to the court of the pagan Brude, or landing from his coracle faced the wild boar of Skye; now he remained behind to show hospitality and preach the Word, in their absence, and to pray for their safeguard from the perils that beset the heralds of the Cross. In many cases the authority of the abbats had the twofold sanction of ecclesiastical pre-eminence and personal rank. Several of them, like Columba himself—such as Fillan, Cormac, Modan, and others—were of princely lineage, and added the claim of hereditary rank to the dignity of spiritual chieftainship.

The Abbat of Iona was the Primate of Scotland, because he was the spiritual chief of the Celts. The other abbats, under that primacy, were, each, the spiritual chieftains of their monasteries, and of the regions around these. The monks were under them like a regiment under its commander, ready to go anywhere or do anything at his command. But when the commander had fallen, or had gone away, or no longer personally led them, the regiment fell into lax and careless ways. The old *esprit de corps* and its accompanying loyalty and irresistible energy were gone. We see this illustrated in the fortunes of the Church in those times in which the Culdees were most numerous, and had gained prominence in the Church. They were times of slow decadence and gradual disorganisation, alike in the old monastic foundations and in the Culdee communities. The old fire had burnt out. The Church wanted *solidarité*, and union within itself. The solitary instance of united action on its part, in the Council of Scone, appears to have originated not with the Culdees or the monks, but with the temporal monarch on the one hand and the head of the gradually advancing body of secular clergy on the other—the king and the Bishop of Alban. The Celtic Church was drooping just because it was Celtic—because it lacked nerve and energy to grapple with the religious wants of a rapidly developing nationality—because it clung to the form of its old monastic methods, after these had lost their spirit and had ceased to be effective, and when the tribal and local peculiarities on which they were based, and to which in earlier times they had been well adapted, were year by year being absorbed in the forms, if not of a higher, yet of a more comprehensive, civilisation.

The religion of Scotland, in fact, instead of owing purity and vigour to the Culdees, was stagnating around their settlements, and was in danger of permanent decay, when God's providence brought into our country a fresh and reviving influence, under which that religion was to recover some, at least, of its former vitality and to renew its life, though the life was to flow in new channels, and to develop under an organisation to which it had not hitherto adapted itself. This change and revival came about towards the end of the eleventh century, and is associated with the saintly name of Margaret, Queen of Malcolm Canmohr.

Out of the mists of legend and fable that lie thick over the heights and levels of that distant era rises, with exceptional distinctness, the figure of Malcolm Canmohr — Malcolm with the big head—the son of "the gracious Duncan." He was but a child at the date of his father's assassination by Macbeth; and many years passed ere time brought about revenge and restitution. Duncan was slain in the year 1040: Malcolm was crowned at Scone on the festival of S. Mark, in April 1057.

The kingdom was beginning to consolidate, though it was yet but limited and disorderly, bounded on the south by lines equivalent to those of the present Border, but on the north and west encroached upon by the petty territories of turbulent earls and mormaers, who maintained an unruly and pugnacious independence. Malcolm discerned the weakness and danger which must threaten both kingdom and dynasty from these restless neighbours; and set himself to reduce their strength, while he concentrated and enlarged the power of the Crown. At the same time, he welcomed to his dominions the exiles whom the strifes and intrigues of the Saxons, and afterwards the advance of the conquering Normans, drove to seek refuge beyond the Tweed. Nor did he fail to take the opportunity, afforded by the intestine troubles of Northumbria, to push his frontier southwards. The region between the Humber and the Tweed was the theatre of perpetual turmoil and bloodshed, amid which Saxon, Dane, Norman, and Scot dealt indiscriminate ravage and slaughter. The victory of Hastings gave Norman William no secure hold over this ill-used debatable land; and it was again and again wasted by Danish piracy, Northumbrian insurrection, and Scottish foray.

On one of his inroads Malcolm met his future queen, as she waited with her disinherited family at Wearmouth, for a fair wind to carry them out of the kingdom her brother had lost. The Scottish king offered the royal fugitives an asylum within his dominions. They had thought of retiring to Hungary, where Edgar's father had found shelter during the tyranny of Canute, and where he and his sisters had been brought up; but they accepted Malcolm's promise of a nearer refuge, and agreed to come to Scotland.

The result was their arrival, by-and-by, at Dunfermline; and finally, Malcolm's asking the Saxon princess to share his throne. Her brother was, against the advice of his friends, averse to her marrying the Scottish king, and at first she recoiled from it herself. She had seen enough of the stormy and distracted world, with its factions and battles, intrigues and murders. Young as she was, she had known the peril and bitterness of exile, of war, of homelessness, of disinheritance, of flight from enemies by land and sea. After all the restless tumult and confusion, the only note of peace was rung in her memory by the convent bells of Hungary. She and her sister made up their minds to seek the calm haven of the Church. Her sister, Christina, carried out her purpose and became the "bride of Christ"; but another destiny was reserved for Margaret. After a brief delay, she yielded to Malcolm's suit. The wedding was celebrated at Dunfermline with all the magnificence which the unrefined Scottish Court could display. This was in the year 1070; Margaret was about twenty-four years of age, and Malcolm some ten years older. They took up their abode at the King's Tower, which was enlarged and beautified, and of which a broken fragment still may be seen within the demesne of Pittencrieff. And from this "city set on a hill"—this stronghold of "grey Dunfermline"—the light of Margaret began to shine, graciously and beneficently, over her husband's realm.

Like all good women, she first shed her influence on her own home. Malcolm lived among his rugged chiefs, with little of the grace or culture of a Court about him or his retainers. Hard fighting and rough living were more familiar to them than domestic quiet or social intercourse. Even the king, though he could speak both the Latin and Saxon tongues, could neither read nor write.

Into this rude and churlish circle Margaret, like a second Una, brought the unconscious charm of her own purity, piety, and refinement. Her religion was the ruling principle of her life; and it was not with her, as it was with the later queen, whose name alone has left a deeper mark on Scottish annals, a ritual and a policy—it was a force, a passion. It was in most of its outward features very different from the religion of our day, which has, perhaps, lost as much in spiritual intensity as it has gained in intellectual breadth. Her love of relics, and special devotion to the jewelled crucifix, with its shred of the true cross, which accompanied her from Hungary, and which was reverenced for generations in Scotland as the "Black Rood"; her washing and kissing the feet of the poor; her night-long vigils in the church, "herself assisting at triple matins—of the Trinity, of the Cross, and of S. Mary—and afterwards repeating the Psalter, with tears bedewing her raiment, and upheaving her breast,"—these bear to us, whose theory and practice are less rigorous and more "enlightened," an aspect of almost superstitious zeal. We are tempted to think of her, as of S. Elizabeth of Hungary, as a morbid devotee: yet the religion thus expressed was of the sincerest and most self-sacrificing character, and fitted to impress the spirit of the age, as no less demonstrative devotion could have impressed it. It wrought upon the bold and generous nature of the king like a humanising spell. Fearless and warlike in the field, and ready as ever to encounter the foe, he set the example in his palace of the decorous and charitable life of a Christian knight. The home of the king of Scotland, under her influence, began for the first time to wear the aspect, never afterwards lost, of the residence, not of a mere chief amidst his retainers, but of a feudal sovereign, surrounded by the chivalry of a settled and polished Court.

In two wide spheres beyond the palace gates the influence of Margaret was soon recognised as "quick and powerful." These were the national policy and the Church.

As regarded the first of these, the two principles she held by were industry and order. It is somewhat difficult after more than seven centuries to distinguish, with exactness, between the measures of Margaret and those of her illustrious and like-minded son David, but we are tolerably certain that the spirit which originated the policy that was carried to its completion by the son was the mother's; and that he, like his father, had learned the truth of the old Saxon belief that " something divine dwelt in the counsels of woman "— and especially of this one woman. While Malcolm strove to consolidate the royal power and to extend the area in which it was supreme, Margaret invited the settlement within that area of her own countrymen, and others from foreign lands, whose industry and skill stimulated those of the natives, and gradually raised the character and the value of Scottish produce and handicraft. She did all that royal patronage could do to encourage traders from Continental ports to visit Scotland. To the impetus thus given to commerce and manufactures is directly referable the growth of those burghs and guilds, to which David afterwards granted charters, and which became the nursing mothers of traffic and enterprise, of civil liberty and popular rights.

Although the formal and regular administration of justice and the construction of a code of laws were, in Margaret's day, still but promises of the future, the idea of them was familiar to her love of order and of peace; and here, too, David was afterwards able to realise the prophetic visions of his mother. We trace to her the beginning and suggestion of the great popular movement, if we may so call it, which by degrees was to substitute the robust and practical civilisation of the Anglo-Saxon for the more visionary and graceful culture of the Celt; to introduce, among the less coherent elements of national life in Scotland, the Norman system of organisation and of feudal interdependence ; and thus out of the cluster of tribes and races over which Malcolm's predecessors had held uncertain sway, to form one homogeneous nation. All this, perfected by David, was commenced by Margaret.

It was, however, as a Church reformer Margaret achieved her greatest work.

The Whitby Conference, from which Colman of Lindisfarne retreated indignantly to Iona, had committed the Anglo-Saxon Church to the discipline and unity of Rome. The Church in Scotland remained true to the traditions of Columba, and long continued to exhibit the Celtic characteristics with which his apostolic force and fervour had imbued it at the first. As Margaret's era approaches, we see the Church still Celtic in character, though more tinged than of old with Roman ideas and practices, and materially strengthened by the possession of substantial endowments. The centres of such religious life and light as existed were beside the Culdee colleges or convents—at St Andrews, Lochleven, Monymusk, Abernethy, Dunkeld, Dunblane, and elsewhere. But the clergy had fallen behind the age. Isolated from the general interests and movements of the Church Catholic, the Scottish Church, which has in its later age been so often rent with schisms, then stood in peril of the sectarianism of tribal and local rivalries, and the blight of an unenlightened provincialism. Usage was lax—authority was vague—life was indolent—thought was unproductive. Not only the Church but religion was in danger, and Margaret set herself to the task of reformation.

One might have expected that the zeal of a queenly devotee would have shown itself in lavish endowments, or benefactions to the clergy. But Margaret and her husband did comparatively little for the Church, in the way of bestowing worldly goods. Her love of the Church and religion was manifested in a more thoughtful way than in mere buildings and gifts. The richer a corrupt Church is, the more infectious grows the corruption. Margaret knew she might leave the endowing of the Church to her children, if she helped to make it worthy of their love and care. Her concern was to reform its usages, and to regulate its orders into harmony with the discipline of Rome. She began with the practical point of erroneous usage. As perhaps was natural in a female reformer, questions of mere ritual were dealt with as earnestly as those of deeper moral meaning. One of her most solemn conferences with the clergy was occupied with the discussion of the right day for beginning the austerities of Lent—in the practice of which the queen was rigidly scrupulous. The king acted as interpreter between her and the Celtic clergy, who knew no Saxon, and for no less than three days " did she employ the sword of the Spirit in combating their errors." "Often," says Turgot enthusiastically, " have I heard her, with admiration, discourse of subtle questions of theology in presence of the most learned men of the kingdom." So gifted a royal disputant was certain to prevail, and Margaret's three days' debate ended in her persuading the clergy to forsake the ancient usage, and to adopt that which Rome had introduced about two hundred years before, of beginning Lent on Ash Wednesday, instead of on the Monday following Quadragesima Sunday.

The Lord's Day had come to be little regarded. The people went about their work and their pleasure on that day as on any other day of the week. The queen remonstrated and urged, until the day was kept with decent propriety, as a day of rest and of religious observance. In Columba's time the "Dies Dominica" was observed as a day of special religious services; but Saturday was still regarded, as by the Jews, as the day of rest—the Sabbath. Thus Columba on the day before his death said, "This day is called the Sabbath; and indeed it is to me a Sabbath, for it is the last day of my laborious life." This usage no doubt accounted for the practice of using Sunday, except as regarded its public solemnities, like any other day, for work or pleasure.

Superstitions about the Lord's Supper, which linger in the Highlands to this day,[1] were rife among the Celtic priests. Some would not celebrate the holy sacrament at all, on the plea of dreading to communicate unworthily. They quoted to Margaret S. Paul's warning against so communicating. "If none but the worthy are to partake," said the queen, "then no one dare, for no one is sinless." Her arguments at this point too prevailed; as also in inducing the clergy to abandon (so at least we gather from Turgot's language) most of those national peculiarities in which theirs differed from the Roman, which to her was the type of the perfect, ritual. The loose system of marriage also felt her correcting hand;

[1] In the Synod of the Free Church of Sutherland and Caithness the Free Church minister at Dornoch stated that in his congregation of 1200 there were only 100 communicants. —'North Star,' 16th April 1896.

and it was no longer possible for a man to wed his stepmother, his brother's widow, or within the like prohibited degrees, as hitherto.

Reforms such as these, touching so closely ecclesiastical usage and domestic life, must have been as difficult as they were necessary, and called for no common firmness, wisdom, and tact, in their execution. But what Margaret, as a Churchwoman, most desired was to do for the Scottish what Wilfrid had done for the Anglo-Saxon Church—to release it from the Columban tradition, and to complete its union with Rome. The lax orders of the Culdees were letting Church property slip away to secular use and possession. The absence of recognised authority was engendering an easy and worldly mode of life. Norman feudalism was close at hand, ready to "grip greedily" the abbey or convent lands, which had lapsed or were lapsing to laymen. The old tribal episcopacy, or the jurisdiction of the Columban abbats, was incapable of ruling a Church into which Saxon and Norman ideas had begun to penetrate. The queen's plan for keeping the ecclesiastical property together, and for providing a regulated government in the Church, for the security both of discipline and faith, was to weld it into the "Catholic" unity, at the head of which stood the successor of S. Peter. Moreover, under a monarchy which, year by year, was surrounding itself more formally with the orderly gradations of rank associated with feudalism and chivalry, a reverend hierarchy tended to lend greater dignity to society and support to the throne than the simple grades of the Culdee communities. Not improbably, besides all this, Margaret, like most pious women, had that secret love and reverence for spiritual authority, which delights in exalting its possessors. Educated too, as she had been, in Hungary, and not unfamiliar with English life, she could not fail to see how widespread and how potent was the influence of the Roman hierarchy and system. Roman ecclesiasticism was destined to mould and govern the Western Churches for the next four hundred years, and Margaret was determined that Scotland should be weaned from its Celtic isolation. Neander laments the sacrifice of local freedom involved in universal submission to the central power; but the loss, she believed, would be compensated by the more uniform order and discipline—the healthier energy—the wider sympathy and community of interest, which were attained by union.[1]

It is noticeable that in her conferences with the clergy, and advocacy of reforms, Margaret never hints at any irregularity in their orders. This is

---

[1] Turgot's Life of Margaret, in the 'Acta Sanctorum,' is reprinted in Dr Metcalfe's edition of Pinkerton's 'Lives of the Scottish Saints,' 1889.

the more remarkable because, both in Hungary and in England, she may very probably have heard doubts expressed as to the apostolic character of the Scotic missionaries and itinerant bishops, and the validity of ordinances as administered in their Church. But if she did, she had too much common-sense to give weight to them. She accepted the ministry of the Church as she found it, though she strove to effect changes in it, as she thought, for the better. At the same time, she showed her veneration for the memory of Columba by rebuilding the monastery of Iona, which the Danes had burnt; and her respect for the true type of the secluded life, where that still survived, in its purity, either in the single cell or the cœnobite group, by kindly and pious intercourse with many of the solitaries, visiting them in their retreats, and bestowing a grant of land on the Culdee fraternity of Lochleven. She was no fanatic, no revolutionary, no irrational prelatist.

The change which she initiated was, however, a vital change; but it was effected without violence, or any visible break in the coherence of the Church's life. There was no forcible revolution—rather we may say, the Church glided out of its sequestered Celticism into the broad stream of Western Romanism, without any rupture of its continuity or erasure of its nationality. For by this time the force of the Celtic element in the life of Scotland had begun to run low. But for the changes that were modifying the character of the people, the queen could never have initiated the changes that were wrought in the character and constitution of the Church. The ecclesiastical and the national life developed together, and in harmony. The Church lost its distinctively Celtic character, which had prevailed for more than four hundred years, simultaneously with the people. The immigration, first of Saxon and then of Norman fugitives, who sought in Scotland shelter from the Conqueror's tyranny, infused new elements of race and character into the nation, hitherto predominantly Celtic. The invasion was a peaceful one: the ecclesiastical revolution that accompanied it was peaceful too. Dioceses were erected, and the rule of the diocesan bishop took the place of that of the abbat. In some cases, as at Dunkeld, the abbat became the bishop. The old Celtic monasteries, which had dwindled down and in some cases been supplanted or succeeded by Culdee settlements, were gradually replaced by regular fraternities, all of foreign origin, into which the members of the ancient order were, in some cases, quietly absorbed—to which, in others, they yielded only after long conflict of claim and jurisdiction. The formation of parishes accompanied and followed that of dioceses; and endowment supplemented parochial division. The Church thus became territorial instead of tribal; episcopal instead of abbatial: it began to own large property in the soil. Above all, it was no longer Celtic in usage and tradition, but Roman. By the end of the thirteenth century the old line of Celtic kings closed in Alexander, and the ecclesiastical transformation was complete. In its rites, doctrines, and government, the Church was much the same as all others that embraced the unity of Rome; although the supremacy of the Pope was hotly disputed by the Scottish kings, and at last only admitted in a fashion, as a protection against the worse evil of the supremacy claimed by the Archbishops of York and Canterbury, each of whom would fain have included Scotland in his province.

The transformation, however, was gradual, and proceeded mainly under the influence of Margaret's sons Alexander and David,—the latter being especially zealous—the profusion of his benefactions earning, as we know, the pithy epithet from one of his less devoted successors, of "a sair sanct for the crown."

Fothad, the last Celtic "Epscop Alban," died in the same year as Queen Margaret; but it was not till fourteen years afterwards (1107) that Alexander saw his way to nominate, for the vacant office, his mother's confessor and biographer, Turgot, Prior of Durham. We are told Turgot was "the choice of the king, the clergy, and the people," though it does not appear how their respective rights were exercised. By the clergy were, no doubt, meant the Culdees, still holding their ground at St Andrews, whom it was the royal policy to conciliate as far as possible. By the people little more can be meant than some such representation of the general opinion as was obtainable on the spot; but this recognition of the people here, as on the previous occasion of the Council at Scone, is significant as showing that in those early days the sacerdotal theory of what constitutes a Church had not established itself in Scotland. The idea of the Church was popular, not clerical; and the right of the people to a share in its management, and their assent to measures affecting its welfare, were respected by the authorities both of Church and State. This and the strongly national sentiment both of clergy and laity stand out, as characteristics marking the Church of the twelfth century as distinctly as that of the nineteenth.

The election of Turgot involved the question of the national independence of the Scottish Church. The Bishop of York, on the strength of certain passages in Pope Gregory's commission to Augustine of Canterbury, claimed that the Bishop of St Andrews, under which title Turgot was to be consecrated, should be one of his suffragans. Alexander refused to concede the claim; the Anglican bishop refused to withdraw it. There were no bishops in Scotland able, according to the now accepted Roman theory, to impart a valid consecration. The king found himself in an embarrassing dilemma; and it was finally agreed that Turgot should be consecrated, without prejudice either to the claims of York or the independence of Scotland. Consecrated he was accordingly at York on 1st August 1109, and thus began that succession of bishops of St Andrews in communion with the Church of Rome which was to last for over four centuries. The date marks the definite line of demarcation between the old Celtic Church and the Scoto-Roman, into which it was now absorbed— the same Church, but under different conditions. From the landing of Columba in Iona in 563 to this consecration of Turgot was 546 years; from the consecration of Turgot to the adoption of the Reformed Confession in 1560 was 451 years, the Celtic epoch of the Church thus exceeding the Roman by almost a century.

A similar Anglican demand was advanced when King David founded the bishopric of Glasgow. This too was claimed as suffragan by York, and the claim was again refused. Papal sanction was added to these English aggressions by a bull of Pope Adrian's, who, in the second year after David's death, charged all the holders of the bishoprics the king had founded to submit to the primacy of York. Not one of them obeyed except the Bishop of Whitherne. The see of Whitherne, owing to its intimate civil connection with England, was regarded as an allowable exception. Probably in recognition of the fact that so stubborn and independent a nationality as that of the Scots was not likely to be coerced, a subsequent Pope, Clement III., in the year 1188 addressed a bull to William the Lion, putting an end to all these Anglican assumptions, and declaring that the Church of Scotland was the "daughter of Rome by special grace, and immediately subject to her."

The right of primacy was asserted by Rome over all the national Churches, and as a rule was tacitly — if not overtly — admitted in the West; but it did not necessarily interfere with their national independence, nor did it impose any of the irritating restrictions, which subordination to a primate in a neighbouring, yet foreign, country would inevitably imply. At a subsequent date, in 1471, the Pope issued a bull erecting St Andrews into a metropolitan see, with the primacy of all Scotland.

The Pope had come to be regarded as the

source of ecclesiastical honour and jurisdiction, and therefore entitled to arrange such matters. His intervention also, as the general arbiter of Christendom, in the decision of questions like those between York and St Andrews, was not resented as an invasion of the rights of the parties interested. It practically served the purpose of a modern arbitration in an international difficulty. But the Pope's interference in the internal affairs of a national Church or State was not so readily acquiesced in, and no nation exhibited less disposition to bow to papal authority than the Scots; or perhaps it would be more accurate to say, no nation showed more determination to maintain its independence, both civil and ecclesiastical. The acknowledgments of the Pope's authority which Scotland, no doubt, made on certain occasions (as when during the disastrous invasion of Edward I. an embassy was despatched to Rome to entreat the mediation of the Holy Father, and was instructed to plead that the kingdom was a fief of the papal see), implied no spirit of submission to the Papacy, but only served a diplomatic purpose in a time of great extremity. There was no objection to own ecclesiastical allegiance to Rome, if doing so would stave off the intolerable usurpations of England; nor was there reluctance to recognise the Bishop of Rome as supreme head of the Church, in the sense of his being the ultimate earthly source of spiritual authority, and as such empowered to ratify or to veto ecclesiastical appointments, to grant dispensations, to issue interdicts, and—generally—to supervise the affairs of Christendom. But any exercise of this authority which trenched on the rights of the crown, the clergy, or the people, or threatened their independence, was resented and resisted. The spirit which withstood Edward and won the battle of Bannockburn was not dormant within the ecclesiastical sphere, and the Church, no less than the State, of Scotland, made good the sturdy motto, "Nemo me impune lacessit."

This note of self-reliant independence, of prompt disregard of any authority which outsteps its proper province and seeks to lord it over a heritage to which it has not a moral title, has always been a characteristic of the Kirk—manifesting itself occasionally, perhaps, with only too emphatic and wilful a decisiveness. There are many instances of it throughout our history, in the papal period of the Church. Let us take one: when in the year 1317 two legates from the Pope, of cardinal rank, arrived in England on the errand of restoring peace between the countries, and sent forward their letters to King Robert, the king refused to receive them because they were not addressed to him under the title of *King*. The letters from the Pope bore the superscription to "Robert Bruce, governor in Scotland." "Among my barons," said the king, "there are many of the name of Robert Bruce, who share in the government of Scotland. These letters may possibly be meant for some of them, but they are not addressed to me, who am KING of Scotland." And he firmly, though with perfect courtesy—"in an affable manner and with a pleasant countenance," reported the cardinals—declined to receive the letters. In spite of this, a subordinate member of the papal mission ventured to proclaim a truce with England and an interdict against the realm; but he was simply warned to get out of the country with all speed, and his proclamation was treated as a nullity. Amid the superstitious deference paid to the Pope and his bulls throughout Christendom, this bold attitude of the Scots says much for their intelligence and self-respect.

At no era of Scottish history was what we may call English influence more direct and potent than in the days of David, who, half an Englishman by birth, was wholly English by education, having up to the age of forty-four, when he succeeded to the Scottish throne, passed most of his life in England. The principal advisers of Margaret and David in their ecclesiastical policy were English prelates; and it was with priests of English birth and training that all the highest offices in the Scottish Church, when first organised on the Roman system, were filled. Indeed so strong were the English influence and element in the changes wrought by David, that the result has been described by a historian, though in exaggerated terms, as an "ecclesiastical revolution in which the Scottish Church was gradually overgrown by an English Church, transplanted to the northern hills, with its clergy, creeds, rites, and institutions."[1] This is an extreme way of putting it; but unquestionably the Anglican modes of thought, of social life, of ecclesiastical organisation, then gained an ascendancy that they never again possessed until after the union of the Legislatures.

Scottish influences had invaded England at a much earlier date, as we have seen, and—until their progress was stemmed at Whitby—bade fair to mould the religious life of that country to their own pattern. At Whitby commenced the reaction, which was in full flood in the reign of Margaret, and reached its height in that

[1] Quarterly Review, vol. lxxxv. p. 116. (Article by the late Joseph Robertson.)

of David. Prelatic and Romanistic principles and practices have always reached Scotland through England. When, after the Reformation, the Scottish Church had reverted to a purer type of government and ritual, we shall find that it was, as before, from England that the reactionary spirit proceeded, and its efforts to reintroduce mediævalism began; and, once more, they reached their height under a monarch who, though Scotch by birth, was, like David, English by education and association. Anglican influence, in fact, has all along been inimical to the primitive simplicity and democratic independence which have always been notes of the National Church in Scotland.

The general establishment of the system of diocesan episcopacy over the whole of Scotland was one of the most serious parts of David's work. He did what he considered was best for the exigencies of the times. The old system of government by abbats and from monasteries, as I have said, had lost its force; and as the population grew less tribal and more homogeneous and settled, it lost also its special adaptation to their circumstances. The emissary of the monastery did noble work as a missionary when Christianity was only making its way against heathenism, and civilisation was still grappling with ubiquitous forces of disorder; but he was less effective when Christianity had prevailed, when education had extended, and savage lawlessness and ignorance had succumbed to intelligence, order, and decency. The secular priest, with his own church to attend to, and his own flock to instruct, was better adapted to the altered conditions. The clearly defined area, to which the bishop's rule was restricted, gave the authority exercised within that area a force and stability, of which the absence of territorial jurisdiction deprived the authority of the abbat. We may regret that the primitive model of churches guided and governed by presbyters acting together, and seeking, when necessary, the advice of a council of the whole Church of their bounds, was not that which was reverted to by Margaret and her sons. But we may question if, among a population not yet wholly united in race and sentiment, and in a thinly peopled country, the Presbyterian system could have been as easily and thoroughly administered as the Episcopal. And, in any event, the tendency to fall into line with the common system and usage of the Church at large was probably too strong to be resisted, had David and his advisers been inclined, as they were not, to resist it.

The benefit he conferred on his kingdom by his profuse patronage of the monkery of the

Roman Church is more questionable. The ultimate failure of the monastic system of Columba, as a mode of government, did not necessarily involve a condemnation of monasticism, as a wise and salutary mode of religious life; but David might have been warned, by the sluggishness and the abuses which had crept into both classes of the older settlements, to pause ere he reintroduced monasticism, and afforded it fresh opportunities of development. At the same time, it must be remembered that, in the twelfth century, monasticism was in its richest flower. Luxury had not as yet debased the lives of the monks of those Roman orders which David domesticated in Scotland. No scandal had been laid at the convent doors. The monasteries were the homes of learning, industry, and charity. The bleak strath became a fertile valley under the conventual agriculture. The rough boors and wild clansmen grew more law-abiding and industrious, as soon as they became the tenants or retainers of the Church. Art and letters, which got but little encouragement in the feudal castle, always found a fostering shelter in the cloister. So that an enlightened, patriotic, and pious prince might not unnaturally be led to do what seemed to be the best he could do for the culture and religion of his subjects, by promoting monasticism through the length and breadth of the land. He erected and endowed the monasteries of Roxburgh, Jedburgh, Kelso, Melrose, Newbattle, Holyrood, Dryburgh, Cambuskenneth, and Kinloss—to name no others—and gave an impetus to the establishment of such houses over all the kingdom which lasted long after he was gone, with the result of rendering the monastic orders in Scotland probably richer and more numerous than in any other European country. By the date of the Reformation it was calculated they owned nearly one-half of the whole wealth of the country, and were the possessors of not less than two hundred monasteries and convents— the larger number of which belonged to the Augustinians, or Black Canons.

Without attempting active suppression, it was David's policy either to supersede the Culdee communities by the erection of the regular establishments, or to absorb their members into the monkish ranks. A nominal primacy over all the Culdees of Scotland was granted to Turgot, on his accession to the bishopric of St Andrews. The language used is, "In his days the whole rights of the Keledei throughout the whole kingdom of Scotland passed to this bishopric." But whatever power this implied was evidently exerted in a very lenient fashion; and in the case of St Andrews itself it was not till the year 1144, or thirty-five years after Turgot's election, that a priory of canons regular of S. Augustin was founded there, in the charter granted to which by David it was stipulated that the canons shall receive the Keledei of Kilrymont into the canonry, with all their possessions and revenues, if they are willing to become canons regular. If they refused, their life-interests were to be respected; but on their demise their revenues were to fall to the canonry, and as many additional canons regular were to be instituted in the Church of St Andrews as there had been Keledei.

To David also we owe the erection of our parishes. The earliest nucleus of the parish was the cell or chapel of the Columban monk, in the spot where he planted the first seeds of the Church, and which — after he was gone — was held in reverence for his sake, and was used as the place of worship for the neighbourhood. Hundreds of parishes still preserve in their names, or in the records of their dedications, the memories of the preachers who first taught in them the faith and the doctrine they had received from Columba, or those who succeeded him in Iona. The other, and later, origin of the parish was the foundation of a church by the owner of the soil. When such a church was built, its founder tithed all, or some of, his lands for its support; and the lands so tithed, or his whole property if not too extended, formed, as a rule, the parish, dependent for religious ordinances on that church. The manor and the parish were thus generally conterminous. As Christianity became more absolutely the national religion, and the Church became more homogeneous throughout the whole country, this mode of founding churches and providing for their support, for the behoof of a definite district attached to each, became more common; and in the deeds of the twelfth century we begin to meet with the term "parish" as one recognised by the law.

Consequent on the establishment of parishes, emerges into view, also in the reign of David, the practice of tithing the land for the support of their clergy. The income of the Columban communities was derived from sources independent of tithes, or, as we call them in Scotland, "teinds." The communities in some cases held lands of their own, as the monastery of Iona held that island; but their more certain and common source of income was the altar offerings, the dues paid for certain church services, and the fines levied for offences against certain laws. The regular and universal grant of tithe, which resulted from the development of the parochial system, formed the pecuniary stronghold of the secular, or parochial, clergy. In Scotland, as in England, where the grants of tithe are of earlier date, the practice of rendering the tenth to the Church originated in no statute or royal decree, but in the freewill of the owners of the soil. It found a Scriptural precedent in the Mosaic law and the usage of the Israelites, and was, indeed, one of the survivals of Judaism. Its adoption in the Scottish Church was spontaneous, and was the voluntary expression of the donor's devotion. It is worth while to remember the fact that no part of the revenue now enjoyed by the Kirk (and which forms but a small fraction of her ancient patrimony) was acquired by State legislation. It was voluntarily gifted, in compliance with a religious idea, with which public opinion was in sympathy.

A practice by-and-by came into vogue, which to a marked extent neutralised King David's laudable design in founding the monasteries. This was the donation of parish churches to the religious orders. Patrons of churches, with the consent of the bishop, conferred them on the great houses of Regulars. The abbot sent down a monk to do the duty of the parish priest, with the result that the interests of the parish were sacrificed to the monastic greed. The officiating monk, or the poorly paid vicar, took care that the tithes and dues were collected, but their destination was the conventual exchequer. As long as they reached that sanctum safely, the superiors made no troublesome inquiry about the "cure of souls." The "extra chalder" was keenly looked after. "The hungry sheep looked up, and were not fed." This abuse was one of the most patent causes of the religious deterioration, both of priest and people, which preceded the Reformation. But this was a development that good King David could not have anticipated.

Another element in the consolidation, and so-called reform, of the Church, which was definitely settled in his reign, was the Ritual. He caused the cathedral churches to fulfil what is one of the most important functions of such establishments — viz., to set the example of a decorous and uniform mode of celebrating public worship. In the Celtic Church there had been, as we have seen, much greater freedom and individuality in the forms of worship than was reconcilable with the strict order of Rome. The Celtic ritual was now disused—not compulsorily, so far as we can ascertain, but it fell out of use as part and parcel of a decaying system. Its place was taken by the Roman missal and breviary, with those modifications which had been adopted in the Cathedral of Salisbury, and which constituted what was called "The Use of Sarum." The ancient use lingered longest in the seat of the Scottish primacy. There the Culdees continued, "in a corner of their church which was very small, to celebrate their own office in their own fashion."[1] But their days, too, were numbered. In 1147 a bull of Pope Eugenius III. deprived them of their hereditary share in electing the Bishop of St Andrews. In 1220 Pope Honorius III. ordered an inquiry to be made into a dispute between the bishop, the prior, and convent of St Andrews, and the "clerics commonly called Keledei," regarding their respective possessions. The Culdee community was then called "the Provost and Culdees of the church of S. Mary." "In course of time the name of Culdee disappeared; and we meet with it for the last time in the year 1332, when their exclusion in the episcopal election is again renewed. After this we hear only of the provost and prebendaries of the church of S. Mary, sometimes styled S. Mary of the Rock." "At the Reformation the provost and twelve prebendaries still remained, the sole Scottish representatives of the once powerful Culdees."[2]

[1] Chronicle of the Picts and Scots, p. 190; Skene's ed.
[2] Bellesheim, vol. i. p. 300, and translator's note.

LECTURE VI.

THE ambition of Rome was satisfied with the success of David's policy. The Scottish Church was Romanised. Its episcopate was conformed to the Roman pattern, under a primate whose consecration had been duly effected according to the Roman canons. The free and national Church of Scotland in both its main branches —the purely Columban, and the British or Cumbrian, in which the tradition of Kentigern lingered —was parcelled into dioceses, under bishops owing allegiance to the Pope—the vicar of Christ, the successor of Peter. What that allegiance meant then, as it means now, cannot be more clearly defined than in the words of the present Pontiff, in his Encyclical of last year (1896): "It must be clearly understood that bishops are deprived of the right and power of ruling, if they deliberately secede from Peter and his successors, because by this secession they separate from the foundation on which the whole edifice itself rests, and for the very reason they are separated from the fold whose leader is the chief pastor. The episcopal order is rightly judged to be in communion with Peter as Christ commanded, if it be subject to and obeys Peter. Otherwise it necessarily becomes a lawless and disorderly crowd. It is not sufficient that the head should merely have been charged with the office of superintendent, but it is absolutely necessary that he should have received real and sovereign authority, which the whole community is bound to obey. The Roman Pontiffs, mindful of their duty, wish above all things that the divine constitution of the Church should be preserved. Therefore, as they have defended with all necessary care and vigilance their own authority, so they have always laboured, and will continue to labour, that the authority of the bishops may be upheld. Yet they look upon whatever honour or obedience is given to the bishops as paid to themselves."

The Scottish Church, however, was never, any more than the Gallican, a complaisant vassal of Rome. The sentiment of national independence was always strong, as was that spirit of freedom which breathes through the chivalrous "Aberbrothock Manifesto," in which the Scottish nobles, protesting against the papal countenance vouchsafed to the English aggressions, tell Pope John XXII. that "not for glory, riches, or honour we fight, but for liberty alone, which no good man loses but with his life."[1] Nor were the Scots blind to the frequent delinquencies and malpractices of the Roman Court —its greed of filthy lucre, its meddlesome interference with national rights, its pretensions to infallible and absolute autocracy. In the great reforming Council of Basel the Scottish Church was represented by two bishops, two abbats, two secular priests, and two friars; and we gather that these deputies supported the liberal principles of which John Gerson was the exponent, and on the critical question of the Pope's superiority to all councils took the side of independence and common-sense. On more than one occasion the intrusion of papal legates was resented, and the exactions of the Papacy were withstood.

The Scots' desire for ecclesiastical independence and autonomy was thwarted by their want of a metropolitan. Without that high functionary the clergy could not meet in council, except at the pleasure of the Pope and by his authority, either exercised by a legate in Scotland or transmitted by rescript from Rome. From the days of King David onwards a few unnoticeable

[1] The Aberbrothock Manifesto—see Appendix II.

legatine councils were held; but in the year 1225 the Pope yielded to the national sentiment, so far as to authorise provincial councils to be held in Scotland without the summons or presence of a legate. The Church at once took advantage of this concession, and the councils acquired a definite importance and national character. The bishops met and ordained that all bishops, abbats, and conventual priors, as the leading ecclesiastical dignitaries and authorities, should henceforth assemble annually, and sit in council, if need be, for three days, under the presidency of a "conservator," elected by the voice of his brother bishops. The conservator presided in the council—opened it by raising the chant "Veni Creator Spiritus," and closed it with the benediction. The opening sermon was preached by the bishops in rotation, the Bishop of St Andrews taking precedence. The conservator summoned the council by a writ addressed to each bishop: he held office from one council to another, with special authority during the interval to deal with transgressions or neglect of the canons; and the record of the Acts of the Council was drawn in the name, and authenticated by the seal, of the "Conservator of the Privileges of the Scottish Church." The conservator was, in fact, for the year of his office, the representative of the Church, and the guardian of

Scottish Councils. 199

her discipline and interests. In this position and prerogative; in his duties as president of the council; in the system of more or less natural selection which guided his appointment, we see distinctly the prototype of the Moderator of the General Assembly. The council, also, in its character, proceedings, and composition, was in several respects an anticipation of the Assembly itself. Although at first only bishops, abbats, and conventual priors were summoned, later the attendance was required of the representatives of the cathedral chapters, of the collegiate churches, and of the conventual clergy; so that it comprised, in point of fact, a very fair and full representation of the Church as a whole, while the State had also its place and voice in the deliberations. Two doctors of the civil law were commissioned to attend on behalf of the king, to communicate his wishes, and to watch over the interests of the Crown and people. Except, however, as thus represented by the head of the State, the laity's right to any share in the councils of the Church was not recognised, and indeed was never urged.

Whether these councils held the required yearly meetings or not cannot be determined. The earliest record of their action which we possess is a code of canons, probably drawn up between 1240 and 1280, and which remained in force, and received little alteration or addition, till near the time of the Reformation. They were read at the beginning of each council after the opening sermon, and after an avowal of adherence to the first four Œcumenical councils—Nice, Constantinople, Ephesus, and Chalcedon—and, laying down certain rules as to the order and constitution of the council itself, they enact that "all the prelates are to hold firmly the catholic and apostolic faith, to instruct those under their jurisdiction in the same, and to urge parents to bring up their children in the knowledge and observance of the Christian religion. The sacraments to be administered according to the form prescribed by the Church. The churches to be built of stone—the nave by the parishioners, and the chancel by the rector; they are to be duly consecrated, and furnished with the proper ornaments, books, and sacred vessels. No church or oratory is to be built, nor the divine office celebrated therein, without consent of the diocesan. Masses not to be said in private places without the bishop's permission. Every parish church to have its proper rector or vicar, who is to exercise the cure of souls either personally or by deputy; and all ecclesiastics are to lead pure and godly lives, or suffer canonical punishment. A sufficient sustentation to be provided for vicars from the churches which they serve, amounting, all burdens deducted, to at least ten marks annually. The clergy to take care that both their mental acquirements and outward habit are such as become their state. No rector or vicar to enter upon any benefice without the consent of his diocesan, or other lawful superior. A proper parsonage-house to be built near every church, within a year's time."

These canons are most wise and wholesome. Of the same tone and tendency are some others, adopted at a diocesan synod held at Musselburgh in 1242, by the good David of Bernham, Bishop of St Andrews—a man of vast zeal, energy, and piety, who in ten years consecrated no less than 140 churches within his diocese. Among the canons of his synod were these, which show how much care was expended, under a good bishop, in the endeavour to have all things in the church done decently and in order. "The churchyards to be properly enclosed and protected against wild animals. The chancel of the church to be kept in repair by the rector, the rest of the building by the parishioners. The clergy to wear a large and conspicuous tonsure, not to eat or drink in taverns except on a journey, not to play dice, and to lead chaste and devout lives. The duty of residence to be strictly observed by the clergy. Marriage not to be contracted save before lawful witnesses. Clerics not to exercise any secular trade or calling; nor to dictate or write a sentence of death. To avoid the inconveniences of frequent clerical changes, no substitute to be appointed for less than a year. Vicars strictly bound to residence. Every rector either to provide a suitable and well-educated priest for his church, or to be himself in orders, on pain of suspension and deprivation of his benefice."

The regular convention of councils was hindered rather than helped by the erection of St Andrews into a metropolitan see in 1471. The theory of ministerial parity, which is known in its full bloom in Presbyterian Churches, was not without its prototype in the medieval Church, in Scotland. Not one of the bishops wished to see a brother elevated to a higher rank than his own. The Bishop of Glasgow especially, as the successor of Kentigern, and representative of the traditions of the British Christianity of Strathclyde, repudiated the primacy of the prelate who could not now be said to have any peculiar right to pose as the "co-arb" of Columba. Each of the bishops had hitherto enjoyed in his turn the rank and prerogative of conservator, and saw with jealousy these submerged in the permanent office of metropolitan. Possibly, also, the growing worldliness and indifference of the bishops and clergy made all alike careless of holding assemblies, which reflected little credit on the

Church, and whose records gave a painful publicity to their own professional shortcomings and neglect of the very canons of their own councils. We hear of no council, summoned or held, for sixty-six years after the creation of the primacy.

The council of 1536 sat under the presidency of Archbishop James Beaton, the uncle of the notorious Cardinal, and was ostensibly called at the instance of the king, James V., who desired that it should ratify and enforce a tax he sought to impose upon ecclesiastical benefices, for the support of his newly instituted Court of Session. This was carried out, to the extent of levying a yearly assessment on the prelates for this object. Another proposal of the king's, the adoption of which would have done much to sweeten the relations of the clergy to the people, was set aside. This was that they should renounce "the corse presents"—the Church cow and the upmost cloth—as the hateful mortuary dues were called, the exaction of which was as unpopular as that of a Welsh tithe in our own days; and further, that they should grant every husbandman a lease of his teinds for a certain fixed payment. Long ere this the teind had lost much of its character of a voluntary benefaction granted by the pious landowner, and had come to be regarded, not, as it really was, a property of the Church, but rather as an impost wrung by the parson from the tiller of the soil. This was partly owing to the fact that its payment had commonly been transferred from the owner to the occupier of the land, and that it was collected by the incumbent personally, who was thus brought into an unpleasant relation with his parishioners, as one who seemed to be not so much drawing the fruits of his own share in the soil as taxing their industry.

The king's sound advice, however, was not accepted; and in the wild days that were coming on, the clergy had bitter reason to regret that they had not taken the opportunity he offered them, of removing the grievances of their taxes on death, and the personal exaction of their teinds. They, possibly, were not altogether inclined to be ruled by the royal counsels, for King James V. made no secret of his impatience of the misdemeanours of their order and his disrespect for its members. The Court of Rome, alarmed lest he should follow the evil example of his powerful kinsman and neighbour the King of England, plied him with every flattery and attention: sent special nuncios to confer with him; sanctioned large subsidies being paid him out of the ecclesiastical revenues, in furtherance of his English war; bestowed on him the mystic cap and sword blessed by the Pope on Christmas night; offered him the title of "Defender of the Christian faith,"—but in spite of these blandishments the king did not even affect a friendliness he did not feel. He encouraged Buchanan to satirise the Mendicant Friars in his play "The Franciscan"; and he sat and listened when Sir David Lyndsay's "Satire of the Three Estates" exposed the clergy and their misdoings, on the public stage, to the frankest popular ridicule; while in an interview with the prelates, in his Court at Linlithgow, he hotly charged them with neglect of duty and the attempt to foment discord between himself and his nobility, and as he warmed with his subject, striking his hand upon the short sword at his belt, he exclaimed— "Wherefore gave my predecessors so many lands and rents to the Kirk? Was it to maintain hawks, dogs, and harlots to a number of idle priests? The King of England burns you, the King of Denmark beheads you; but I shall stick you with this same whinger."

At the time he uttered this fierce invective the clergy of Scotland had fallen low in the moral scale. The enjoyment of near four centuries' "Catholic" apostolic succession had failed to sustain and invigorate their apostolic character. Never was their lineal descent from the source of Catholic unity and authority, in S. Peter, technically more unimpeachable; never was the boasted threefold ministry more hopelessly unlike that of the apostles. At no period in the history of the Scottish Church do its records reveal a baser type of character and conduct in the clergy—a more scandalous neglect of duty—a more sacrilegious worldliness and profane immorality on the part of almost all who held high office in the Church, or concerned themselves in its affairs.

There were no doubt some good men both among the bishops and the priests; but they were lights shining in dark places. That Kennedy, Archbishop of St Andrews, wise, learned, and devout, was, when he died in 1466, "lamented as a public parent,"[1] is the testimony of so keen a Protestant and partisan as George Buchanan. Reid of Orkney and Douglas of Dunkeld were both men who had imbibed the spirit of the New Learning, to which their Church at large was stupidly indifferent. The one beautified the massive Cathedral of Kirkwall, and provided the first endowment for the University of Edinburgh; the other "gave to rude Scotland Virgil's page," and—"noble, valiant, learned, and an excellent poet"—left behind him, as the historian of his illustrious family records, "great approbation of his virtues and love of his person, in the hearts of all good men."[2] Gavin Dunbar, Bishop of

---

[1] Buchanan's History, book xii. 23.
[2] Hume of Godscroft, Hist. of the Douglases.

Aberdeen from 1518 to 1532, pious, generous, and enlightened — the friend of Hector Boece the historian of Scotland—is said to have spent the whole revenues of his see in works of charity and public utility. His predecessor, Elphinstone, the founder of King's College, was at once a man of letters, a statesman, and a true overseer of the Church—whether as an ambassador abroad, or in the Parliament and in his cathedral at home, doing his devoir as a public-spirited and patriotic servant of the Church and State.

Among the humbler churchmen, too, there were men of God who mourned the evils of the times, and held closely to the truth as they understood it, — such as Ninian Winzet, schoolmaster at Linlithgow, and ultimately Abbot of S. James's, Regensburg, erudite and honest, a lover of the ancient ways, but grieving over "the decline of the true faith" and the ignorance and vice of his brethren in the priesthood,—"Alas!" he says, "we are right sorry that it is true for the most part or more, that they are unworthy of the name of pastors":[1] such as Thomas Forret, vicar of Dollar—kind and tender to the poor of his flock—a diligent pastor and faithful preacher — faithful to the death, for because of

---

[1] Winzet's Tractates: with introduction, notes, &c., by J. K. Hewison, M.A., F.S.A.Scot., Minister of Rothesay. Scottish Text Society.

his fidelity his end was to be burned. These, however, were the rare exceptions. When we look beyond them we behold a turbid sea of harlotry, simony, ignorance, superstition, mere worldliness and carnality, into whose foul waters the stately fabric of the Church is sinking lower and lower, as into an abyss of shame and ruin.

To take a few examples. Of the last two primates of St Andrews one was the persecuting Beaton, notorious for his amours. So debauched was the moral feeling of the time that this most reverend father in God thought it no shame to attend publicly the nuptials of one of his daughters and the Earl of Crawford, which were performed, says Archbishop Spottiswoode, "with an exceeding pomp and magnificence." The other, himself a bastard son of the Earl of Arran, was the father of three bastards. The last Bishop of Aberdeen is described by Spottiswoode as "a very epicure, spending all his time in drinking and whoring," and wasting great part of the revenues of the Church on his lemans and their children. The last Bishop of Moray made away fraudulently with the revenues of his see, and did not deny the charge of having thirteen concubines. Chisholm, the penultimate Bishop of Dunblane, robbed the revenues of the Church to enrich his three illegitimate sons. Of the four bishops of Argyll, from the beginning of the sixteenth century to the year 1558, two were illegitimate members of noble families; and one had himself illegitimate offspring. But one need not multiply instances of the clerical degeneracy. The preamble of the canons of the Provincial Council, held in Edinburgh in 1549, frankly declared that the two chief causes of the existing troubles and heresies in the Church were the "crassa ignorantia" and "profana obscenitas vitæ" of the general body of the churchmen. They stood condemned by their own tribunal.

Yet with all this clerical criminality, it is not just to pass such a severe sentence on the religious condition of Scotland as is pronounced by Dr M'Crie, the biographer of Knox, who is but one of a class of zealous Protestant writers who can see no good thing in the pre-Reformation Nazareth. "The corruptions," says Dr M'Crie, "by which the Christian religion was universally distinguished before the Reformation, had grown to a greater height in Scotland than in any other nation within the pale of the Western Church."[1] This is not accurate. Beaton was cruel and profligate, but he was also a genuine patriot and able statesman. Scotland might breed a Beaton and a Chisholm, but she produced no parallel to Pope Alexander VI. and

[1] Life of Knox, Period 1st.

his son, "the monster steeped in every crime." The Scottish feuds and factions were embittered and unrelenting; but the country never exhibited such scenes of savage fanaticism and brutal inhumanity as rendered the religious wars of Bohemia and Hungary a horror and scandal to Christendom; nor had the holy office of the Inquisition ever established itself and practised its diabolical arts within the Scottish border. Moreover, education in Scotland had gained a high level. The Papacy discouraged popular education; but the Scottish Government and the medieval Scottish Church, always independent in its spirit, fostered learning in spite of the Papacy. We find the proof of this in the scholastic system established in this country as early as the thirteenth century, and maintained in efficiency until broken up by the storms which burst upon the Church in the sixteenth.

From early times we distinguish in Scotland three classes of schools—"Sang schools," which were connected with the cathedrals or the more important churches, and whose primary intention was to train singers for their musical services; "Grammar schools," which were founded in most of the burghs; and "Monastic schools," which were attached to the monasteries. All these had this in common, that the education they afforded was under the charge of the Church, and of the monastic orders specially; and the method of management adopted was generally to appoint a single monk as director or inspector of the schools of a burgh or of a district, under whose superintendence other monks taught. The interest in education, which had distinguished the Columban Church, was not seriously impaired by its amalgamation with the Church of Rome. It survived in active force; and before the foundation of any of the existing public schools of England (the oldest of which is Winchester, founded in 1387), we find the charge of the schools of Roxburgh intrusted in 1241 to the monks of Kelso, over whom was an official called "the Rector of the Schools." In 1256 the statutes of the church of Aberdeen imposed on the chancellor of the cathedral chapter the duty of supervising the discipline, and teaching of the schools, of that city.

Of the three classes of schools the sang schools were the most rudimentary — teaching music, reading, and grammar. They, indeed supplied the place of a system of primary schools, so far as they went. Their close connection with the Church tended to insure their extinction when the Reformation came; and in 1579, when the mischief had been done, an Act was passed ordaining that sang schools should be provided in burghs for the instruction of the youths in music and singing, which, says the Act, "is like to fall in great decay without timeous remeid be provided." But an Act of the Scots Parliament could not restore the school in the cathedral cloister, and the tuneful monks who had taught it; and Scottish sacred song has only now begun to regain its voice. In the grammar schools the course embraced Latin, thoroughly taught, and whatever was included under the terms "grammar and logic," with instruction in some of the modern languages, and in the principles and practice of arithmetic. The monastic schools were of a still higher grade, and appear to have been intended chiefly for the education of candidates for the priesthood, and for the sons of the nobility and greater landowners. These schools virtually supplied the place of the universities ere these arose. Those only were received into them who had already passed through the grammar or secondary schools, or had acquired instruction equivalent to theirs. One of the requirements was "perfect Latin," which we suspect would nowadays rather thin the list of entrants to our colleges, and even to our Divinity Halls; and the curriculum included philosophy and law.

It is evident that such was the education given in the monastic schools that men were able to go direct from them, and take that place among Continental scholars and thinkers taken in the fourteenth century by John of Duns, in the fifteenth by John Mair and Hector Boece, and in the sixteenth by George Buchanan.

The general culture which prevailed, at least in every class above the rank of the rural peasantry, may be inferred from many indications in the Scottish life of the fifteenth and sixteenth centuries. Thus a commission was issued in Buchanan's day, of which he was president, to rectify the inconveniencies arising from the use of different grammars in the schools. The existence of such a multiplicity of grammars, as to call for a commission of the kind, is a proof of no little educational activity. It is obvious that French was familiarly known and spoken in Scotland from the thirteenth century. In many of the grammar schools no language was allowed to be used but Latin. When the Reformation dawned there was an eager demand for the Reformation literature; and though by that time the corruption of the clergy had become notorious, and the Church had lost much of its native spirit of independence, education was still very generally diffused; and the Reformers' charge against the priests and monks was not that they left the people ignorant of their letters, but that they never instructed them in the veriest elements of religious truth.

Had religious instruction been offered them, the people were ready to receive and benefit by it. They were sufficiently educated to read books, and to understand intelligent teaching. Sir David Lyndsay says he wrote not for scholars, but "for colliers, carters, and for cooks"; and his works, with those of Dunbar, passed through several editions in the sixteenth century. Luther's writings, smuggled across from Holland, were eagerly sought. In 1542 the Scots Parliament authorised the use of the Scriptures in the vernacular tongue, and John Knox testifies "there might have been seen the Bible lying upon almost every gentleman's table. The New Testament was borne about in many men's hands."

But those who should have been the religious instructors of the people had no instruction to give them. They were illiterate, and ignorant of theology. The bishop never preached; the parish priest seldom. Such preaching as was to be heard was from the mouths of the monks and mendicant friars, and it was, as a rule, but little to edification. There was no private or catechetical tuition. The ministry had utterly broken down, and failed as a means of grace—as an instrument of religious teaching—as a guardian of morals—as the custodian of the apostles' doctrine and fellowship. "Even among the higher clergy," a Roman Catholic historian testifies,

Degeneracy of Clergy. 215

"too many were more than suspected of leading lives the reverse of edifying; while the inferior ecclesiastics were lamentably deficient in that trained theological learning which alone could meet and overcome the dominant errors of the time. Above all, it is impossible to doubt that the knowledge which the people at large possessed of the doctrines of their religion was insufficient to enable them to cope successfully with the coming storm. 'There,' said Bishop Leslie, speaking of the causes which led to the overthrow of the faith in Scotland — 'there is the source and origin of the evil, that the people, neglected by the clergy, and uninstructed in the Catechism in their tender years, had no sure and certain belief.' "[1]

The hideous excesses of outrage and sacrilege, which followed in the track of the " Lords of the Congregation," proved too plainly how wholly the populace had become demoralised under a worthless priesthood, and how thoroughly all respect for religion, its ordinances, its holy things and places, had been rooted out of the popular mind. Like priest, like people. The general *morale* was pitiably low. The " horrible crimes " which abounded in the realm, and which ecclesiastical discipline had left unchecked, formed one of the earliest subjects on which the Reformers

[1] Bellesheim, vol. ii. p. 322. Hunter Blair's translation.

appealed to the Government. The reader of the 'Book of the Universal Kirk' will see how constantly the Church, when awakened from her torpor, strove to arrest the prevalent crimes and vices.

The great religious revolution, in which Luther's trumpet blew the first note of war, had changed the whole constitution of the Church in many kingdoms of the Continent, and had worn itself out in England, ere yet Scotland felt its force. The remoteness of our country from the central scenes of conflict; the weakness of the Government; the turbulence of the nobles; and the emigration of the flower of the Scottish scholars, acted as a barrier between Scotland and the revolutionary influences. It grew plain, however, as the reign of James V. passed on, that Scotland must sooner or later be involved in the general crisis. Had any prelate or ruler of the Church been able by skill, diplomacy, strength of will, and firmness of administration, to postpone the evil day, it would have been Cardinal Beaton, who in 1539 became Primate, and in Church and State the foremost man in Scotland. But even under his sway the spirit of freedom and reform grew stronger; and he and the clergy began to think of putting their house in order. The swell of the far-off Continental storm was reverberating on the Scottish shore: they could scarcely hope that the tempest would pass away and leave untouched the churches and cathedrals, the monasteries and manses, of Scotland. Beaton was too sagacious not to see that there must be two measures for the safety of the Church—the one the repression of heresy, the other the reform of morals. But, in a convention of the clergy and bishops held at Edinburgh in 1546, the discussion of these subjects was postponed to the exigencies of the war with England. The English had crossed the Border, and already Melrose, Kelso, Dryburgh, and Jedburgh had been burnt. The convention voted a liberal subsidy—to be levied on benefices of more than £40 in annual value. The repulse of Henry and the maintenance of the French alliance were to the clergy of such vital moment, that many of them are said to have fought in person at Pinkie, under a banner bearing the legend "Afflictæ sponsæ ne obliviscaris." Indeed the political combinations, necessary to thwart the English and reforming party, appear to have engrossed Beaton's attention more than any attempts at Church reform. If indeed that matter was debated at all, there was no result as regarded the all-important point of restraint of the abounding clerical immorality.

Beaton was murdered; but under his successor, Hamilton, council after council was summoned to devise schemes of reform, and plans for the repression of "heresy." If highly moral canons could have extinguished immorality, the Scottish priesthood would have been a pattern to Christendom. Could ecclesiastical thunderbolts have demolished heresy, Scottish orthodoxy would have rivalled that of Athanasius. But it was too late. There is an eagerness, half ludicrous half pathetic, in the solicitude with which the moribund ecclesiastical system looks round for causes of scandal, and proclaims its correctives and antidotes, persuading itself that the time for their application is not really over and gone. And yet no one appears to have really understood the fatal depth of the Church's fall from its early purity, its wholesome discipline and government, its high standard of duty and self-denial on the part of its clergy. Demoralised by long familiarity with wrong, and blinded by devotion to the Vicar of Christ, the clergy—ignorant and worldly—did not apprehend, like the angel of the Church of Ephesus, "from whence they had fallen." They evidently did not see the fatal contrast between themselves and their predecessors in the Celtic era of the Church, which even in its decadence had never shown the gracelessness, the impurity, the sluggish decrepitude, the collapse of decency, of discipline, of self-

General Decadence. 219

respect, which marked the close of the Roman era.

The old Celtic delight in the Word of God, and constant study of the Scriptures, had given place to their complete disuse and prohibition. The once hearty services had dwindled down to perfunctory masses scantily attended. The careful preparation of candidates for the ministry had succumbed to a glaring system of nepotism, favouritism, and simony, which scattered office in the priesthood and the Episcopate among the baseborn, the greedy, the licentious, the incompetent and illiterate. The rigid discipline and careful order of the monastic Church had lapsed into the self-indulgence which made the so-called fast-days mere objects of popular ridicule, and the irreverence which turned the sacred ritual into general contempt. The Celtic combination of devoted loyalty to the ecclesiastical chief, and free play of individual zeal and genius, had long since died down into apathetic and sluggish formalism and routine. The people had no longer any share in the choice of their spiritual overseers; nor was there any conscientious oversight. The authority of the revered abbat had been superseded by the nominal rule of the bishop, whom—in nine cases out of ten—nobody revered or could revere. The Church had fallen, and no ingenious canons of alarmed councils, no archbishop's Catechisms or "Godly Exhortations," no professions or promises, could lift her out of her Slough of Despond.

The Provincial Council of 1559 received from "the Lords of the Congregation," as those who had assumed the lead in the reforming movement were called, certain articles of reformation, indispensable, they maintained, to the welfare of the Church. These were, amendment of the lives and habits of the clergy; satisfactory examination and proof of the requisite qualifications before admission to orders; that there should be a sermon delivered in every parish church on every Sunday, and if not also on every holiday, at least on Christmas, Easter, and Whitsunday; that after mass the common prayer and litanies should be read in the vernacular; and that no one should be allowed to dishonour, or speak irreverently of, or connive at the irregular celebration of, the sacraments, or to despoil or injure church, chapel, or religious house. These and other equally reasonable demands were not altogether satisfactorily answered. The request that the common prayers should be read in the vulgar tongue was refused; but strict rules were laid down for the frequent preaching of the parish priest and the due instruction of the people, for the abolition of certain irritating exactions on the part of the clergy, and for the speedy reform of their loose ways of living—as well as for the regulation of pluralities, the examination of presentees to benefices, and the visitation of monasteries and nunneries. The scheme of improvement, by which the exigency of the crisis and the claims of the new ideas were to be met with safety, was, on the whole, respectable as a scheme, except in that particular of denying the use of the vernacular; but it was a scheme on paper merely. The council could write it out, but could not translate it into action. And so far from reforming the Church, it has been affirmed, and probably with a measure of truth, that this set of reforming canons, instead of being a strength to the Church, accelerated the very catastrophe it was designed to avert. For the rigorous statutes of this council, and the obligations and restraints they imposed, were so distasteful to the younger clergy, that the dread of the novel discipline with which they were threatened inclined them to take their chance of greater liberty among the ranks of the Reformed, and to desert the old communion in its last extremity. Certainly among the many members of the clerical order who adopted the principles of the Reformation, all were not actuated by religious motives.

The last act of the Provincial Council of 1559 was to appoint another, to be held at Edinburgh in the following year, to make inquiry as to the due execution of the canons, and take counsel as to any further questions of ecclesiastical discipline that might arise in the meantime. That council never met. It was summoned for the 11th February 1560. By that date John Knox had arrived from Geneva, and had inflamed the popular passions to the pitch of zeal, at which the godly congregation and the "rascal multitude" dealt indiscriminate devastation to the most venerable and historical edifices in their country. The noble churches and monasteries of Perth, the stately Palace and Abbey of Scone, the glorious Cathedral of St Andrews, the High Kirk and the royal Abbey of Edinburgh, with many more, had been sacked and ruined. The Government of the queen regent had been openly defied, and a rival power—that of the so-called "Lords of the Congregation"—had entered into negotiations with Elizabeth, a foreign sovereign, in which she engaged to assist them in an alliance, offensive and defensive, against France. In pursuance of these negotiations, the Treaty of Berwick was concluded about the very time the council should have been sitting; in virtue of which an English army of 8000 men entered Scotland, and, attacking the Scots and French forces of the Crown, proceeded to promote the cause of religious reform with the sword. Then followed the death of the regent, the proclamation of peace between the Government and the Congregation, and the virtual triumph of the Reforming party, resulting in the proscription of the mass, the downfall of the Roman hierarchy, and the adoption of the Reformed Confession by the Parliament of 1560.

The catastrophe was startling in its suddenness, its completeness, and its revelation of the prevailing ill-will towards the Church, and the undisciplined violence of party and sectarian passion, which marked the progress of a movement that was, in its earlier stages at least, more a political revolution than a religious reformation. Other causes were at work, in making the way of the movement plain, than that dissoluteness of the clergy and those ecclesiastical abuses to which I have directed your attention. One of these, and the most essentially religious of them, was the presence of that leaven of Wycliffite doctrine in the Lowlands, which no rigour of persecution had been able to eradicate. In their days of peril, some of Wycliffe's "poor priests" had found shelter there; and witnesses for the simple Gospel they preached had never been wanting. Many had sealed their testimony with their blood; but the persecution of the "heretics" begat that which it sought to destroy. In Scotland, as elsewhere, the blood of the martyrs was the seed of the Church, but not of the Church that did homage to Rome. The spectacle of the martyrdoms of Patrick Hamilton, of George Wishart, of Thomas Forret, and of Walter Mylne, hardened the people's hearts against the bigoted hierarchy, and embittered the silent rage with which those who loved liberty and truth marked its inhuman tyranny. The goodwill of the middle class—mainly the burghers and traders—which included most of the intelligence, the sagacity, and the religious principle of the community, was hopelessly alienated from the secular clergy, bishops and priests alike. They saw in them no toleration of free thought—no belief in those truths of the Gospel which Wycliffe and Luther had taught them to value, and which bore to them the promise of liberty, reform, progress, in every department of life, thought, and action.

To all this the regular clergy were as hostile as the secular. The popular favour had fallen away from the monasteries. These for several generations had enjoyed a just popularity. But luxury and laxity had made their way into the cloisters. The wealth and power of the great abbeys and monastic houses by-and-by rivalled, if they did not exceed, those of the principal nobles. The mitred abbat sat in Parliament, and was an important social and political personage, the equal of the bishop and the peer. Much as the monks had done for the people, they were doing comparatively little when Henry VIII. began to dissolve the great English houses and to plunder their revenues. The news of what went on south of the Tweed no doubt was familiar in the north; and the popular envy and cupidity, engendered by the sight of the riches and splendour of the abbeys and monasteries, were not counterbalanced by any deep sense of gratitude for good works done and pious services rendered to the people by their owners. The pride which any intelligent and educated Scot must have felt at the mention of their famous names was probably little, if at all, shared by the multitude, and was not even a strong sentiment with the more cultivated class. We can mark few signs of the reverence which ought to have been inspired by the aspect and traditions of the abbatial and cathedral churches. The churches of either order were unusually grand in their architecture and wealthy in their possessions. And yet, so estranged was the common feeling from those who took charge of these historical temples, that no general effort was made to save them from the violence of the mob that roamed the country at the heels of the preachers and the "Lords of the Congregation." And not only so, but the angriest passions of these disorderly innovators expended themselves in working havoc among the very noblest of those

P

buildings. The devastation could not have been possible had not popular respect and affection become wholly detached from the monasteries—had there not been a deep-seated jealousy of the wealth and splendour of the great dignitaries, and a desire to level those who had hitherto held their heads so high.

Yet another, and a very potent, factor in the ecclesiastical revolution, was the character of the Scottish nobles. Nowhere was the title of noble less appropriate than to the great majority of the members of the Scottish peerage. They were poor, mean, greedy, and unprincipled. Again and again, in the reigns of the Jameses, they had showed themselves treacherous to their country and disloyal to the Crown. Some were in the pay of England; some in the pay of France. A disinterested and honest patriot was hard to find amongst the whole gang. They had long cherished a grudge against the Church, because it generally—if not always—took the side of the Crown in the monarch's frequent encounters with the factions of the nobility. They had long envied the Churchmen their large possessions, their well-cultivated farms, steady feudal tenants, and costly church furniture of silver and gold, more splendid and precious than any they could display in their own ancestral halls. They had long, also, regarded whatever material profit they could make out of the Church as fair spoil. In this they had been fatally encouraged by the example of the Crown, and by the criminal laxity of the Church itself. When James IV. appointed his natural son, Alexander Stuart, Archbishop of St Andrews, at the age of eighteen, and took him with him to the field of Flodden, he was only giving a more than usually conspicuous illustration of a system which had treated royal and noble bastardy as a title to ecclesiastical promotion, and had looked on office in the Church as no bar to civil or even military employment. And this system was unblushingly connived at by the Church.

For three hundred years before the Reformation, we may say, the Scottish bishops had never made the previous admission to orders an indispensable preliminary to admission to a benefice. Those of them who had a proper respect for their profession, and for the character of the clergy, might try to make this qualification imperative; but they tried in vain. They could not cope with the insatiable desire of the beggarly nobles to provide for their kindred or dependents at the Kirk's expense. They could not withstand the monarch's thrifty purpose of endowing his illegitimate offspring out of the ecclesiastical revenues. The records of the diocesan and provincial councils bear frequent witness that rectories and other offices were filled by men who were not clerics. And it is acknowledged, with shame, by the best champions of the Roman Church in her conflict with the Reformers, that rich livings, with the cure of thousands of souls, were held by persons utterly incompetent and unqualified. The root of this laxity may probably be traced to the loose practices of the Culdees in sanctioning the hereditary tenure of benefices, and in allowing their endowments to lapse into lay hands: but the laxity had never been properly repressed; and it grew with the growth of the Church, till, on the eve of the Reformation, it had gained a rampant and indecent notoriety.

All these abuses had whetted the nobles' appetite for the plunder of the Church. As long as she stood secure and unassailed, fortified by the august authority of Rome and the protection of the law, it was easy, by intrigue or evasion of canon or statute, to grasp at a benefice here and there; but it was impossible to appropriate, with the wholesale audacity of Henry VIII., the general possessions of abbey, cathedral, and well-dowered rectory. But, let the religious passions of the people only be stirred to the needful fervour, then the bishops might be driven off, the monks unfrocked, the parish priest frightened into submission, and the goodly heritage of the Church would be the prey of the strongest of the depredators. There can be little doubt that the nobles argued thus;—that their reforming zeal was in most cases the mere stalking-horse of their wolfish avarice, and that their desire to rob the Church was one of the most efficient causes of the religious revolution called the Scottish Reformation. In no country were the various elements which combined to produce the religious revolution of the sixteenth century of a more complex kind; but certainly in none did the movement, as a whole, owe less to that class which should have set the example of disinterested patriotism, to say nothing of religious principle.

I have spoken of those causes which helped to accelerate this great reforming movement, when it at last reached Scotland, and to secure its rapid and irresistible progress. In every such movement, however, the crowning impetus and final direction, which determine not only its success but stamp it with its special character, is a personal force. It was so here: the personal force was John Knox, next to Columba the most striking figure and most creative influence in Scottish history.

LECTURE VII.

THE character, influence, and career of John Knox have been so often and so ably discussed and expounded by historians and critics, from many and different points of view, that I do not propose entering on a field already fully occupied.[1] I wish merely to indicate the nature of his work as the leader of the Scottish Reformation.

To become the leader of any national movement in Scotland was no easy undertaking. For generations the country had been divided, politically and ecclesiastically, between three factions: the faction of the king and the nobles who stood by him; the faction of the nobles who were in revolt or opposition; and the faction of the Church, which not unsuccessfully

---

[1] And most recently, and in a very thorough and exhaustive manner, by Mr Hume Brown in his biography of the Reformer; and by Mrs MacCunn in her brilliant contribution to the series of "Leaders of Religion."

held its own between the other two, and which was upon the whole, although spiritually tyrannical, not unkindly in its relations to the people. The difficulty of initiating and carrying out any general scheme of policy or reform, in a nation so disrupted, was seriously aggravated by the presence, in its northern regions, of a race differing in language and in its degree of civilisation from its neighbours, and full of warlike and predatory instincts. Knox's achievement was that he, a man sprung from the middle class, and a simple member of the common priesthood, taking his own independent way, became the national leader. In spite of the anger of the Crown, the false friendship and the selfish duplicity of the majority of the nobles, the indifference of some and the unenlightened zeal of others of the commonalty, he was able to inspire the national mind with higher moral ideals than it had hitherto been conscious of, with a self-respecting desire for liberty of life and thought, and a consequent detestation of the unspiritual oppression of the Roman Church; and so to combine and direct towards the great end of national enfranchisement all those feelings, desires, and forces, which were in sympathy with the world-movement of the Reformation.

That his ways were often rude and his manners harsh and churlish, we do not deny; nor, remembering that he had spent eighteen months of his manhood among the galley-slaves in a French galley, do we greatly wonder at it. That he was bigoted and intolerant is scarcely to be imputed to him for unrighteousness. Bigotry and intolerance were inextricably woven into the ideas of a time in which tolerance was an almost impossible virtue. Elijah on Mount Carmel could not tolerate the priests of Baal, if he was to overthrow the idolatry of Israel; Knox in Edinburgh could not tolerate the mass, if he was to win civil and religious freedom for Scotland. So at least it appeared to him. The more liberal and tolerant spirit of Maitland of Lethington (as has been recently urged with singular ability in Mr Skelton's admirable book)[1] desired a policy of comprehension, if not of compromise, theoretically more humane and just than Knox's policy of "Thorough"; but such a policy, at such a time, was thrown away on the Irreconcilables whom it would fain have reconciled. Knox took a rougher but directer road. He fought intolerance with its own weapons. Any others would not have even dinted the breastplates of the foe. He had been less touched than any other reformer with the humane charm of the New Learning. He

[1] Maitland of Lethington and the Scotland of Mary Stuart. By John Skelton, LL.D., C.B.

had none of the "sweet reasonableness" of Melanchthon, none of Zwingli's urbane sense of civic equity and social charity. He was not troubled with humanitarian scruples about using the sword of the Lord and of Gideon, when he saw an enemy or evil-doer, however stalwart or pretentious, before him. His life's battle was against the enemies of Christ's Church, and in that battle he feared God and knew no other fear. "If Knox," says Dr Schaff—that historian and scholar, Swiss by birth, American by adoption, whose removal the whole Reformed Church deplores—"if Knox lacked the sweet and lovely traits of Christian character, it should be remembered that God wisely distributes His gifts. Neither the polished culture of Erasmus, nor the gentle spirit of Melanchthon, nor the cautious measures of Cranmer, could have accomplished the mighty change in Scotland. Knox was, beyond doubt, the providential man for his country. . . . Such fearless and faithful heroes are among the best gifts of God to the world."

And just as truly says Mr Froude, who alone among English writers has shown a hearty appreciation of the character of the man he calls "the grandest figure in the entire history of the British Reformation,"—" Toleration is a good thing in its place, but you cannot tolerate what will not tolerate you and is trying to cut your throat. . . . Knox and the Covenanters fought the fight and won the victory; and not till then came the David Humes with their essays on miracles, and the Adam Smiths with their political economies, and steam-engines and railroads, and philosophical institutions, and all the other blessed or unblessed fruits of liberty." And this is all the truer because, though animated throughout by the highest religious principle, and originating in the effort to reform the doctrine and practice of religion as then established in his native land, the mission of Knox was much deeper in its meaning, and wider in its scope, than any purely religious or mere dogmatic or ecclesiastical enterprise could ever be. His merit and power lay in this, that he recognised, more clearly perhaps than any other reformer, the essential character of the Reformation as the revolt of humanity against dominant oppression—the assertion of the human right to liberty of life, intellectual, moral, political.

In Scotland, as in Switzerland especially, the Reformation was the assertion and vindication of what may be broadly called "popular rights."

And notwithstanding all the rudeness of the methods—the coarseness and violence, at this point or that, in the struggle to clear the way— the Scottish Reformation, as led by Knox, was a long and resolute step in the upward path of light and liberty. It involved much destruction of that which might have been reasonably held sacred from assault; the desecration of much which old association and reverence had consecrated; the waste of much that might have been saved for the highest ends of national welfare. The reckless overturn of many things that should have been the objects of popular respect, engendered a hardness of sentiment and a roughness of manner which have survived long enough to become a kind of national reproach; but, rough and ugly as the process of transition from the old to the new and the means of emancipation from the ancient *régime* were, the work in itself was substantially righteous and salutary. It probably could not have been wrought out more delicately, nor accomplished except at the cost of all the pain and travail, which must accompany moral, social, and political, new birth.

"It was not a smooth business," as Carlyle says,[1] "but it was welcome surely, and cheap at that price—had it been far rougher on the whole, cheap at any price, as life is." The tradition of ecclesiastical dignity and influence was broken; the prerogative of the Crown was boldly questioned; the rights and privileges of the nobles were freely invaded; the old bonds and usages of society were loosed, and knocked about; but

[1] Essays on Heroes : The Hero as Priest.

the people began to live a higher life, and a coherent Scottish realm became a possibility.

Knox had imbibed at Geneva a large share of the spirit of austere discipline and relentless severity which characterised the administration and the theology of Calvin. "The Lord thy God is a jealous God, visiting the iniquities of the fathers upon the children," was an aspect of the Almighty's character much more to his mind than "the Lord retaineth not anger for ever, because He delighteth in mercy." Jael, the wife of Heber the Kenite, who drove her inhospitable spike through the temples of her sleeping guest, was in his eyes a nobler type of womanhood than Mary with her box of ointment, which was not sold for 300 pence and given to the poor. An intense conviction of the rectitude of his own course, and the truth of his own doctrine — a gloomy certainty of the hopeless perdition destined for his gainsayers and opponents—a prevailing sense of the justice and inevitability of God's ways and judgments,—these, coupled with an inexorable standard of morality, gave Knox a strong and stern hold upon the general mind and conscience; but they also imparted to his influence that character of hard-heartedness and uncharitableness, of Puritanic austerity and self-righteousness, which has too long infected the religion of Scotland. The same influence was

General Morale. 237

unfavourable to the growth of a pure *morale*. Ethical purity and integrity will never result from laws of unmerciful stringency and discipline of unrelenting vigour; and from the many lamentations which we find in the post-Reformation literature over the prevalence of crimes and vices of a flagrant sort, it is evident that the old corruptions had been by no means wholly rooted out of the general community. How little the upper and governing classes, the men of rank and estate, were swayed by religious principle in the part they played during the reforming period—how wholly selfish and partisan their motives were—how devoid they, on the whole, were of honesty and honour, is proved, as I have already indicated, by their frequent treacheries, by their lives, in many cases of gross licentiousness, and by their unscrupulous robbery of the patrimony of the Kirk. It is not among the mere peasantry on the one hand, nor the nobility and great landowners on the other, that we find the fruits of righteousness during the lifetime of Knox and his successors in the sixteenth century; but rather among the lesser landowners, and the members of the middle class, whose growth in general influence and rise in political and social power the Reformation did much to promote.

Those who maintain the necessity of a threefold order in the Christian ministry, and deny the right of any Church not owning that order to be regarded as a true branch of the Church catholic, represent the reformation in Scotland as the close of the Scottish Church's ecclesiastical existence, the collapse of its apostolic ministry, and the institution of a new form of schism in that country.[1] Such a representation has no warrant in the facts of the case.

I showed you, in my first lecture, that the threefold order of bishop, priest, and deacon is no part of the constitution of the apostolic Church; that the only two orders recognised in the New Testament are those of the elder or overseer and the deacon; that the episcopate emerged from the presbyterate, in post-apostolic times, by a natural evolution; and that the congregational episcopacy of the early Church was essentially different from the diocesan episcopacy of the medieval. Further, I pointed out that the catholicity and apostolicity of a Church could not depend on its owning a certain mode of government; but on its spirit and character, its holding the true faith, and possessing an

---

[1] "Churchmen," to avoid the wrong done to their principles by calling the Church of Scotland by its proper name, use the term "Kirk" (which comes exactly to the same thing); but sometimes their "object is attained by the more splenetic periphrasis of 'that form of schism which is established in Scotland.'"—Duke of Argyll, Presbytery Examined, Preface.

orderly and properly authenticated ministry.
Moreover, we saw that, in the original idea of
the Church, prominence was given to the great
principle of the priesthood of the Christian
people—the principle which strikes at the root
of all sacerdotalist pretension and superstition.
The history of the primitive Church had been
long forgotten in Scotland, its principles had
been ignored. That embodiment of them in
the Columban Church, to which the country
was indebted for its peculiar type of religious
worship, life, church government, and organisation, had been overlaid by the cumbrous
paraphernalia imported from Rome; and the
results had been what I described in my last
lecture. The task that Knox and his coadjutors
had to face was not the invention of any
novelties: it was simply the removal of the
accumulated abuses of ages, and the reassertion
of the truths and rights which these had hidden
out of sight—the clearing away of lumber and
litter, that the ancient foundations and venerable walls of the house of God might be restored to view. In the whole process there was
no schism. To renounce "the usurped authority
of the Roman antichrist"[1] was not schismatic.

[1] The King's Covenant of 1580—known afterwards as "The National Covenant," and as such subscribed in 1590, 1638, 1639, and by King Charles II. in 1650 and 1651.

It was a necessary vindication of national independence. No national Church can be schismatic so long as it holds the Catholic faith.

Rome is not the centre and crown of Christian unity; nor is the Pope the vicar of Christ, in any sense in which any faithful minister of His Word and bishop of a flock is not His vicar. It was not the spirit of schism, but the spirit of purity, freedom, and truth, that compelled the Church of Scotland to sever its communion with that of Rome, and to abjure its unworthy allegiance to the Roman bishop. In doing so, and in readjusting the conditions of the National Church, the reformers reverted to primitive and apostolic principles and models. They restored to the "brethren" (the general body of the faithful) their long-withheld rights as members of the Church, and their share in its self-government. They abolished the bloated and unapostolic prelacy, which had too long lorded it over God's heritage. They cleansed the worship of the congregations from the superstitious and unscriptural accretions which had disfigured the once purer ritual of our fathers, and they gave its former place in that ritual to the reading and preaching of the Word. While retaining unaltered the Œcumenical creeds of the Apostles and of Nicæa, they drew up and obtained legislative sanction for a confession of the faith as held, in its in-

Extent of Changes Made. 241

tegrity, by themselves and the rest of the reformed Churches.

All this was not accomplished without some concomitant outbursts of popular fanaticism and excitement, and selfish obstruction from professed friends of reform, much to be deplored; but the work was attended with less disturbance in the external circumstances of the Church, and less change in the *personnel* of its clergy, than might have been expected. Though the Church lands and other endowments were freely plundered, her territorial position remained unassailed. The churches, manses, and glebes were let alone. Her parishes were not meddled with. The ruling power of the Church was transferred from the bishops to the General Assembly, which was only a modification of an institution already familiar in Scotland. Ever since the year 1225, when the clergy obtained the Pope's sanction to their holding provincial councils, these, as we have seen, had sat from time to time, and regulated the affairs of the Church. The General Assembly was the counterpart of those old councils, which had helped to preserve the Church's independence; but the introduction of the laity to a share of their deliberations made the reformed conventions at once more truly national, and liker to the primitive model of the Ecclesiastical Synod.

The change in the actual composition of the clerical body, effected by the Reformation, was slighter than is commonly supposed. The first General Assembly, or National Reformed Church Council, was held in 1560, and numbered but forty-two members, of whom only six were ministers, and of these six four were reformed priests. To them the national voice, speaking through the Parliament, intrusted the task of framing anew the constitution of the Church. It was done so ably and thoroughly, that in seven years the staff of the Church included five superintendents, 289 ministers, and 715 "readers"—over 1000 in all. These must have been found for the most part among the Romanist clergy. They were not foreigners; and among the natives of Scotland the clergy were almost the only possessors, though by no means generally the possessors, of the qualifications necessary for the duties of minister, preacher, and reader.

Five of the Romish bishops—those of Orkney, Caithness, Argyll, the Isles, and Galloway — adopted the principles of the Reformation: but Roman Catholic writers question whether some of these had been validly consecrated under papal sanction; and our information as to their position and functions in the communion of the Reformed is very vague. There is no doubt, however, that a considerable number of the secular clergy, and not a few of the regulars also, conformed. Some of the former remained in their old parishes, as ministers: others were appointed at the discretion of the General Assembly, as readers, and were promoted from that office to the full ministry, when pronounced "most qualified for ministering the Word and sacraments." In the 115 parishes in the Synod of Perth and Stirling, Dr Hew Scott's[1] researches in their records discovered at least thirteen appointments of those who had certainly been in Roman orders, and many more of those who presumably had been so. The proportion was probably not less in other districts. The fact is interesting, as illustrating the spontaneity of the process by which the Church reformed herself from within, and without any violent rupture of the continuity of her ministry. Those who take a natural interest in tracing the regular sequence of office and order in the Church, and who attribute a proper value to the element of a true apostolical succession, find with satisfaction that the great transformation, which passed upon the Kirk in the sixteenth century, thus involved no break in that sequence and succession. The old order changed, giving place to the new; but between the two there was no

[1] Author of the 'Fasti Ecclesiæ Scoticanæ.'

absolute disruption. Out of the Romanist emerged the Reformed ministry. As, four hundred years before, the Celtic Church had been amalgamated with the Church of Rome, so now, though the passage was more rapid and stormy, the Romanist was in part absorbed into, in part superseded by, the Reformed.

The Church, from the days of David to those of Mary, had been under that government of bishops, in which the members of the Church in general had no share. The bishops were subservient to a foreign authority at Rome. This government was now set aside, and with it was discarded the sacerdotal conception of the Church on which it rested. The Reformers reverted to the apostolic conception of the Church, as the Christian community in the completeness of its whole membership. The government was vested in an assembly which, like the first Christian councils, contained both clergy and laity — "elders" and "brethren." Under this General Assembly other courts were instituted, not immediately, but as the process of the Church's development and consolidation permitted. The lowest of these was the kirk-session, the next was the presbytery, the third the synod. The session consisted of the minister, elders, and deacons of one parish; the presbytery of a minister and elder from each of a group of parishes; the synod of a minister and elder from each parish of the several presbyteries within the synodical bounds. Admission to the ministry had, under the Roman *régime*, been at the pleasure of the bishops. The old scrupulous preparation and conscientious training of the Celtic Church had been utterly relinquished; and ordination had been profaned and bartered, while the people's right to a voice in the appointment of their spiritual teachers and guides had been habitually flouted. All this was now amended. The "call" of the Christian congregation was recognised as the primary basis of admission to the cure of souls. Before the person so called could be admitted he must be strictly examined by the presbytery, or—before the definite erection of presbyteries — by the ministers of a district acting together in a presbyterial capacity, who must satisfy themselves as to his adequate learning, good character, and general capacity for the work of the ministry. If he stood the examination, he might then be ordained—not otherwise. At first, and for a few years after 1560, the laying on of the hands of the presbytery, which was the visible sign of the commission granted to the candidate, was disused. This abrupt departure from apostolic usage was justified in the 'First Book of Discipline' by the curious plea, "Albeit the apostles used imposition of hands, yet seeing the miracle is ceased, the using of the ceremony we judge not necessary." Knox and the other authors of that book were evidently under the impression that the apostles, by the imposition of hands, imparted some miraculous gift — a superstition they ought to have rid themselves of when they bade farewell to "the works of men's invention," such as—to use Knox's own words—"pilgrimages, pardons, and other sic baggage."[1] They might have remembered that of the earliest of all ordinations it is recorded that Moses was commanded to lay his hand on Joshua—not that he might receive the Spirit, but—because the Spirit was already in him.[2]

It is in connection with the reformed use in ordination, and the transference of the act from the bishop to the presbytery, that the charge is brought against the Church of having thereby separated itself from the Church Catholic. We cannot admit the charge as valid. The "laying on of the hands of the Presbytery," to which S. Paul refers as the warrant of Timothy's ministry,[3] had gradually given way, as we have seen, to the laying on of the hands of the president of the presbyters, as the essential element in ordination. The old rite now recovered its original form. The diocesan bishop no

[1] History, book i.   [2] Num. xxvii. 18.   [3] 1 Tim. iv. 14.

longer was allowed to usurp the privilege of admitting whomsoever he would to the ministry. The congregational bishops, acting together in a recognised and orderly court, resumed their control of the function which guarded the sacred portal of the sanctuary, but which had been grievously abused. The episcopate, being a mere post-apostolic development from the presbyterate, could have no exclusive claim to appropriate a right of which the presbyterate was the original depositary, and to exercise a power which presbyters had exercised before bishops, as distinct from presbyters, had been heard of. The theory of episcopal apologists that, while the apostles "ordained" in all the churches presbyters, who had no authority to confer ordination in their turn, they "consecrated" a few chosen men to a rank higher than the presbyters and equal to their own, "qualifying them to ordain deacons and presbyters, and, when necessary, to impart their full commission to others,"[1] is a theory merely, without historical support.

In the Roman Church ordination of a priest is a sacrament; consecration of a bishop is not. Whatever peculiar and efficacious grace resides in the sacrament, must therefore be held, by that Church, to belong to the priest, not to the bishop. The bishop, at least, receives no fresh or

[1] Dean Hook, Church Dictionary, p. 727.

greater share of the sacramental grace, through his (non-sacramental) consecration. This fact marks the priesthood as the order in which the sacred deposit of grace and authority, originally committed by the apostles to their successors (whatever that may amount to), is actually to be found.[1] The Scottish presbyters who arranged the organisation of the Reformed Church had no scruple in acting upon this principle. At the call of the people they examined a man's fitness for the ministry,—if fit, they ordained him. Having no more faith in episcopal government than in episcopal ordination, they vested the Church's administration in duly formed courts,

[1] "To test the matter practically—the credentials of the apostles were the ability to cure diseases, to take up serpents, and to drink of deadly poison without harm: power was also given them to pardon sins. It is recorded in holy Scripture that they did actually cure diseases, and of one of them it is recorded that the bite of a venomous reptile did him no harm; but they seem to have seldom or never pardoned sins. Now, any who claim to be successors of the apostles by apostolical succession, and who claim by that succession to be possessed of similar graces and powers, should surely therefore show the credentials of apostles. Will they, then, cure diseases? No! Will they, then, handle the deadly rattlesnake?. No! Will they drink of poison? No! Will they pardon sins? Yes!—they, and those of the inferior grade of presbyters, will pardon sins. That is to say, that they cannot do what the apostles did, but profess to be able to do what the apostles seem not to have done—and that an easy matter, which any one can *say* he can do. According, then, to this Scriptural test, any who claim to be as the apostles of Jesus Christ, by apostolical succession, are but false apostles, and the doctrine a blasphemous figment."—Tod's Protestant Episcopacy in relation to Apostolical Succession, p. 22.

in which the representatives of the people, called the elders, as well as the deacons, acted along with the ministers in all matters affecting the interests of the Church and congregation, except in the ministry of the Word and sacraments. The only orders recognised were two, those of the presbyter or minister and the deacon. The deacon now resumed his proper place in the Church, not as a subordinate assistant in the services and aspirant to the priesthood, but as the Church's almoner, or "distributor," intrusted with the care of the poor, and of the properties and goods of the Church. He sat in the kirk-session, but had not the governing voice and vote there allowed to the elders; who, in the Reformed Church, held a place peculiar to themselves, the true significance of which has been obscured by the attempt, repeatedly made, to invest their office with a spiritual character, which it does not properly possess or historically claim.[1]

The name of these officials is Scriptural, but the office itself was an outcome of the reforming policy which had originated in Switzerland. There, and especially in Zurich, under Zwingli, the relation of Church and State was pre-emi-

[1] For an example of this attempt, which has no doubt some sanction in the 'Second Book of Discipline,' see 'The Eldership of the Church of Scotland,' by the Rev. J. G. Lorimer. For an able and learned exposition of the opposite view, see 'The Ruling Eldership,' by the late Principal P. C. Campbell, D.D.

nently intimate, and the representatives of the people had a place and power in the administration of the Church, unknown either in the East or West since the apostolic and earliest patristic times. Scotland was in so much the disciple of Switzerland, that it need not surprise us to find this special mode of according full recognition to the lay element in Church government reproduced in our ecclesiastical constitution. The elders of the Kirk were the embodiment of the apostolic principle that the Church was the whole body of the faithful, and of the Swiss practice of associating certain men with the pastors in the government of the Church, as the representatives of that whole body. The elders were not "presbyters" in the sense in which that word is identical with *bishops* or *ministers*: they were the "elders of the people," in the sense in which the term was used in Old Testament times to designate those who, by reason of age, station, or character, were regarded as worthy representatives of the rest of the community. The elder is defined in the 'First Book of Discipline' as a man of good life and godly conversation; without blame and all suspicion; careful for the flock; wise, and above all things fearing God. His office is defined as consisting in governing along with the ministers, in consulting, admonishing, correcting, and ordering all things appertaining to the state of the congregation; and as differing from the office of the ministers, in that it includes neither preaching the Word nor ministering the sacraments. The elder's co-operation with the clergy included all administrative business. The elder at first, as also the deacon, held office only for a year at a time, but later this restriction was removed.

Another functionary who obtained a vocation in the remodelled system was the Reader. For this also there was primitive warrant. His office was one well known in the early Church. In Cyprian's days the reader was appointed to read to the congregation from the Scriptures or other permitted writings, such as the Pastor of Hermas and the Epistles of Clement of Rome. The office was then regarded, and coveted, as forming a stepping-stone to the priesthood. The Scottish reader was deputed to places where there was no settled ministry, that he might read the common prayers and Scriptures before the congregation, and sometimes even add a word of exhortation. The office might be held by a deacon if he were qualified; but it was intended to be, as a general rule, only a temporary one, and a substitute for that of the settled minister. The readers were commonly chosen, as I have said, from the ranks of the conforming priests; and from the carefulness with which evidence of their ability to discharge the duty is required, it is plain that the office of the priest in the unreformed Kirk was often held by a man who could not read the English language intelligibly, and whose literary acquirements presumably extended no further than to such an acquaintance with the missal as enabled him to stumble through the celebration of the mass. The readers (with what appears to be the ineradicable desire of unlicensed persons to usurp the office of the licentiate — a desire commonly strongest in those whose incapacity renders its indulgence least desirable) proved a somewhat intractable set of functionaries, and again and again we find the General Assembly discharging them from the assumption of ministerial duties beyond their own sphere.

It would be a mistake to suppose that the government of the Reformed Church of Scotland was settled on a *dogmatic* basis, or in accordance with a preconceived theory of the *jus divinum* of Presbytery. There is, on the contrary, clear evidence that the first Reformers had no dogmatic hatred of Episcopacy, or attachment to Presbytery. Among the reforms which the Lords of the Congregation craved in their first petition, abolition of Episcopacy was not included, or even named. The episcopal function was continued in the appointment of the reformed Superintendents; and the Episcopal order, as an order, was regarded with tolerance, if not with respect, by those who rebelled against the domination and the doctrines of Rome. What brought Episcopacy into discredit was the character of the prelates, who represented it in Scotland before and at the date of the Reformation, and the tenacity with which they clung to the Roman connection, when the nation had made up its mind to renounce what the reforming Act of Parliament called "the Pope of Rome and his usurped authority." The bishops' fidelity to Rome destroyed their influence in Scotland, where popular sympathy and reverence had already been alienated by their worldly lives, their neglect of duty, their preference of the interests of the Roman Church to those of the Scottish nation, and the many ecclesiastical abuses which they had connived at and encouraged. Thus, when the destructive stage of the Reforming movement was passed, and men began to reconstruct a somewhat shattered system, there was no effort made to adapt the old episcopate to reformed conditions. At the same time, the expediency of the episcopal function was too apparent to allow that function to be discarded. One of the first reconstructive acts of the Reformers was, therefore, to perpetuate it, through the appointment of those who were called "Superintendents"—a name exactly equivalent to that of bishop or overseer; and designating an official who, under reformed conditions, would supply to the Church all that was best in the function of the Celtic abbat or the "Catholic" bishop.

The Reformers were not hampered in this by any theory either for or against the episcopal order. They did not believe it was of divine institution; they did not believe it was of satanic origin. What was useful and apostolic in the discredited office they would preserve. They would have wise and good men acting as overseers of the churches, the advisers of their brethren—the superintendents of their work—not in virtue of an authority vested in a traditional hierarchy, and exercised at the dictation of a foreign potentate, but an authority conferred by the Church itself in order to meet its own necessities, and for the proper exercise of which those clothed with it were to be responsible to the Church, as represented by its General Assembly. Those who have imbibed Andrew Melville's ideas as to the inherent mischief of Episcopacy, and the inherent virtue of Presbytery — ideas unknown to Knox and his coadjutors—have made a practice of representing the office of superintendent as a mere temporary expedient, and an excrescence on the Presbyterian system. In point of fact, it was one of the earliest and most carefully devised institutions of the Reformed Church — adapted to be permanent, and held, as it was, at the will of the great governing council, regarded as perfectly in accordance with Presbyterian theory and practice.

For Presbytery, we must remember, does not mean the simple assertion of that questionable entity called "Presbyterian parity." It means the government of the Church by presbyters—by the whole body of the ministry and those associated with them for purposes of government, and not by bishops or the members of a special class, claiming to govern not as the representatives of the whole body of the Church, but in virtue of an alleged divine commission. That parity, which insists on holding that every presbyter shall be considered the equal of every other, and that there shall be no ascending scale of office or function in the ecclesiastical body, and which has therefore rejected the order of superintendents, is practically untenable. It is not exhibited even in the Church of which it is supposed to be a distinctive principle. Apart from the imparities created by individual character and genius, there are the imparities unavoidable under any active and intelligent organisation. He who is *primus inter pares* is for the time being as much *cæteris impar* as if they were not his peers. The Moderator of a presbytery or Assembly is the temporary president, with powers belonging as specially to his office as if he were a superintendent. The difference between the prerogatives of the minister of a parish and those of the minister of an unendowed chapel is as distinct as if the one and the other belonged to a separate order of ecclesiastics. If Presbyterian parity exist at all in more than in name, it is as much infringed by a commission of the General Assembly being empowered to exercise, occasionally, and inconveniently, those duties of supervision which were discharged regularly and without friction or offence by the duly constituted superintendents of the Church of the Reformation. There is no reason to believe that those who instituted the office contemplated its early abolition. That abolition was owing to the development of extreme theories, and the illegitimate revival of that pretended Episcopacy which the nobility set up to serve their own rapacious purposes. But two of the most prominent features of the reformed system of Church government, as organised by Knox and those who acted with him, were the governing General Assembly of the Church; and under it and responsible to it the superintendent.

The system of superintendency was never carried out in the fulness of its design. The only districts or dioceses which were actually planted were those of Glasgow; Angus and Mearns; Argyll and the Isles; Lothian; and Fife.

But the intention was to provide superintendents also for Orkney; Ross; Aberdeen; St Andrews; Jedburgh; and Dumfries; and thus to occupy the whole area of the Church.

In the appointment of a superintendent, the ministers, elders, and deacons of the chief town in the province or diocese, along with the magistrates and council, nominated two or three of "the most learned and godly ministers within the whole realm"; and every church in the province was at liberty to do the same. Public intimation of the names was duly made, and after thirty days, all the nominees were subjected to a searching examination, at the hands of the clergy of the province and certain of the already appointed superintendents. After this a vote was taken—proxies from absent ministers being allowed—and he for whom the majority voted was set apart, in a solemn service, to the office of superintendent. He was not required to resign his parochial charge, but obtained assistance in it, that he might not be hindered in his episcopal work. The appointment of ministers began with the "call" of the people, on which followed strict examination by the other presbyters of the bounds: after which, if found duly qualified, the candidate was by them solemnly ordained.

In the appointment of elders the minister and kirk-session drew up a "leet" for the people to choose from. So also in the case of the deacons.

One of the wholly new features of ecclesiastical arrangement, to which prominence is given in the First Book of Discipline, was the institution of the "Exercise," as it was called. It was one of the healthiest of the marks of the Church's abandonment of sacerdotalist traditions. It was an emphatic assertion of her belief in the great truth of the priesthood of the whole Christian family. The exercise was a kind of general or congregational assemblage, which was to be held once a-week, with the express object of bringing the members of the Church together on a basis of social union, for mutual edification, and for the exercise of the individual "gift" which each might possess. The object in view was "that the Kirk have judgment and knowledge of the graces, gifts, and utterances of every man within their body; the simple and such as have somewhat profited shall be encouraged daily to study and to prove in knowledge, and the whole Kirk shall be edified. . . . Every man shall have liberty to utter and declare his mind." It was, though new in the Scottish Church, but a reversion to the apostolic usage, the proper rules for which S. Paul suggests to the Corinthians;[1] and was singularly well adapted for knitting the Church together in

[1] 1 Cor. xiv.

friendly intimacy, and in religious and intellectual intercourse. The conventionality, which took the place of sacerdotal tradition, and stiffened the development of the Reformed Church, gradually transformed this free and intelligent conference—wherein all took an equal part—into a more formal meeting, in which the minister gradually assumed the lead, if he did not indeed monopolise the whole functions; so that, to use the words of Edward Irving, "our church meetings" (and he does not exclude those of the Lord's Day), "from being for edification of the brethren by the Holy Ghost showing Himself in the variously gifted persons, have become merely places for preaching the Gospel, and not for edifying the Church." The revival of the earlier custom of a free meeting, for united worship and open conference and discussion, could not fail to be interesting and profitable to any congregation attempting it. Where the ordinary so-called "prayer-meeting"—which is not really a prayer-meeting so much as a preach-meeting—is found to be dull and unattractive, this attempt to freshen it and give it life might be worth a trial. The discontinuance of the "exercise"—which is not referred to even in the Second Book of Discipline—is only one out of many instances of the contraction, rather than expansion, in freedom and variety of development which early began to narrow and impair the life of our Reformed Church.

In those details of order and organisation which I have put before you, we have the constituent elements in the government and administration of the Reformed Church: the minister of the Word and Sacraments standing at the centre of the whole organisation, whether in his more individual relation to one congregation as pastor and teacher, or in his larger relation to a group of congregations as superintendent; the deacon, in charge of the patrimony and the alms of the church; the elder, or representative of the brethren, acting along with the minister and deacon in counselling, ruling, and applying the discipline of the Church. Over all these was the General Assembly, or National Ecclesiastical Council—the supreme depositary of authority and instrument of government. The Presbytery and the Synod were later developments of the Presbyterian polity. In its earliest stages it exhibits only the two extremes—the kirk-session, or council of the minister with his elders and deacons, on the one hand; and the General Assembly, or council of the whole Church, on the other. The constitution of the Assembly, at first and for a long time, was of a civil, quite as much as of an ecclesiastical, type—that is to say, we find its membership determined by civil as well as by ecclesiastical qualifications. The nobles and great landowners sat in it in virtue of their rank and territorial influence; and of those members who were called "commissioners of kirks" we have no reason to believe that all were office-bearers. The Reformed Assembly was, in a sense and a degree in which the Roman councils had never been, fairly and fully representative of the nation in its religious convictions and polity. The whole system, of which the Assembly was the crown, was, in its theory and organisation, the very antithesis of the system which had grown up under the sombre shadow of Rome. It dealt a death-blow to the sacerdotalism which was the vital principle of the Roman Church. It released the Christian ministry and the government of Christ's Church from the thraldom of priestcraft, and set them upright on a rational, as opposed to a traditional and sacerdotal, basis.

It may be questioned whether so complete a change as the establishment of the reformed order implied was necessary; whether, for example, the supremacy of the General Assembly might not have been asserted and maintained quite as fully, though some of its members had borne the ancient name of bishop instead of the modern title of superintendent; whether the theory of Presbyterian parity might not have flourished under a system which, while recognising the episcopate as an office, refused to recognise it as a distinct order? But, on the whole, it is doubtful if less thorough measures would have served the essential purpose. Every step taken could refer to Scriptural sanction or primitive example. The time was not one for half-measures and bland compromises. The necessities of the case left no leisure for Fabian tactics — for prolonged deliberation and warily cautious choice of means and methods. The Church had to be purified, reformed, and re-established promptly on a more stable foundation, and the system of reformation that Continental experience had tested and approved appeared the best and soundest to the Scots Reformers. Even "the judicious Hooker," determined apologist of Episcopacy as he was, recognised that the argument of a present and pressing necessity might override a theory and a tradition of Church government. "This device," says he, speaking of that scheme of ecclesiastical polity which Calvin established in Geneva, and whose principles Knox reproduced in Scotland, "I see not how the wisest at that time living could have bettered, if we duly consider what the present estate of Geneva did then require."[1] If the best that could be

[1] Ecclesiastical Polity, Preface, ii. 4.

The Books of Discipline. 263

devised for the time at Geneva, and if it worked well and secured the orderly administration of the Church's worship and discipline there (as Hooker acknowledges it did), why should it be discarded, after experience had approved it, in order to revert to another polity which Geneva had found to be profitable neither for religion and morals, nor for the civil welfare of her citizens? Why should its efficacy not be tried in Scotland, and, as in Geneva, be justified by its results?

The new polity, as I have pointed out, did not emerge whole and complete in all its parts from the mint of the First Book of Discipline. It received its fuller elaboration in the Second Book, and at the hands of Andrew Melville. He gave it the new impetus, under which it expanded and developed into its perfect organisation of kirk - sessions, presbyteries, synods, and assemblies, each of these being, like all healthy organisms, a natural growth. The principles at the root of the growth were the sufficiency of the order of presbyters for all purposes of discipline, order, and government; and the right of the people to a voice in the affairs of the Church.

The first foe that the Reformed Church had to fight was Prelacy, the earliest development of which was, as we shall see, the creation of the "tulchan" bishops, who were mere channels through which the revenues flowed into the coffers of the nobles. The tulchans were knocked on the head by Andrew Melville in 1580. Again in 1598 the Episcopal title was revived, that under cover of it churchmen might be once more admitted to Parliament; and in 1610 Anglican consecration was bestowed on the parliamentary prelates, whose reign lasted till 1638, when their office and order were rudely overthrown. Renewed again at the Restoration, Prelacy was finally abolished at the Revolution. Through all these years of conflict it was the symbol of despotism and wrong. Under guise of Prelacy the Church was cozened out of its revenues; the liberties and consciences of the people were violated; the absolutism of the Stewarts was advanced. This, more than anything in the office of bishop itself, made "black Prelacy" so abhorrent to the commonalty of Scotland; and, identifying Presbytery with freedom of life and thought, deepened their attachment to the polity of the Reformation. And all through these years of conflict that polity remained substantially unchanged. Bishops were set up and were pulled down, but from the days of Knox to those of Carstares the doctrine, discipline, and government of the Church continued practically unaltered. The

Assembly and the Presbytery had the real power; the bishop had little, if any, except what the support of the arm of flesh gave him. The records of Synods and Presbyteries during the time when Prelacy was most vigorously enforced —from 1662 to 1688—record the inner life of the Church in much the same terms as those in which it might be recorded now, except that the Synod had a permanent moderator, who was present and took the lead at every ordination. The ecclesiastical name, and a part of the form, might be changed; but throughout, the life and character were essentially Presbyterian, as the regular succession of the ministry was Presbyterian. The presbyterate never had to seek renewal from foreign sources; but the parliamentary prelates of James I. and the nominees of Charles II. had alike to travel to Westminster, to knit up there the ravelled line of the disorganised Episcopate.

We may note, at this point, that not only did the Church never lose that essentially Presbyterian character which was stamped on it at its Reformation, but that the changes which more than once were temporarily made in its form of government were in the main so political and external, that they did not even affect the mass of the clergy sufficiently to break their connection with the Church. We have seen how the great body of the Celtic clergy became Romanist; how numbers of the Romanist became Reformed. Similarly the great body of the parochial clergy at the Restoration accepted, without resistance, the imposition of Episcopacy; and a large majority of the parochial clergy at the Revolution accepted, in the same way, the re-establishment of Presbytery. Several of them lived quietly on in their parishes through both changes, — some, perhaps, because they were men of peace, like Leighton or Laurence Charteris; some, no doubt, because they were of the same mind as Andrew Gray, of Coull, whose epitaph bore that

> "He had a church without a roof,
> A conscience that was cannon-proof:
> He was Prelatick first; and then
> Became a Presbyterian;
> Episcopal once more he turned,
> And yet for neither would be burned." [1]

Or of Gavin Young, who, being asked how he reconciled his conscience to remaining minister of Ruthwell, through all the changes of Church government from 1617 to 1671, ingenuously replied, "Wha wad quarrel wi' their brose for a mote in them?"

At the Restoration, and at the Revolution, the clergy numbered about 1000. Of these,

[1] Fasti, p. 528.

less than 300 were put out, or removed themselves at the Restoration; about 400 at the Revolution. In each case the majority remained. That majority at the Revolution was composed chiefly of men who had been Episcopally ordained—as, at the Restoration, it was composed of men who had been Presbyterially ordained — and from whose ranks the bishops between 1662 and 1688 were chosen and consecrated, without previous re-ordination. The stream of orders flowed on in a current, at first somewhat mingled, but which gradually cleared itself, as the Episcopally ordained remnant died out, and the Presbyterate became once more —as in the primitive Church—the sole channel of ordination.

Since the end of the seventeenth century no convulsion of any kind has disturbed the peaceful progress of the Church. Changes have passed upon it, as they pass upon all bodies whose life is in themselves, but they have not been forced upon it by any external pressure,—they have been the natural developments of the Christian consciousness of the body of Christ. There have been certain modifications in methods of administration; in ritual; in the general cast of doctrine and interpretation of Scripture; but there has been no change in the system of presbyterial government, in the common order of our reformed worship, and in the authorised standards of belief. Almost all the principles of the First Book of Discipline have remained throughout all her vicissitudes the distinctive principles of the Church. In the end of the nineteenth century she retains the essentially Presbyterian type of polity devised for her by Knox and the Reformers of the sixteenth.

LECTURE VIII.

IN no country was the scheme of reformation, as drafted by the Reformers, more symmetrical and complete than in ours; in none was its accomplishment more hampered and thwarted by the mean rapacity and traitorous disloyalty of the governing class. Knox's statesmanlike idea of an apportionment of the ecclesiastical revenues between the proper support of the ministry, of the poor, and of a comprehensive system of graduated national education, was never realised, simply because the politicians who pretended to be zealous for Protestant truth and reformed principles were knaves and robbers, destitute alike of religion and of patriotism. It was the misfortune of the Episcopal form of government that it became first the tool, and then the ally, of their treachery and greed. First, as I have said, arose the "tulchan" episcopate, the channel through which the rents of the Church flowed into the pockets of the spoilers. Next came the *quasi*-episcopate of Spottiswoode and the other Presbyterian ministers who, though without Episcopal ordination, and equally without any election by people or cathedral chapter, and simply at the mandate of the Crown, were illegitimately consecrated by three English bishops at London; and who imposed on the Church, at King James's bidding, the episcopate which, after an existence of barely thirty years, was abolished by the General Assembly of 1638. One evil of the introduction of these irregular overseers was that the orderly supervision of the Church by its own superintendents fell into abeyance, and the nominees of the Court usurped the offices of the elect of the Church, and yet never discharged them faithfully.

But though a kind of nominal episcopacy was thus created, the essentially Presbyterian character of the Church remained intact; and its courts, formally constituted and ratified as courts of the realm as they had been by the Acts of 1592, assumed the jurisdiction and the national position which they still retain. This reversion to, and chartered adoption of, a scheme of government founded on primitive principles, was accompanied by a notable change in the character of the ministry. The former inefficiency and immoralities disappeared. The ranks of the conforming priests and monks were carefully weeded, before any were pronounced qualified for office in the remodelled Church. All other candidates were only admitted after anxious scrutiny. The result was the formation of a clerical body, whose purity of life and personal good fame even the mendacious tongue of sectarian slander did not venture to asperse. The satiric literature, which had nothing but the bitterest gibes for the priesthood, stopped its railing. It found no food for libel or lampoon among the Protestant clergy. Even had it found such material, the satirist would have been slow to use it. The clergy now held a place in the reverence of the people the priests had never gained. As time went on, and the party of the Court and the Episcopate assumed an attitude progressively hostile to popular rights and liberties, the defence of these and the assertion of the principles which lay under them were, with an ever-increasing reliance, intrusted to the ministers. They were the true leaders and champions of the people; and the people repaid the clergy's independence and patriotism with their own confidence and respect.

The clergy, no doubt, were too often ready to use the pulpit for purposes more polemical and political than became the house of God; but their excuse was the absence of a free press, and of any other available means of appealing to the general mass of their fellow-citizens, and of exposing before them the misdoings of the civil rulers and ecclesiastical usurpers. No suspicion of time-serving or self-seeking impaired their honourable influence. They had a fair title to "stand so high in all the people's hearts." The name of Knox has a place of its own in the roll of the worthies of the reforming era; but Craig, Bruce, Durie, Douglas, and Andrew Melville are not unworthy compeers. Melville's name, in particular, is associated with the completer development of the Presbyterian polity and the construction of the Second Book of Discipline. The First Book was virtually the work of Knox, and laid down the polity of the Church on broad and liberal lines. It specified five offices (but only two orders) in the Church — minister, superintendent, elder, deacon, reader. It sketched out a large educational scheme. It directed that the Holy Communion should be celebrated at least four times in the year; that there should be two public services on Sundays—the second to include catechetical instruction of the young; that there was to be daily service (reading and prayers) in the towns. The service-book to be employed was the version of the Genevan liturgy which Knox had used abroad, and now introduced in Scotland as the 'Book of Common Order.' It demanded that "the whole rents of the Kirk" should be intrusted to the Kirk for the behoof of the ministry, of the poor, and of education.

This first Book of Discipline was accepted by the General Assembly of 1560, but not by the Parliament, where its generous ideal of the reconstructed Kirk was sneered at as a "devout imagination." The Second Book was accepted by the Assembly in 1581, and was virtually approved, though not formally sanctioned, by the Parliament of 1592 in the Acts known as "the Charter of the Church." It differs at some points from the First; and we note in it, specially, the more dogmatic tone; the strict injunction of the imposition of hands as a necessary element in ordination; the omission in the list of ecclesiastical offices of the superintendent and the reader, with the addition of the doctor or teacher as an ordinary function, distinct from the minister, pastor, or bishop; and also the definition of the eldership as "a spiritual office." The hand of Melville is easily recognisable in these two changes—the distinction between the doctor and the minister, and the assertion of the spirituality of the elder's office. His humanistic devotion to learning prompted the one; and possibly a desire to erect, over against the threefold ministry of the Episcopalians — bishop, priest, and deacon—a Presbyterian triad, minister, elder, and deacon, of equal validity, may have suggested the second. Each, however, was an error and innovation.

The office of the "doctor" never obtained

definite sanction in the Church; but Melville's theory of the eldership gained very common assent, and has injuriously affected the tenure of that office for three centuries. It has led to unfortunate confusion in the general conception of the primitive presbyter (elder, minister, bishop) and of the reformed representative of the brethren; and, engendering erroneous ideas of the position and duty of the latter, has often deterred excellent and eligible men from becoming members of the kirk-session. Melville's bitter experience of the character of the civil Government, and the dangers that beset the Church's relation to it, when wielded by such men as the Regent Morton, and of the insidious recrudescence of Prelacy under the covert of tulchanism, betrays itself in an elaborate article on the civil magistrate, and an absolute condemnation of the episcopal title and office, for neither of which the earlier manifesto afforded a precedent.

This is only one indication of a process which went on throughout the closing years of the sixteenth, and, one might say, nearly the whole of the seventeenth century. The insane determination of the Stuarts to force their ecclesiastical crotchets upon a free people and a "stubborn Kirk"[1] begot a jealousy and resentment, and narrowness of view, which poisoned the general

[1] King James VI.'s own phrase.

stream of public life and thought. Time and energy, that might have occupied themselves in working out large schemes of educational progress, of civic and social reform, of commercial and industrial advancement, were taken up in withstanding the arbitrary aggressions of absolute power and defending the simplest rights of a civilised community. Instead of devoting themselves to theological investigation, to perfecting the "platform" of the Reformed Church, to fostering the general interests of humanity and religion, the clergy had to spend their lives in the bare effort to make good whatever advantage had accrued from the overthrow of Popery, to maintain the merest liberty of worship, and to secure the scantiest provision for their own daily sustenance. Intensity of irritated feeling—concentration of ill-will against "the troublers of Israel"—contraction of sympathies—exaggerated importance attributed to secondary causes of dispute—while the great primary verities and duties fell into the background,—all this was the natural result.

The ecclesiastical atmosphere had become somewhat calmer and the horizon clearer at the time of King James's death. The bishops were not given to intermeddling. The people were, on the whole, fairly quiescent. Compliance with the obnoxious Articles of Perth was not stringently insisted on; and of these the only one that was thoroughly disliked was the kneeling at Holy Communion. Odium attached to this, because it suggested the false doctrine of the corporeal presence, and was utterly unlike the apostolic use. The other four — private baptism, private communion, confirmation of children when eight years old, and the observance of Christmas, Good Friday, Easter, Ascension, and Whitsunday—were objects of comparative indifference, and generally disregarded. But with the accession of Charles everything went wrong. His gloomy fanaticism would be content with nothing short of the thorough suppression of Presbyterian principle, order, and usage, and the complete subjugation of the Scottish Church to the Anglican yoke and model. In the struggle which ensued, between royal absolutism and the freedom of the Church and the nation, the victory lay with the " stubborn Kirk " ; but it was gained at a heavy price. The resistance to the policy of Charles and Laud, which found its ablest and most constitutional exponent in Alexander Henderson, the Moderator of the Assembly which in 1638 expelled the bishops, was not always under a control so sagacious and temperate as his. The enthusiasm of the Covenant passed, from a patriotic and public-spirited defiance of arbitrary encroachments on the liberty of the subject and the rights of the Church, into a quixotic enterprise for extirpating Prelacy and propagating Presbytery beyond the bounds of Scotland, and enforcing a uniformity of creed, ritual, and Church government throughout the three kingdoms. This enterprise was the motive of the international compact known as "The Solemn League and Covenant," and of the deliberations of the famous Westminster "Assembly of Divines." Both were conspicuous illustrations of the apparently unalterable law, by which ill-regulated action is counterpoised by reaction, generally ending in the "madness of extremes." Both, as has been well said, "unfortunately were a copy *reversed* of the plan of James VI. in 1606, and of Charles in 1633, which had been so fruitful of misery, from the opposite side."[1] Subscription of this League and Covenant was demanded from all sorts and conditions of men, on pain not only of ecclesiastical censure but of civil penalty. Whoever objected to declare himself in favour of "the extirpation of popery, prelacy, superstition, heresy, and schism," and to assist in "the discovery of all such as have been, or shall be, incendiaries, malignant, or evil instruments," because of their refusal to sign the portentous document, was regarded as himself a malignant.

[1] Rev. J. Rankin, D.D., in 'Church of Scotland, Past and Present,' vol. ii. p. 520.

The Solemn League and Covenant was well received in most districts of the country, except in Aberdeen. That city was the seat of a school of divines whose theology was of a type which was only now trying to root itself in the Scottish soil. The general development of doctrine throughout the kingdom, up to the second decade of the seventeenth century, had been on distinctly Calvinistic lines. During that decade a reaction towards a freer and fuller Gospel set in, and it continued to advance till 1638; but the " Purging Committee," which was one embodiment of the zeal of the Assembly of that year, made short work of " the Aberdeen doctors," as these divines had come to be called. They were all deprived and deposed; and the theology of the Synod of Dort triumphed over the nascent efforts of native thought.

The very foremost of these victims of irrational sectarianism (for that policy deserves no other name which drove good and learned men out of their churches or chairs, simply because their theological system had more in common with that of Pelagius and Arminius than with that of Augustine and Calvin, and their ecclesiastical sympathies leant to Episcopacy rather than to Presbytery) was Dr John Forbes, son of Bishop Patrick Forbes. The bishop was one of King James's creations; but, unlike most of them, was a man wise, earnest, and learned, who made it his aim to draw to the churches and University of Aberdeen the ablest scholars and clerics whom he could find. Amongst them was his second son. Like almost all the leading scholars and divines of Scotland, John Forbes completed his education on the Continent, Scottish intercourse with which was much more free and constant in those days than it has ever been since. He studied at Melanchthon's university as well as at others in Germany; and on one occasion at the Swedish university of Upsala, he maintained a public disputation against the Lutherans and their archbishop. Returning to his own country, he was appointed Professor of Divinity and Church History in King's College, an office he held until Covenanting fervour succeeded in ousting him from it, after which, his elder brother having died, he retired to the paternal estate of Corse, and occupied himself in completing his great work, ' Instructiones Historico-Theologicæ," which he published at Amsterdam in 1645, with a preface which contained a formal recommendation of the work by the theological faculties of Leyden, Franeker, and Utrecht.

In this book, as in his professorial lectures, Forbes strove to supply what he recognised as a pressing want of the time—the want of a historical treatment of theological questions. The

Roman Catholic reaction was in full swing on the Continent, and controversialists, subsidised from Rome, were busy, even in Scotland, appealing to the historical sentiment. They maintained that all Catholic antiquity was on the side of the ancient Church, and that the Reformed Confession and ritual were mushroom growths of the revolutionary sixteenth century, which could trace their descent no farther back than to Luther, Zwingli, or Calvin. This propaganda was not without its effect on the public mind; and Forbes felt it was inadequately met by the ordinary method of combating it, which was to make appeal to Scripture, as the main if not indeed the sole warrant of the reformed doctrine. He adopted the method of treating doctrine in its historical continuity, establishing it first from Scripture as its basis, and then tracing its history from age to age, marking where it maintained its purity, and where it became stained with Roman error or warped with heretical perversion. But he, and all such quiet and peace-loving workers in the field of religious speculation and research, were pushed aside and silenced by the heady disputants who involved the country in bitter quarrel over questions of government and order, and the intrigues and shibboleths of embittered parties, political and ecclesiastical.

The Scots politicians of Charles I. and of the

Protectorate were no great improvement upon those who had preceded them. The Churchmen, with few exceptions, were men of narrower view and less commanding power. Between the " Resolutioners " and the " Protesters," as the two factions that divided the Church, after the Glasgow Assembly, were named, its higher life was all but strangled. The Church lost its intellectual freedom, as under the Roman priesthood it had lost its moral character.

One fatal effect of the constant wranglings was the dispersion of many of the finest elements in the national life, among foreign churches and universities. Men of free spirit and active mind would not stay at home, to be subjected to clerical inquisition and tyranny because of their opinions on religion or politics. So, to escape from the intestine turmoils of the Church, when under Cromwell Resolutioner and Protester were defying each other, and Puritanism was subverting the sound foundations on which the Reformed Church had been established; and afterwards when, under Charles II., " black Prelacy " was again for a time in the ascendant, refugees were constantly flying over-sea, to friendlier shores and less distracted societies than those of Scotland. (In the calendar of the University of Sedan alone we find, during the seventeenth century, the names of seven Scots professors.) Their native country was impoverished by its own feuds, while others were enriched. This depletion accounts in some degree for the decay of native influence in our domestic affairs at this disordered time. The controlling impulses came from England, as they had come in the days of Margaret and David, and found no coherent national sentiment and conviction to oppose them.

It was after James could issue his ukases from London, with the Anglican Church at his back, that his episcopal propaganda became really efficient. It was from Lambeth that the policy was dictated which, overshooting its mark, roused the Scots to their successful assault upon the Jacobean Prelacy. But, *en revanche*, it was in the Jerusalem Chamber that the scheme was hatched which deprived the Scots of their native Confession of Faith and 'Book of Common Order,' and foisted on the Kirk a Confession, a Catechism, a Directory for Worship, and a Psalm-Book, compiled by an English Assembly in which Scotland had only a fragmentary representation. This misfortune would have been impossible had not the nation, divided against itself, been debilitated by a constant and feverish recurrence of sectarian squabbles and rancorous jealousies, the blame of which must primarily rest on that party which had, from 1572 to 1638, been obstinately on the side of absolutism, and had persistently done its best to crush the civil liberties and thwart the religious inclinations of the people. Over a country so rent and weakened Cromwell gained an easy mastery. As he had turned the English Parliament out of doors in April, so in July, 1653, he dismissed the General Assembly. Deprived of its governing body, the Church became more and more distracted and disunited, and, under the ægis of the Protector, that section of it acquired malign preponderance which had most in common with the principles, religious and political, of the English Independents. Another influence, whose advent this faction welcomed, travelled northward with the republicans, and changed some of the familiar features of Scottish religion. This was the influence of the grim and illiberal Puritanism of the southern sectaries. Theirs was no longer the noble love of pure worship and spiritual and civic freedom, which had animated their predecessors in the days of Elizabeth and James. Their spirit had deteriorated. They had grown rudely regardless of catholic usage; and, inflated with exaggerated conceptions of individual liberty, contemned the decent traditions of public worship, and the sober proprieties of ritual. The excesses in fervour of extempore prayer and controversial preaching, which they delighted in, were not native to Scotland.

The Scottish Church had from 1560 been accustomed to the ritual of the 'Book of Common Order,' and was, on the whole, contented with it, though some improvements in it had been contemplated, and no doubt would have been introduced, had not the whole question of the Church's worship been turned topsy-turvy by the reckless folly of Charles and Laud. The 'Westminster Directory' would never have been sought or desired by Scotland, had it not been pushed on for the sake of a visionary uniformity, under the pressure of the Assembly of Divines, in which English Presbyterianism, Independency, and Puritanism were in the ascendant. To that ascendancy is due, in the main, the gradual deterioration of the theory and practice of the Church's ritual, and the adoption of peculiarities ignorantly supposed, by those who know no better, to be of native growth. Thus the curious custom of reading out the verses of the psalms to be sung, line by line, was introduced, against the wishes of the Scots Commissioners in the Westminster Assembly, because the English considered it convenient where "many cannot read." A concession to English illiteracy. Again and again Baillie complains of the opposition offered by the Brownists to the use of the Lord's Prayer, the Doxology, and the minister's kneeling in the pulpit for private prayer. But the Brownists did not stand alone in discarding pious usage. Henderson, in his sermon before the Glasgow Assembly called "The Bishops' Doom," specifies among the other transgressions of the prelates their "interdicting" the daily morning and evening prayers, and their private celebration of marriages—offensive departures from the more excellent way of the first Reformers.

When the General Assembly accepted the Directory, it did not set aside the national Prayer-Book; but that book was, as I have said elsewhere,[1] "virtually superseded by the Act of 1645, imposing the Directory. And this must have been felt as a grievous necessity by many of the best leaders of the Kirk. For these were men utterly opposed to Puritanic disregard of forms and usages in worship, however much their political sympathies might draw them towards the Puritans. The Assemblies of 1639, 1640, and 1641 passed Acts against innovations in public worship, directed not against prelatic but puritanic changes. Burnet speaks of a letter issued by one of these Assemblies, specially addressed to those who, 'in a spirit of innovation and hunting after popularity,' were trying to abolish such 'laudable practices,' hitherto in use, as the Lord's Prayer, the Doxology after the Psalms, and the minister's kneel-

[1] The Reformed Ritual in Scotland, p. 28.

ing for private devotion on entering the pulpit: and the great Henderson, on being invited by the Assembly to prepare new forms of worship 'wherein possibly England might agree,' declared that he could not take upon him to 'set down other forms of prayer than we have in our Psalm-Book, penned by our great and divine Reformers.' But 'uniformity' was the watchword; and in the Westminster Assembly the preponderating influence was that of English Presbyterianism and Independency, of a distinctly puritanic caste, and not that of the Scottish type of religion, which had retained much of the Catholic spirit and reverence for ecclesiastical usage, inherited from intercourse with the Reformed communions of the Continent.

"The nursing-mother of the extempore harangues which took the place of prayers of the old liturgical model, of the interminable discourses, of the graceless practices which began to deform the decent order of public worship, was English Independency. From it, and not from our Scottish ancestors, descended to us the ungainly heritage of meagre rite and unseemly negligence in the conduct of the public worship of God.

"Already, in Scotland, the tendency to subordinate the devotional to the intellectual element in divine service, and to allow the individual minister to colour the whole with the hues of his own prejudice or passion, had asserted itself with an emphasis distasteful to men of the wide culture and sober piety of Henderson and Baillie; but no Scotch Presbyterian had as yet exhibited this characteristic in the abnormal extremes witnessed in England. The tendency must, however, have been infectious, for we find Baillie thus complacently recording his experiences of a day with the brethren at Westminster: 'We spent from nine to five very graciously. After Dr Twiss had begun with a brief prayer, Mr Marshall prayed large two hours, most divinely confessing the sins of the members of the Assembly, in a wonderful pathetic and prudent way. Afterwards Mr Arrowsmith preached an hour; then a psalm; thereafter Mr Vines prayed near two hours, and Mr Palmer preached an hour, and Mr Seaman prayed near two hours. After Mr Henderson had brought us to a sweet conference of faults to be remedied, Dr Twiss closed with a short prayer and blessing.' This interminable prolixity was not an exceptional exuberance. Dr Calamy tells us that on the days of public fasting, which were frequent, Mr Howe would go on from nine in the morning till four in the afternoon, with only an interval of about a quarter of an hour, during which he took some material refreshment, and the people allowed themselves the more spiritual restorative of psalmody. The spirit which prompted religious services of this type grew with the growth of Independency in England, and spread northwards with the advance of the principles of the Commonwealth. By slow but sure degrees the old constitutional party in the Scottish Church lost their hold on the people, and the fervid and fanatical 'Protesters' gained theirs. Internal strifes tended to develop the loose practices and rhapsodical utterances, to which all forms and rubrics were an Egyptian bondage; and the vagaries of the preacher were deferred to as the irrestrainable movements of the free spirit."

These tendencies, impairing the Church's unity, marring her worship, sapping her strength, and denationalising her character, gathered force as the crisis of the Restoration approached, and secured an easy triumph for the low treachery and breach of faith which reintroduced the bishops, fortified—on this occasion—with Anglican ordination as well as consecration. But their reign was short. They were set up in 1662, and in 1689 the Scots Parliament finally abolished them; and in 1690 it re-established the Presbytery, which had been established after the accomplishment of the Reformation of 1560, by the Parliament of 1567. Then the land had rest from the gross oppression under which it had groaned during the despotism of the second Charles and his brother; and the Church, firmly secured in its constitutional liberties and prerogatives, began to repair its desolations, to fill its waste places, and gather together the flocks which persecution had scattered. The "glorious Revolution" of 1688, which delivered the nation from its political thraldom, rendered this restoration of the Reformed Church's original constitution and government possible, and secured its permanency. The displacement of the bishops was all that, in point of fact, was necessary. Their presence had not interfered with the Presbyterian administration of the Church, in all its subordinate departments. Their absence, and the consequent recall of the General Assembly, removed an inconvenient and objectionable anomaly, and reinstated the supreme court in its proper position and authority. No other change was required. The Caroline Episcopate had introduced no novelties, save the novelty of an unrelenting persecution for conscience' sake; in comparison with which the intolerance of the Covenanters appears but a misdirected excess of zeal.

The ritual of the Church had not been purged of the elements which had begun to infect it during the Protectorate, and remained substantially on the Puritanic level. "We," says Sir George Mackenzie—"the bloody Mackenzie"—"had no

T

ceremonies, surplice, altars, cross in baptism, nor the meanest of those things which would be allowed in England, by the dissenters, in way of accommodation." The old Catholic features of the worship—the regular repetition of the Lord's Prayer and the Apostles' Creed—the responsive Amen—and the attitude of kneeling at prayer, had dropped out of use along with the 'Book of Common Order'; and the Caroline bishops and curates did nothing to raise the character of the public services of the Church. Even the kneeling at Communion, about which King James had made such a pother, was not renewed. Nothing marks the Episcopate of this time so distinctly as being the mere creature of a court, and a party indifferent to religion if only they could enforce a form of Church government amenable to the designs of absolutism, than its misuse of its rare opportunity of imparting a higher tone to the national ritual. Had the bishops had the true interests of religion at heart, they could not have let it slip from their hands. The old liturgy was laid aside. A fresh attempt to introduce the Anglican was hopeless; but they might have drawn up and gained acceptance for an order which would have commended itself to the minds of the devout, by providing services at once less elaborate and less tinctured with Romish alloy than those of the English Prayer-Book, and less controversial, dogmatic, and vehement in substance and style than those of Knox's compilation.

In the mind of the author of the 'Book of Common Order' the dread of retaining any form, or phrase, or ceremony, which had been in any degree a covert of Romish superstition, overbore the due sense of what was reverend and devout in the ancient usages, and an impartial estimate of the measure of beauty and solemnity proper in the various offices of public worship. Antagonism to Rome was with Knox the absorbing principle—we might almost say, the mastering passion. I do not call the antagonism unreasonable; but its manifestations were exaggerated and excessive. It stamped on the religion which he helped, more than any other man, to mould, a character of combative intensity, of negation and protest, which had more in common with the mental attitude of Joshua at Jericho than with that of S. Paul on the Areopagus. It specially marked the ritual of the Church with a note of harshness in form and sectarianism in feeling, which were unfavourable to the development of a devotional and catholic spirit in the people—nay, tended to repress it,— a repressive tendency which was not counteracted, but increased, by the undue prominence given to "the preaching of the Word." The clergy of the Restoration, who failed to improve the prayers of the Church, were little able to give any higher qualities to its preaching.¹

Strange, that with the restoration of the three-fold order of ministers, and the creation of a staff of bishops regularly consecrated (which the Kirk had never possessed since its reformation a hundred years before), there should be no unmistakable renewal and invigoration of her life, no palpable elevation of the standard of ministerial character and efficiency, no emanation of more gracious influence from every function of the rehabilitated priesthood, under the paternal care of the apostolic episcopate. Strange, that the signs of apostolicity—the lips touched with fire from the altar, the self-forgetful devotion, the ardent zeal, the cheerful endurance of labour and travail, the hardy encounter of perils on every side, the courage nothing could daunt, the faith that never failed—were not to be seen among the men who let no revolutions shake the tenacity of their hold on manse and glebe and teind, nor those who stepped into the places which others had vacated for conscience' sake, nor those who

---

[1] Of those here referred to (the men who took the places of the ministers who refused to conform to Episcopacy) Bishop Burnet says: "They were generally very mean and despicable in all respects; the worst preachers I ever heard, ignorant to a reproach, and many of them openly vicious. They were a disgrace to their order, and were indeed the dregs and refuse of the northern parts." —History of His own Time, i. 260.

from the hand of a profligate king had accepted the bishop's mitre, but among those whom loyalty to the principles of their Reformed Church exposed, some to exile, some to the dungeon, and some to the scaffold—all to persecution. Again the threefold ministry failed to vindicate its claim to special validity and sanctity. It was no more holy in character, catholic in spirit, and apostolic in powers and gifts under Charles II. and James VII., than it had been under James V. and Mary.

The one outstanding personality in the dreary years between the Restoration and the Revolution is Leighton's. And Leighton had written those works which keep his memory green, whose intellectual breadth and spiritual philosophy had such a charm for Coleridge, while he was the Presbyterian minister of Newbattle and the Principal of the College of Edinburgh. The Episcopal office, which he accepted in the vain hope of healing wounds and promoting peace, he resigned in wearied heartsickness, after twelve years' discouraging experiment, to die in voluntary exile.

The General Assembly met in 1690, for the first time since Colonel Cotterel's dragoons had escorted it out of Edinburgh in 1653. Its clerical members were the survivors of the clergy outed in 1662, for refusing to own the authority of the bishops. There were only about sixty of them: by Act of Parliament of the same year they had been restored to their former charges. Parliament had already ratified the Confession of Faith, and confirmed the Presbyterian government, now finally reinstated in its entirety. The original Scots' Confession was thus at last definitely set aside, and its place legally given to that of Westminster. This was matter of great regret—the old Confession being less exactly Calvinistic, less complex and particular, more Catholic in spirit and temperate in statement, than the new, which exaggerates the doctrine of the divine sovereignty, disparages that of human responsibility, and conceals the truth of God's universal fatherhood and goodwill to men behind its dogma of an arbitrary election. But the puritanic impetus of the Protectorate had pushed the Westminster symbol into a position from which no one now thought of dislodging it.

Its effect upon Scottish theology has been repressive, reinforced as adherence to it was by stringent formulas of subscription, invented originally not so much in the interests of rigid Calvinism as of anti-Jacobite fidelity to the Revolution Settlement. It was supposed that Episcopalians would refuse such formulas. Possibly at a later date, and when the connection between Episcopacy and Jacobitism had displayed itself more unmistakably, such a supposition was correct; but at the date of the Revolution Settlement, the Episcopalians showed no aversion from pledging themselves to subscribe the Confession. Before the revolutionary storm the bishops fled like their predecessors in 1638 — they became "the Kirk invisible," as Claverhouse said, with disdainful sarcasm, deserting their flocks—but they left behind them a large contingent of the clergy who were content to remain in the Church under its altered conditions. A hundred and eighty of them, with Dr Canaries— a prominent divine of somewhat dubious reputation—at their head, appealed to the General Assembly to be allowed to sign the Confession and an engagement to submit to the Presbyterian government, on the ground that they desired to be "permitted to act as presbyters in presbyteries, synods, and General Assemblies, in concurrence with the Presbyterian ministers, in the government of the Church as now by law established."

Grave suspicions of the motives of some of these conformists, and of their loyalty to the reigning sovereigns, required the exaction of stricter declarations; and for some time commissions of the Assembly had much to do in deciding upon claims of recognition, cases of desertion, and of illegal retention, of benefices. In every case the Church took care that no unlicensed or irregularly ordained person should take advantage of a time of confusion and urgency to make his way into the ministry.[1]

As for the Episcopal clergy, the treatment of all who were doing their ministerial duty well, and who honestly agreed to behave as loyal subjects, was fair, and in many instances generous, —many men being left undisturbed in their manses who yet had never taken the oaths to Government. That this lenity was often ill returned—especially in districts of the Highlands where Jacobite feeling was strong and sectarian passion took the place of religious principle—appears from several scenes of uproarious, and even

---

[1] "We have an unbroken ministerial succession from the ancient Scottish Church. The latest blunder in connection with this subject which I have noticed is one made by the Rev. Cosmo G. Lang. In a pamphlet recertly published, on 'The Future of the Church in Scotland,' by way of throwing doubts on our succession, he says: 'One of the first Acts of the first General Assembly, after the Revolution, was to admit to their communion, without any ordination, three Cameronian preachers.' . . . It is pathetic to think of how the 'persecuted remnant,' who, according to their lights, were loyal at all costs to the King of Zion, and the Prince of the kings of the earth, amid almost insuperable difficulties and not without scruples of conscience, because of the festival days of the Dutch Church, sent their most promising youths from the moorlands of Galloway and Dumfries, to study in the universities of Holland, and to be ordained by Dutch '*classes*' (*i.e.*, presbyteries), rather than that men without a lawful commission should minister to them in holy things; and of how, after they were cut off from this stream of succession, they remained for more than twenty years without a ministry at all, rather than violate the holy order of God's house."—Rev. G. W. Sprott, D.D., in 'Scottish Church Society Conferences,' 2d series, vol. ii. p. 64.

murderous, violence, attending the settlement of Presbyterian ministers, in parishes where the Episcopal incumbents had been left during their life in unmolested possession. Thus—to take an example—in the parish of Knockbain, in the year 1711, after the appointment of Mr John Grant, —the new minister, on the following Sunday, accompanied by one of his heritors, went by a boat to church, "and when at a small distance from the boat they were surrounded by a great many men and women (about two hundred), who lay in ambush. Some of them had their faces blackened, and a few were in women's clothes, some armed with swords (durks) and heavy battons; all the women had battons. Mr G. had his hat knocked off and torn in pieces, his head sadly cut, and was dragged by his cravats till almost choked, the mob still pursuing in back, sides, &c., with their staves, to get them to travel harder (more nimbly). The mob also tore a suit of fine clothes to rags; his outer coat, black coat and vest, with all his linens (were likewise) stole out of his pocket, and after a terrible effusion of his blood, and casting cold water upon his wounds, they carried him to the top of a hill, and resolved to have killed him, had not some, more tender-hearted, opposed this, and rescued him. Mr John M'Kenzie, who preached in the Episcopal meeting (-house) for that and neighbouring parishes, stood on a rising ground, feeding his eyes with their barbarous usage, and thereafter preached to the mob, most of them having pieces of Mr Grant's clothes tied or pinned to the most open parts of their bodies as trophies of victory."[1]

Scenes of a similar kind have been witnessed in more than one district of the country since the close of the revolutionary epoch, but originating in a different cause than the substitution of a Presbyterian for an Episcopal incumbent. These arose from the operation of the law of patronage. The Reformers had asserted the principle, which they traced to the apostolic era, of the Christian people's right to "call" their ministers. "It appertaineth," said the First Book of Discipline, "to the people, and to every several congregation, to elect their ministers." But, like some other points in that book, this was not included in the Church's legal constitution. By the Act of Parliament of 1567, which established the Church on its reformed basis, it was "statute and ordained" that while the examination and induction of ministers belonged only to "the Kirk now openly and publicly professed," the "presentation of laic patronages" should be reserved for "the just and ancient patrons." "Knox and the other Reformers accepted establishment on these terms; and

[1] Fasti, v. 283.

we cannot for a moment fancy they would have done so had they considered it anti-Scriptural."[1]

Up to the Reformation the patronage was vested in the landowners, in the Crown, in the bishop or the abbat, never in the people. After the Reformation it was clearly understood, as a principle, that no minister should be intruded on an unwilling congregation; but it did not necessarily follow that the people should choose him. The strong position, taken up in the First Book of Discipline, was not maintained in the Second, which gave the initiative to the "eldership," not to the congregation. It defines a minister's election as consisting in the choosing of a person "most able" for the vacant office, "by the judgment of the eldership and consent of the congregation." By the Revolution Settlement patronage is conferred on the (Protestant) heritors and the elders, who are "to name and propose a person to the whole congregation, to be either approven or disapproven by them"—the presbytery to decide, if objections be made, as to their validity, and to ordain and induct, or forbear, as they think proper. For the call of the congregation was thus substituted the right of offering objection only, to which, if reasonable, the presbytery

---

[1] Our National Church, p. 52—a remarkably able little work—"an Appeal against Disestablishment addressed to the common-sense and Christian spirit of lay Presbyterians in Scotland." 5th ed.

must give effect. As compensation for the loss of their right of patronage, the patrons were to receive from the heritors and liferenters of each parish a sum of 600 merks, or in sterling money £33, 6s. 8d. After the lapse of twenty years it was found that only four parishes had produced this compensation.[1] Seeing that the right of patronage was so little valued by those to whom it had been transferred, and that the new way of appointing ministers had "occasioned great heats and divisions," it was resolved that in all parishes in which the 600 merks had not been paid the patronage should be placed on its old footing; and this was accordingly done by the Act of 1712.

This restoration, though in one aspect an act of justice to the patrons, was undoubtedly alien to the ideas of the Scottish people, inconsistent, in its virtual annulment of the popular call, with apostolic precedent, and, in the general opinion, a violation of the sacred international stipulations of the Act of Union. It did not put an end to "heats and divisions," but rather increased them, and became the parent of not a few demonstrations, as discreditable to religion as that which occurred at Knockbain in 1711. "Disputed settlements," where no call approved the patron's choice, and all objections were set aside by the

[1] Cadder, Old Monkland, New Monkland, Strathblane.

presbytery, were too frequent, and often attended with riot and violence. The policy of the Church in regarding the call as of no account, and enforcing the appointment of the patron's presentee—a policy of which Robertson the historian was the strenuous and consistent assertor — tended to weaken the Church's hold upon the people during a long period of the eighteenth century, and was the cause of the two considerable secessions of that century, as it may be said to have been of the still larger one of 1843. The wisdom of waiting for the growth of opinion and development of events, and the unwisdom of seeking the remedy of ecclesiastical grievances in schism, are illustrated by the fact that patronage (relief from which was the motive of these three secessions), having been legally abolished, no longer exists within the Church; and the theory of the first reformers, after the uncertainties and delays of three centuries, has at last been realised.

Questions of patronage could in no way involve that of the orders of the clergy. Everything connected with orders lay within the Church's sphere of purely spiritual jurisdiction. The State, which secured the Church in her patrimonial rights, and protected the independence of her courts, only stipulated that no one should be admitted to the ministry except after due examination, and by the solemn ordination of his presbytery. The attempt of a party in the Church to strip presbyteries of this right, by enacting, in the " Veto Law" of 1834, that the judgment of a majority of the "male heads of families being communicants" was to supersede that of the presbytery as to the fitness of a presentee to a parish, was defeated by the decision of the House of Lords that such a radical change in the ecclesiastical constitution could not be effected, by the General Assembly, without the concurrence of Parliament.

The exercise of patronage, however, had much to do with the people's loyalty to the Church, and reverence for her government; and these were undoubtedly strained by the way in which the so-called "Moderate" party ruled the Church, postponing, as was commonly thought, the rights of congregations to the pleasure of patrons. There was among this party a good deal of that easy compliance with the ways of the world, that lack of spiritual-mindedness, and that philosophical indifference to deep religious questions, which were popularly summed up in the one word "Moderatism." This tended to make their ministerial labours unfruitful. It rendered their Church policy unnecessarily provocative of opposition, because suggesting that it was careless of the religious sentiments of the people.

The period when this Moderatism was at its height was one in which theology, as a science or a literature, was, in Scotland, absolutely silent and barren. It kept strictly within its statutory limits. As far as preaching was concerned, if on the Moderate side there was a good deal of adust morality, there was on the Evangelical side a compensating quantity of equally dry Calvinistic orthodoxy. But this was the very time when the Scottish Church, as represented both by her clergy and her laity, came forward to occupy a field in which they felt no fetters cramp their freedom, and to hold a foremost rank in British literature. Robertson himself, the Moderate leader, took a place second only to Gibbon's as a historian. Blair's Lectures on Rhetoric caused the foundation of the Chair of English Language and Literature in the University of Edinburgh; and his sermons—though in no sense a contribution to theology—were so famous that they were translated into almost every European language; and, what is perhaps more remarkable, earned their author a pension from royalty of £200 a-year. Principal Campbell of Aberdeen, author of 'The Philosophy of Rhetoric,' gained an almost equal reputation by his reply to Hume's essay on 'Miracles.' John Home's tragedy of 'Douglas' acquired an immense contemporary renown. Thomas Reid, Adam Ferguson, Dugald Stewart, and Adam Smith forced men to listen to the voice of Scottish Philosophy.

The influences under which Scottish intellect now began to devote itself to letters were not those of any new revival of learning throughout Europe, such as had marked the period of the Renaissance. They were not the product of any immigration of foreign scholars, such as had followed the fall of Constantinople. They were mainly two: the repressive tendency of the statutory Calvinism on the one hand, and the liberalising stimulus of the larger intercourse with England, which resulted from the Union, on the other. These combined to produce a non-theological literature of great power and brilliancy.

Another fact tended in the same direction. The development of the Church, in the eighteenth century, differed entirely from that in all previous epochs since the Reformation, in this respect—that it was dissociated from any question connected, directly or indirectly, with Episcopacy. *That*, as a factor in Scottish ecclesiastical affairs, as an influence on Scottish theological thought, disappears before the second quarter of the eighteenth century, and does not reappear again. When this fruitful source of ecclesiastical contention and theological discussion vanished, no other arose to take its place, or to engross the intellectual energies which, throughout the whole of the seventeenth century, we may say, had expended themselves in the strifes of presbyter and prelate. It was when Episcopacy was thus shelved that the narcotic influence of the Westminster Confession, backed by its exacting formula, made itself acutely felt. Theology had no room within its narrow barriers for speculative movement. Thus all mental energy and expanding genius turned from the strait enclosure, strictly guarded by the Confession, to wider and more open arenas. But the day of a revived theology was sure to come. The preaching of the post-Revolution period continued to be of the same type as that of Samuel Rutherford and the zealots of the Covenant,—a harsh and stolid Calvinism. Thomas Boston exhibits a fair specimen of its characteristics in his 'Fourfold State': life not an education, but a severe probation, on which depend irrevocable issues of eternal bliss or eternal torment; an iron " decree " absolutely determining who shall be saved, and who damned; a view of the worthlessness of "works" which could only benumb all moral instincts and sense of personal responsibility.

The inevitable reaction from teaching of this sort was the preaching of morality rather than of doctrine. But the Moderate discoursing on morality was not nutritive. It begat no spiritual enthusiasm, no glow of religious sentiment, no energy of religious life. It was certain to retreat into the background, or to find its oracles deserted, as soon as any stronger and more passionate force should press forward, startling the general conscience—arresting the general attention—awakening the inner consciousness which had been more than half asleep. And this force came into the sleepy hollow of the Kirk, in the shape of the resolute Calvinism and warm evangelical fervour which marked the preaching of Rowland Hill and the brothers Haldane. Hill was an English clergyman, the Haldanes were Scottish laymen; but all three had their share in breaking up the dull and not always decorous stagnation of religious thought and life in Scotland.

What has been called the "Evangelical Revival" began, Calvinistic,—but without the inhuman extremes and limitations of predestinarianism which had marked the theology of Rutherford, Halyburton, and Boston. But this Evangelicalism, though warm and earnest, was not to some minds more sufficient as a basis of reasonable faith than the Moderatism which it displaced. It tended to foster the growth of a religion which dealt in severe and curious self-inspection, and search for "assurance of salvation" in its own frames and feelings, and lacked broad and healthy sympathy. It begot a selfish individualism, and obscured the great central fact of God's fatherly relation to all, by teaching an austerely limited atonement, and formally forensic explanations of its relation to mankind. A more direct and personal application of the Gospel than the ordinary preaching commonly offered, and — as the only true warrant and source of this—an exposition of the Atonement which should evolve a deeper moral and spiritual meaning than that of the ordinary doctrine, became a felt necessity. Neither the scheme of "satisfaction," which was the favourite Puritan theory; nor the "rectoral" hypothesis, which regarded Christ's sufferings and death as, in the main, an exhibition of divine justice and vindication of God's character as the moral governor of the world, met the needs of the deepening spiritual consciousness which Evangelicalism failed to satisfy, and which could not accept, as a veracious theory of the Atonement, one which excluded from its scope the vast majority of human beings. The earliest, and in some respects the most deeply spiritual and original, representative of this unrest and wider outlook was a layman, Thomas Erskine of Linlathen.

We cannot enter now on an examination of Erskine's teaching, and of that of his friend and fellow-labourer in the field of a deeper and freer theology, John Macleod Campbell. I name them here as the pioneers of the movement, which has ultimately broken the gloomy dominion of the theology that had been so cramped in its growth by the shackles of Westminster that its continued influence would have, sooner or later, extinguished the spiritual and intellectual liberty without which an apostolic ministry becomes impossible. "Where the Spirit of the Lord is, there is liberty." This liberty, too, like that won at Marathon or Leuctra, has its martyrs and confessors. Campbell's deposition was the price which had to be paid to the spirit of purblind bigotry, dominant in the General Assembly of his day, for his assertion of the freedom of the Gospel. The Church has long repented of its act of narrow-minded injustice, and has recognised the truth of the teaching which, sixty years ago, it branded as unsound. Thus the thoughts of Churches widen with the process of the suns, and the "heresy" of one generation becomes the accepted dogma of another, which does not always remember whose conflict displaced the error, or through whose sacrifice the advance was gained.

"Thus it is the brave man chooses, while the coward stands aside,
Doubting in his abject spirit, till his Lord is crucified,
And the multitude makes virtue of the faith they had denied."

The liberty of prophesying, of which Campbell was the pioneer, is now the Church's secure possession.

Church Discipline. 309

In other departments of her life we can mark a similar enfranchisement from time-worn bonds. Till within living memory her discipline proceeded upon principles and methods in many particulars not far removed from those of her Roman period. An inquisitive scrutiny of morals was conducted by kirk-sessions; and penalties, little differing from penances, were prescribed to delinquents, with the intention of "satisfying the Kirk." The practical benefit of all this was very questionable. In as far as it might engender in the minds both of ministers and people a keener sense of the obligation of pure morality, it would do good. But it was more likely, in most cases, to foster a system of spying and informing on the one hand, and of deception and pietistic pretension on the other—alike fatal to the practice of Christian charity and to the growth of a salutary and manly public opinion. It is open to debate whether the confessional of the Popish priest, or the surveillance of the Protestant minister and kirk-session, was the more injurious to that self-respect and spirit of personal liberty which are inseparable from all true morality. The exercise of discipline still requires reform on the lines of definite principle and uniform application; but the disuse of the former devices of secret investigation and public penance is a distinct deliverance from an oppressive system.

The ritual of the Church, during the eighteenth and the earlier part of the nineteenth century, was bald and unimpressive in the extreme, disfigured by many of the roughest features of the irreverent Puritanism of the Protectorate. The spirit of enlightened and liberal progress has to a large extent transformed it, so that it has now regained some, at least, of the catholic usages and proprieties in which, three hundred years ago, it was at one with all the Reformed Churches.

The Church's conception of her duty, as a national institution, has also expanded in breadth and comprehensiveness. Sectarian sentiment, engendered by long periods of party strife and quarrel over secondary questions, has given place to a healthy conviction, at once devout and patriotic, of the primary necessity of caring for the nation as a whole, and holding her establishment, with all its privileges and endowments, in trust for the general good—moral, intellectual, social—of all the people. To realise this great conception of her position and duty, the Church needs all the self-devotion and power her ministry can supply. Nothing could help her more, in so worthy a work, than the restoration to their proper places of an order and an office, which have not held these places since the Reformation.

The order is the Diaconate. Well known and expressly recognised then, as the second order in the apostolic ministry, it has been partly superseded by the eldership (invested, through the ill-starred definition of the Second Book of Discipline, with a character not its own), and partly disused, through a strange and unpardonable laxity. Never wholly dormant, it has been of late revived in several parishes. In others it is still in abeyance. It ought to be revived in all in which it has been allowed to lapse, and the apostolic ministry thus restored to its original completeness.

The office is the Superintendency. Without this in well-organised operation there can be no thorough, impartial, and effective supervision of parochial and presbyterial functions, and no responsible guarantee of adequate discharge of duty. It is fortunate for the Church that, in again choosing, from the ranks of her ministry, men able to exercise this office, she would be introducing no innovation, but simply reverting to the wise practice of the fathers of the Reformation.

The Church has a noble future before her. She will best adapt herself to its necessities by the reverent study of a noble Past. We have seen, as we have reviewed a history full of vicissitudes of war and peace, of storm and calm, of conflict and of victory, many a passage that records the temporary triumph of autocratic tyranny over popular rights, of superstition over the power of love and of a sound mind, of knavish statecraft over unselfish patriotism; the disastrous results of irrational devotion to wrong principles, and of the maintenance of just principles upon untenable grounds; the loss of spiritual power consequent on the base enjoyment of carnal security and ease; but at no point in that history have we failed to mark—even amid its deepest gloom and confusion—some clear sign of the presence of that Divine Spirit which the Church's Head has promised shall abide with her for ever. He has never left Himself without a witness. In the unworldly simplicity and flaming zeal of the Celtic apostles—in the pious lives of the best of the Roman clergy—in the martyrs and confessors of the Reformation and of the Covenant—in the faithful remnant who began to rebuild the battered walls after the deliverance from the bondage of the Stuarts—in the prolonged array of faithful men who until now have preserved unimpaired the succession of the ministry, the testimony of the Christian creed, the sacred line of that life of which the Cross is the inspiration, we see sufficient evidence that this Church is a true plant of the divine husbandman's planting, and that "the holy seed is the substance thereof." Should the day again come, as it has come often in the past, when she shall find herself deserted by false friends, assailed by envious foes, "fallen on evil tongues and evil times, and compassed round with darkness and with danger," the consciousness of this will be her strength and stay; will encourage her people to uphold, and to hand on to generations yet unborn, her righteous claim to the title of the National Church of Scotland; and will nerve her pastors and teachers to make full proof of their Apostolic Ministry.

APPENDIX I.

THE TENURE OF THE SCOLLOGS.

"THE actual tenants of the lands were those who officiated; but, like so much else, the lands in no long time came to be secularised, the tenants paying so much to provide choristers, known as 'Scollogs,' 'Scolocs'— ('Scolofthes' seems to be the most ancient spelling): their lands, as well as many others in E., were under the superiority of St Andrews. There is record of them being leased in 1265. A century and a quarter later (1387), when the Bishop of St Andrews, in person, held an inquest at E. into his rights and belongings there, among other matters, it was renewed or confirmed upon the Scoloc lands that they had to provide four choristers, and with sufficient robes, to sing in the church. This service had likely gone on till the Reformation, though with the laxity that had crawled into all else. It had never, apparently, nor anything in its place, been resumed in the Reformed Church—it would have been reckoned rank idolatry. Nevertheless, in the E. charters, in the sasines or infeftments of heirs, there is mentioned for a century and a half after the Reformation the burden on the Scoloc lands of providing four singers—in one deed, which is in the common tongue, they are called 'clarks-sangsters.' . . .

"What have you got now for these valuable acres, granted so long ago to the 'dark-attired Culdee'? Gradually leased away with the burden upon them of supplying the four 'sangsters,' who had been paid ever more and more niggardly, while the acres increased in value, even this due was allowed to lapse; but the illusion was carried on upon parchment for a century or two longer, until it vanished in air. Truly you have been 'let down' gently—'with the process of the suns'—over these thousand years or thereby,—but of a verity 'let down.'"

The above, from an obliging correspondent, is an illustration of the tenure on which the Scollogs held their lands and rendered their services, and of the ecclesiastical laxity and secular trickery by which the Church has been, in so many cases, cozened out of her property.

APPENDIX II.

THE ABERBROTHOCK MANIFESTO:

A LETTER FROM THE SCOTS BARONS TO THE POPE
(NATIONAL MSS., Part II.)

" To the most Holy Father in Christ our Lord, the Lord John, by Divine Providence of the Holy Roman and Catholic Church Supreme Pontiff, his humble and devoted sons, Duncan Earl of Fyf, Thomas Ranulf Earl of Moray Lord of Man and of Annandale, Patrick of Dunbar Earl of March, Malise Earl of Stratheryne, Malcolm Earl of Lennox, William Earl of Ross, Magnus Earl of Caithness and Orkney, and William Earl of Sutherland, Walter Steward of Scotland, William de Soulis Butler of Scotland, James Lord of Douglas, Roger de Mowbray, David Lord of Brechyn, David de Graham, Ingeram de Umfravill, John de Menetethe, Warden of the Earldom of Menetethe, Alexander Fraser, Gilbert de Hay, Constable of Scotland, Robert de Keith, Mareschall of Scotland, Henry de St Clair, John de Graham, David de Lindsay, William Olifaunt, Patrick de Graham, John de Fentoun, William de Abernethy, David de Wemys, William de Montefisco, Fergus de Ardrossane, Eustace de Maxwell, William de Ramsay, William de Montealto, Alan de Moravia, Donald Cambell, John Cambena, Reginald le Chen, Alexander le Setoun, Andrew de Lescelyn, and Alexander de Streaton and other Barons and free tenants, and the whole community of the kingdom of Scotland, send all manner of filial reverence, with devout kisses of your blessed feet. We know, most Holy Father and Lord, and from the chronicles and books of the ancients gather, that among other illustrious nations, ours, to wit the nation of the Scots, has been distinguished by many honours; which passing from the greater Scythia through the Mediterranean Sea and the Pillars of Hercules, and sojourning in Spain, among the most savage tribes, through a long course of time, could nowhere be subjugated by any people, however barbarous; and coming thence, one thousand two hundred years after the outgoing of the people of Israel, they by many victories and infinite toil acquired for themselves the possessions in the west which they now hold, after expelling the Britons, and completely destroying the Picts, and although very often assailed by the Norwegians, the Danes, and the English, always kept them free from all servitude, as the histories of the ancients testify. In their kingdom one hundred and thirteen kings of their own royal stock, no stranger intervening, have reigned, whose nobility and merits, if they were not clear otherwise, yet shine out plainly enough from this, that the King of kings, even our Lord Jesus Christ, after His passion and resurrection, called them, though situated at the uttermost parts of the earth, almost the first to His most holy faith, nor would He have them confirmed in this faith by any one less than His first Apostle, although in rank second or third, to wit, Andrew the most meek, the brother of Saint Peter, whom he would have always preside over them, as their Patron.

"Moreover, the most holy fathers your predecessors, considering these things with anxious mind, endowed the said kingdom and people as the peculiar charge of the brother of Saint Peter, with many favours and very many privileges: So that our nation, under their protection, has hitherto continued free and peaceful, until that Prince, the mighty King of the English, Edward, the father of him who now is, under the semblance of a friend and ally, in most unfriendly wise harassed our kingdom, then without a head, and our people conscious of no guilt or guile, and at that time unaccustomed to wars and attacks; and the injuries, slaughters, deeds of violence, plunderings, burnings, imprisonments of prelates, firing of monasteries, spoliations and murders of men of religion, as well as other outrages which this prince perpetrated on the said people, sparing no age or sex, religion or order, no one could describe or fully understand but he who has learnt it from experience. From these evils innumerable, by the help of Him who, after wounding, heals and restores to health, we were freed by our most gallant Prince, King and Lord, our Lord Robert, who, to rescue his people and heritage from the hands of enemies, like another Maccabæus or Joshua, endured toil and weariness, hunger and danger, with a cheerful mind; him also the Divine Providence, and according to our laws and customs, which we will maintain even to the death, the succession of right and the due consent and assent of us all, have made our Prince and King; to whom as to him by whom deliverance has been wrought for our people, we for the defence of our liberty are bound, both by right and by his deserts, and are determined in all things to adhere. But, if he were to desist from what he has begun, wishing to subject us or our kingdom to the King of England or the English, we would immediately endeavour to expel him as our enemy, and the subverter of his own rights and ours, and make another our King, who should be able to defend us; for, so long as a hundred remain alive, we never will in any degree be subject to the dominion of the English. Since not for glory, riches, or honours we fight, but for liberty alone, which no good man loses but with his life. Hence it is, Reverend Father and Lord, that we beseech your Holiness, with all urgency of entreaty, on the bended knees of our hearts, that you, reflecting with sincere heart and pious mind how, with Him whose place on earth you hold, there is no respect of persons, nor distinction of Jew or Greek, Scots or English, and looking with fatherly eyes on the sufferings and straits brought on us and the Church of God by the English, would deign to admonish and exhort the King of the English, for whom that which he possesses ought to suffice, seeing that of old England used to be enough for seven kings or more, to leave in peace us Scots, dwelling in this little Scotland, beyond which there is no human abode, and desiring nothing but our own; and for procuring peace we are heartily willing to render him whatever we can, having regard to our estate; for it concerns you, Holy Father, thus to do, who seest the cruelty of the heathens raging against the Christians, whose sins demand such punishment, and the bounds of the Christians narrowed day by day; and how much it would derogate from the memory of your Holiness if, which God forbid, the

Church in any part of it suffer in your times eclipse or scandal, judge ye. Stir up, therefore, the Christian Princes, who, alleging no real cause, pretend that they cannot go to the succour of the Holy Land on account of the wars which they have with their neighbours, of which impediment the truer cause is, that in the subjugation of their smaller neighbours they reckon the advantage nearer and the resistance feebler. But with how joyful heart our said Lord and King, and we, if the King of England leave us in peace, would go thither, He who knows all things knows well.

"This we declare and testify to you the vicar of Christ and to all Christendom; and if, trusting too much to the reports of the English, your Holiness do not give to this implicit belief, and abstain from favouring them to our confusion, the loss of life, the ruin of souls, and other evils that will follow, which they will inflict on us, and we on them, will, we believe, be laid to your charge by the Most High. Wherefore we are and shall be, in those things wherever we are bound, as sons of obedience, to do your pleasure in all things as His vicar; and to Him, as the supreme King and Judge, we commit the defence of our cause, casting our care on Him, and firmly trusting that He will give courage to us, and bring our enemies to naught. May the Most High long preserve your Holiness in health to His Holy Church.

"Given at the monastery of Abirbrothoc in Scotland the sixth day of April, in the year of Grace one thousand three hundred and twenty, and of the reign of the King above-mentioned, the fifteenth."

INDEX.

Abbat, importance of the office of, under Columba, 82—a presbyter, not a bishop, 84—primacy of the Columban monasteries vested in the, 119—privilege granted to the, to sit in Parliament, 224.
Aberbrothock Manifesto, the, 196—Appendix II., 317-321.
Aberdeen, the Breviary of, quoted, 43—opposition to the Solemn League and Covenant at, 278—new school of theology at, *ib*.
Abernethy, church of Columba at, 64—the bishopric at, 120—seat of primacy of the Columban Church, *ib*.
Adamnan, Life of Columba by, 60—account of the closing years of Columba by, 67—on the ritual of the Columban Church, 87.
Agilbert, leads the Roman party at the Whitby Conference, 105.
Aidan, mission to Northumbria of, 99—establishes a church on Lindisfarne, 100.
Alban, Bishop of, title of primate of the Columban Church, 120.
Alban, S., martyrdom of, 36.
Alchfrid, King of Northumbria, opposes the teaching of the Celtic monks, 101.
"Altus," the, 52, 138.
Anchorites. See Eremites.
Anglican Articles, the, 6.
Antioch, "prophets and teachers" at, 8.
Antony, S., account of the life of,

72—effect of certain words of Christ upon, *ib*.—hermit life of, 73—develops the cœnobite life, *ib*.
Apostolic Ministry, definition of an, 4—essential note of, *ib*.—view of, in the Scottish Church, *ib*.
"Archimandrite," the title of, 74.
'Armagh, Book of,' the, 79.
Armagh, foundation of the primacy of, 80.
Armenian Church. See Church.
Asaph, S., successor to Kentigern in Wales, 47.
Ascension, observance of, 276.
Assembly, the General, modelled on the early provincial council, 241—when first held, 242—original constitution of, 260—Acts passed by, on innovations, 285—meeting of, in 1690, 293.
Augustine, mission to Britain of, 96.
Augustine, S., theology of, 93.

Baillie, account of a day at the Westminster Assembly by, 287.
Baird, Mr, warm patriotism and zealous churchmanship of, 2.
"Baird Lectureship," terms of endowment of the, 1.
Basel, representatives of the Scottish Church at the Council of, 197.
Beaton, Cardinal, profligacy of, 208—ability of, 209, 216.
Bede, on conversions by Ninian, 41—quoted as to Christianity in Northumbria, 97—on efficient

ministry in the Celtic Church, 110, 112.
Bernard, S., on irregularities in the Irish Church, 81.
Bernham, David of, canons drawn up by, 201.
Bishop, no trace of distinction in the New Testament between "elder" and, 20—emergence of the office of, 22—no trace of divine institution of the office of, *ib.*— growth of the distinction between the elder and the, 27—the parish the diocese of the, 30—subordination of the, in the Columban Church, 80, 82.
Bishops, creation of the Caroline, 292—appeal to the General Assembly by, 295.
Blanc, missionary devotion of, 62.
Boece, Hector, 153, 213.
'Book of Common Order, The,' the Scottish Church and, 284—drops out of use, 290—opinion of the author of, 291.
'Book of Discipline, First,' the, on the laying on of hands, 245—definition of an elder in, 250—institution of the "Exercise" suggested in, 258 — specific offices mentioned in, 272—on the Holy Communion, *ib.*—on the liturgy, *ib.*—on the revenue of the Church, *ib.* — accepted by the General Assembly, 273 — sneered at by Parliament, *ib.* —on the election of ministers, 298.
'Book of Discipline, Second,' the, accepted by the General Assembly, 273—approved by Parliament, *ib.*—how it differs from the 'First Book of Discipline,' *ib.*—the hand of Andrew Melville easily recognisable, *ib.*—on the election of ministers, 299.
'Book of the Universal Kirk,' the, 216.
Boston, Thomas, the 'Fourfold State' by, 305.
Brendan, S., incident in connection with the death of, 87.
Britain, the introduction of Christianity into, 35—how the Church was first formed in, 36—influence of Iona throughout, 95.
Brownists, opposition to certain parts of the Scottish ritual by the, 284.
Bruce, King Robert, firm attitude to the Pope taken by, 183.
Brude, King, opposition to Columba by, 60 — encouraged by the Druids, *ib.* — converted by Columba, 61—death of, 64.
Buchanan, George, 153, 213.
Burnet, Bishop, quoted regarding innovations, 285.
Bute, Marquess of, edition of the "Altus" by, 52.

Calamy, Dr, account by, of a church service during public fasting, 287.
Campbell, John Macleod, pioneer of a freer theology, 307 — deposition of, 308.
"Candida Casa," the building of, 39.
Canons, read at the provincial councils, 199 — on the sacraments, 200—on church architecture, *ib.*—on masses, *ib.*—David of Bernham's, 201 — on the tonsure, *ib.*—on the conduct of the clergy, *ib.*—on marriage, *ib.* —on the work of the clergy, 202 —on vicars, *ib.*—on troubles and heresies in the Church, 209.
Carey, a true follower of the primitive Church, 91.
Carthage, Synod of, enactments by the, 26.
Cassian, visit to the Egyptian monasteries by, 74—an opponent of Augustine, 76.
Catholic Church. See Church.
Cedd, Bishop, interpreter at the conference at Whitby, 106—conforms to the Roman order, 109.
Celebrad, the, 135.
Celtic Church same as Columban Church. See Church.
Charles I., fanaticism of, 276—Scots politicians of, 280—reckless treatment of the question of worship in the Scottish Church by, 284.

Charles II., Scotland during the reign of, 281.
Christmas, observance of, 276.
Chrodigang, Bishop, founds the institution of "secular canons," 156.
Church, Armenian, characteristics of the, 3.
Church, Indo-Syrian, features of the, resembling the Celtic Church, 113, 114.
Church, the, no special class of ministry in, 11 — popular and social characteristics of, *ib.*—not an order, but a society, 13, 14—decay of apostolic character of the, 14—sacerdotal development within, *ib.*—the dark period in, 23—early Presbyterian features in, *ib.*
Church, the Catholic, the Church of Scotland a branch of, 3—examples of Churches that do not so form part of, *ib.*—sacerdotalism and, 16.
Church, the Columban, distinct idea in the government of, 83—observance of the yearly festivals in, 85—the tonsure in, *ib.*—absence of Mariolatry in, 86—ecclesiastical type in, *ib.*—doctrines held in, *ib.*—ritual in, 87—celebration of mass in, *ib.*—connection with the East of, 88—beautiful simplicity of, 89—influence of, upon later times, 90—primitive spirit of, 91 — little affected by Patristic tradition, 92—theology of, *ib.* — purity and validity of the orders of, 110—transference of the primacy of, to Dunkeld, 118—succession of abbats ended, *ib.*—the monastery at Iona burnt, 119—primacy of, removed to Abernethy, 120—assumes a national character, 122—not the same multiplicity of bishops as in Ireland, 124—choice and power of the abbat in, *ib.*—special distinction of the bishops in, *ib.*—idea of the ministry in, 125—duty incumbent on an aspirant to the ministry in, 126—ministry of the *Diseartach*

(man of the desert), 127—the *Soscelaighte* or gospeller, *ib.*—common worship of the members of, 135—the "Celebrad," *ib.*—the "Oiffrenn," *ib.*—rule of faith in, 136—use and value of the Psalter in, 137—prominence of music in, *ib.*—hymns freely used in, 138—the "Altus," *ib.*—Responsories, *ib.*—order of service in, *ib.*—ritual of, *ib.*—the prayer of Intercession, 139—the Eucharist, *ib.*, 141—the Immolation, 141-144 — sacrament of baptism in, 145—language of the services in, 146—most distinctive characteristics of, 149—loss of early characteristics by, 151—stamped with the Celtic character, 161—causes of decay in, 162, 163—interest in education of, 211.
Church, the Scottish, never a complaisant vassal of Rome, 196—representatives of, at the Council of Basel, 197—provincial councils held in, 198—discipline in, 309—improved ritual of, 310—expanded conception of her duty, *ib.*—has a noble future, 311.
Cleirich Mainistrich, the, 129.
Clement, Epistles of, on the president of the Christian community, 23.
Clergy, the, how esteemed by the people after the Reformation, 271.
Clonard, Columba at the school of, 52—ordination of Columba at, 53.
Cœnobium, constitution of a, 74.
Colman, succeeds Finan at Lindisfarne, 100 — represents the Celtic clergy at the conference at Whitby, 105—arguments of, there, 106, 107—abandons Lindisfarne, 109.
Columba, S., legendary meeting between Kentigern and, 48—arrival in Scotland of, 52—boyhood of, *ib.* — literary training of, *ib.* — Celtic poems attributed to, *ib.* — schools attended by, 53 — ordination of, *ib.*—the greatest monasteries of, 54—a master of

the art of copying and illuminating MSS., *ib.*—dispute with Finnian, *ib.*, 55—retires to Inismurray, 56 — excommunicated by the Irish Church, *ib.* — induced by Molassius to leave Ireland, *ib.* — sails to Iona, 57 — Iona bestowed upon, by King Connal, 59 — choice of headquarters at Iona, *ib.*—first efforts at, *ib.*—missionary idea of, *ib.*—enters on the conversion of the Northern Picts, 60—force of personal ascendancy in, 61—marvellous voice of, *ib.*—founder of the Scottish Church, 62—assistants of, *ib.*—individual liberty under the sway of, 63—mission into the East and Midlands of, 64—influence of, 65—author of the independence of Dalriada, 66—character of, 67 — Adamnan's account of the death of, *ib.*, 68—efficiency and permanence of the work of, 69 — principle of the Church of, 72 — observance of the yearly festivals by, 85—the most conspicuous example of the itinerant preacher, 128 — princely lineage of, 162.

Columban Church. See Church.

Columbanus, missionary following of, 94.

Comgall, accompanies Columba from Ireland, 62—two types of ministry combined in, 128.

Communion, Holy, the, the First Book of Discipline on, 272—the custom of kneeling at, 276.

Confession, not made in private in the Celtic Church, 146.

Confession, the first Scots', 6—on Apostolic Ministry, *ib.* — definitely set aside, 294.

Confession, the Westminster, legally adopted in the Scottish Church, 294.

Cooldrevny, battle of, 55.

Cormac, adventurous missionary voyages of, 62.

Corman, unsuccessful mission to the Angles by, 99.

Councils, provincial, established in the Church of Scotland, 198—order of proceedings in, *ib.*—the system an anticipation of the General Assembly, 199—canons read at, *ib.*

Covenant, Solemn League and, motive of, 277 — conditions of subscription to, *ib.*

Cromwell, dismissal of the General Assembly by, 283.

Culdees, the, antiquarian interest attached to, 152—controversy as to meaning of the name, *ib.*—preferable etymology of the name, 153 — earliest instance of the appearance of, 154—prevalence of such societies, 155—characteristics of, *ib.*—references by Wyntoun to, 156—included the cœnobite, 157—their priests married men, 158—possessed of no great centre or standard of authority, 159 — an example of affairs in the churches of, 160 —description of, 194—decay of the order of, *ib.*

Cuthbert, S., sanctity and devotion of, 115—withdraws to Farne, *ib.* —ascetic habits of, *ib.*—marks a transition, 116—churches dedicated to, 117—two types of ministry combined in, 128.

Cyprian, sacerdotal theory held by, 16—a typical High Churchman, 29.

Cyril, theology of, 93.

Dalriada, Columba's choice of a king for, 65—influence of Columba in, *ib.*—the real germ of the kingdom of Scotland, *ib.*—made independent of the kings of Ireland, 67.

David I., English prelates the advisers of, 185—establishes a general system of diocesan episcopacy, 186 — questionable patronage of the Roman Church by, 188 — monasteries erected and endowed by, 189—founds the priory of St Andrews, 190—institutes parishes, *ib.*—origin of "teinds" in the reign of, 191—settlement of ritual during the reign of, 193.

Deacon, inauguration of the office of, 7—change of office of the, 14—position of, in the Reformed Church, 249, 260.
Deacons, mode of appointment of, 258.
Diaconate, the, traces of, within the apostolic age, 22—leading idea of, *ib.*—importance of the revival of, 311.
Didaché, no trace of the episcopate in the, 25.
Discipline, exercised in the Scottish Church, 309.
Diseartach, the, 127.
Doctor, the office of, 273.
Douglas, Gawain, general contemporary esteem of, 206.
Druidism, conversion of the Picts from, 65.
Druimcli, the, 131.
Drumceatt, Columba at the assembly of, 68.
Dunbar, Gavin, Bishop of Aberdeen, admirable character of, 207.
Dunbarton, importance of, in the fourth century, 78.
Dunfermline, marriage of Malcolm Canmohr and Margaret at, 166 — Queen Margaret's work at, 167.
Dunkeld, transference of the primacy of the Columban Church to, 118—King Kenneth builds a church at, 119—primacy of the Columban Church vested in the abbat of, *ib.*—title of the bishop of, 120.

Easter, debate at Whitby as to the celebration of, 103, 104—defeat of the Celtic view regarding, 108.
Egyptian monasticism, the germ of the Columban Church, 72.
Elder, title of, exchanged for priest, 14 — no distinction between "bishop" and, 18, 20—Bishop Lightfoot and Dr Hatch on the office of, 19—Dr Hatch's view criticised, 21—gradual distinction between "bishop" and, 26 — how defined in the 'First Book of Discipline,' 250—duties of, in the Reformed Church, 260.
Elders, appointment of, a natural step in the Christian Church, 18 —ordained by S. Paul, *ib.*—a name used by S. Paul interchangeably with "bishops," *ib.* —first indication of corporate action by, 19—special duties of the, 83—peculiar place of, in the Reformed Church, 249, 250.
Elphinstone, Bishop of Aberdeen, admirable character of, 207.
Encyclical, Popish (1896), quoted, 195, 196.
Episcopacy, first appearance of, 23—nature of, in the Ignatian Epistles, 26—Ignatius the first advocate of, 27.
Episcopate, the, emergence from the presbyterate, 19—Dr Hatch on, 20, 21—not apart from the presbyterate, 22 — wide divergence from the simplicity of the early Church in, 31 — no exclusive claim over the presbyterate, 247 — imposition of, by James VI., 270.
Episcopos, duties of a Presbyterian minister simply those of the, 24.
"Eremites," the societies of, 72.
Erskine, Thomas, of Linlathen, work in theology of, 307.
Eucharist, celebration of the, in the Celtic Church, 139-141.
Evangelist, Philip describes himself as an, 7—Timothy urged by S. Paul to do the work of an, 9.
"Exercise," the, nature of, 258— object of, *ib.* — discontinuance of, *ib.*

Fasts, frequent in the Columban Church, 86.
Festivals, observance by Columba of, 85.
Finan, succeeds Aidan at Lindisfarne, 100.
Finnian, probably visited Ninian, 43—Columba at the school of, 52—quarrels with Columba, 54, 55.
Forbes, Dr John, a pupil of Melanchthon, 279—the 'Instruc-

tiones' of, *ib.*—aim of the book by, *ib.*
Forbes, Patrick, Bishop of Aberdeen, wisdom and learning of, 278.
Forret, Thomas, vicar of Dollar, faithful ministry of, 207—martyrdom of, 224.
Fortrenn, Bishop of, title of primate of the Celtic Church, 120.
French, spoken in Scotland from the thirteenth century, 213.
Froude, Mr, on John Knox, 233.

Gallus, missionary following of, 94.
Gemman, literary training imparted to Columba by, 52.
Gnostics, instance of influence of the, 31.
Grammar schools, 210—the course taught at, 212.
Gray, Rev. Andrew, curious epitaph of, 266.

Haldane, evangelical preaching of the brothers, 306.
Hamilton, Patrick, martyrdom of, 224.
Hampden, Bishop, on the institution of the Lord's Supper, 33.
Hatch, Dr, on the office of "elder," 19—view of, criticised, 21.
Hebrides, the, Irish missionaries in, 58—Culdee cells in, 154.
Henderson, Alexander, sermon by, on prelatic errors, referred to, 285—on the question of ritual, 286.
Highlands, violence attending the settlement of Presbyterian ministers in certain districts of the, 297.
Hilda, Abbess of Whitby, agrees to the conference at her monastery between representatives of the Anglo-Saxon and Columban Churches, 105.
Hill, Rowland, evangelical preaching of, 306.
Honorat, S., the island of, the original seat of Egyptian monasticism in Europe, 76.
Hooker, on Church government, 262.

Ignatian Epistles, the, no approach to prelatic claims in, 26—views of Church government in, 27—letter to the Church at Smyrna, 28—letter to the Magnesians, *ib.*—letter to the Philadelphian Christians, *ib.*—letter to Polycarp, *ib.*—maxim of, 29.
Incense, not used in the Celtic ritual, 146.
Independents, English, influence of on the Scottish Church, 283.
Indo-Syrian Church. See Church.
Inismurray, Columba retires to the island of, 56.
Iona bestowed upon Columba, 59—activity of Columba's followers at, 69—an educative and missionary centre, 70—cradle of the National Church of Scotland, 71—characteristics of the Church at, *ib.*—features of the establishment at, 84—perfect guilelessness of religious life at, 89—ascetic simplicity practised at, 94—influence of, throughout Britain, 95—college of elders at, 112—the monastery burnt, 119—the monastery restored by Queen Margaret, 176.
Ireland, Columba maintains regular intercourse with, 67.
Irish monks, skill of the, in copying and illuminating MSS., 54.
Irving, Edward, on Church meetings, 259.

James, S., description of his own office by, 10.
James V., anxiety of the Roman Church authorities to please, 204—offered title of "Defender of the Christian Faith," 205—Buchanan and Lyndsay encouraged by, *ib.*
James VI., episcopal propaganda of, 282.
Jamieson, Dr, on the Culdees, 132.
Jews, Hellenist, quarrels between Jews of Palestine and, 7.
Jocelin, not a safe historical guide, 46—account of Kentigern by, 48—stories of Columba by, *ib.*

John, S., description of his own office by, 10.
Judaism, the sacerdotal element in, 15.
Jude, S., description of himself as a bond-servant, 10.

Keledei. See Culdees.
Kells, primacy of the Columban monasteries in Ireland vested in the abbat of, 119.
Kennedy, Archbishop of St Andrews, 206.
Kenneth, King, the monarchy of, 66.
Kenneth, missionary devotion of, 62.
Kent, Roman missionaries in, 96.
Kentigern, S., story of the youth of, 44—travels of, 45—extent of the diocese of, 46—character of the ministry of, 47—migrates to Wales, *ib.*—returns to the North, *ib.*—ceases from his missionary labours, 49—death of, *ib.*—churches dedicated to, under his name of "Mungo," *ib.*—good results of the work of, 51.
Kirk-session, institution of the, 244.
Knockbain, violence attending the settlement of a Presbyterian minister at, 297.
Knox, John, nature of the work of, 230—inspiration to the national mind by, 231—intolerance of, 232—policy of, *ib.*—little touched by the new learning, *ib.*—Dr Schaff on, 233—Mr Froude on, *ib.*—effect of Calvin's theology upon, 236—sources of the influence of, *ib.*—defects in the character of, *ib.*—the task set before, 239—view of the imposition of hands, 246—keen antagonism to Rome of, 291.

Latin, the language used in the services of the Celtic Church, 146—taught in the monastic schools in the fifteenth and sixteen centuries, 212, 213.
Leighton, Archbishop, outstanding personality of, 293—works by,
ib.—tenure of episcopal office by, *ib.*
Lerins, community of ascetics in the isles of, 76.
Lightfoot, Bishop, on the office of elder, 19.
Lindisfarne, headquarters of the Anglo-Celtic Church, 100.
Lord's Supper, the, Scriptural ideas of, 32—more restricted to sacerdotal functionaries, *ib.*—wide departure from the original institution, 33—Bishop Hampden on, *ib.*, 34—superstitions as to, among the Celtic priests, 173—Queen Margaret's view regarding, *ib.*
Lords of the Congregation, the, certain articles of reformation proposed by, 220—alliance with Queen Elizabeth against France, 222—mob following of, 225.
Lyndsay, Sir David, James V. present at a performance of "The Three Estates" by, 205—whom he wrote for, 214.

M'Crie, Dr, severe judgment pronounced by, on pre-Reformation Scotland, 209.
MacGregor, Rev. Duncan, quoted on the Celtic Church, 126—quoted on mode of operations of Columba, 128—the Lee Lecture by, 134—on the administration of the Eucharist in the Celtic Church, 141—on the language used in the services of the Celtic Church, 147.
Machar, missionary devotion of, 62.
Mackenzie, Sir George, on ritual in the Scottish Church, 289.
Maelrubha, missionary devotion of, 133.
Magnesians, letter of Ignatius to the, 28.
Maitland of Lethington, policy of, 232.
Malcolm Canmohr, the kingdom of, 164—first meets Queen Margaret, 165.
Manifesto, the Aberbrothock, 199, Appendix II., 317-321.

Margaret, Queen, reviving influence introduced into the Scottish Church by, 163—meets Malcolm Canmohr, 165—destined for a convent, 166—marries Malcolm Canmohr, *ib.*—work at Dunfermline of, *ib.*—religion the ruling principle of, 167—religious zeal of, *ib.*—effect upon national policy and the Church of, 168—two principles of, in national policy, *ib.*—Church reform the greatest work of, 170—scrupulous in keeping of Lent, 172—urges the keeping of the Lord's day, *ib.*—adheres to the Roman ritual, 173—views on marriage of, *ib.*—rebuilds the monastery of Iona, 176—bestows land upon the Culdees of Lochleven, *ib.*—vital change in the Church effected by, *ib.*

Martin, S., of Tours, repute of, 39—story of the conversion of, *ib.*, 40.

Martyr, Justin, mention of the episcopate by, 23—description of a communion service by, 24—no trace of the episcopate in, 26.

Meath, King of, arbitrates in the dispute between Columba and Finnian, 54.

Melville, Andrew, development of Presbyterian polity by, 263—abolishes "tulchans," 264.

Mercia, evangelisation of, 100.

Ministry, value and efficiency of a, 5—loses its simple apostolic character, 14—lofty Celtic ideal of a, 125—admission to the, after the Reformation, 245—the "call" the primary basis of, *ib.*—the laying on of hands, *ib.*, 246.

Moderatism, unfortunate results of, 302—Robertson the historian and, 303—Dr Blair and, *ib.*

Molassius, induces Columba to leave Ireland, 56.

"Monastic schools," virtually in place of the universities, 212.

Monks, three classes of, at Iona, 85.

Montalembert, quoted regarding the introduction of Christianity into Northumbria, 98—quoted on the work of Wilfrid, 110.

Mundus or Mun, missionary devotion of, 63—rule left his followers by, 133.

Mungo, S. See Kentigern.

Mylne, Walter, martyrdom of, 224.

Nectan, King of the Picts, expels all Columban monks from his territory, 118.

Nice, Council of, decision of, as to the celebration of Easter, 103.

Ninian, S., baptism of, 37—visit to Rome of, 38—object of the journey to Rome by, 39—consecrated a bishop, *ib.*—visits Martin of Tours, *ib.*—builds "Candida Casa," *ib.*—monastery of, at Whithern, 40—religious ministry of, 41—where he mainly carried on his mission, *ib.*—travels of, *ib.*—number of churches dedicated to, *ib.*—transitory effect of the work of, 42—repute in Ireland of his training-school of Whithern, *ib.*—death of, 43—fate of the work of, 51.

Nobles, the Scottish, disloyal character of, 226—desirous to plunder the Church, 228.

Northumbria, evangelisation of, 97, 100.

Oblation, the Great, 143.

Odran, missionary devotion of, 133.

Oiffrenn, the, 135.

Ollamh, the, 131.

Ordination, rite of, in the Reformed Church, 246—privilege of, withdrawn from the diocesan bishop, *ib.*—theory of episcopal apologists on, 247—in the Roman Catholic Church, *ib.*

Oronsay, Columba lands at, 57.

Oswald, King, consolidates Northumbria, 98—appeals to Iona for missionaries, *ib.*—death of, 100.

Oswy, King, succeeds to the throne of Northumbria, 100—instructed by Scottish monks, 101—presides at the conference at Whitby, 106.

Pachomius, monastic institution of, 74—admirers of the ascetic life of, *ib.*

Paganism, revival of the superstitions of, 14.

Palladius, mission to Scotland of, 43—tradition regarding Serf and, *ib.*

Parishes, institution of, 190.

Patrick, S., obscure history of, 77—birthplace of, 78—early life of, *ib.*—sold into slavery, *ib.*—studies at Lerins, *ib.*—returns to Ireland, 79—missionary practice of, 80—virtually Christianised Ireland, *ib.*—most distinctive feature in the organisation by, *ib.*—ordained bishop, 81—reverence for the Word of God by, 137.

Patronage, Act of Parliament regarding, 298—up to the time of the Reformation, 299—understanding as to, after the Reformation, *ib.*—the Second Book of Discipline on, *ib.*—compensation for loss of the right of, *ib.*—placed on its original footing, 300—restoration of, alien to the ideas of the Scottish people, *ib.*—frequent disputed settlements because of, *ib.*—error of the enforcement of, *ib.*—enforcement by the Church, 301—the "Veto Law" of 1834, 302.

Paul, S., silent regarding Church offices, 9—only titles applied to himself, *ib.*—exhortation to Timothy by, on a preacher's duty, *ib.*—instructions to Titus by, *ib.*—usage of, as to the terms "elder" and "bishop," 10—injunctions of, as to the eldership, 18—on the action of elders, 19—on the "laying on of hands," 246.

Pelagius, ideas of, probably existent among the monks of Iona, 86.

Penda, King of Mercia, carries on war against Northumbria, 97, 100.

Perth, the Articles of, 275.

Peter, S., description of his own office by, 10.

Philadelphian Christians, letter of Ignatius to the, 28.

Philip, the preaching of, 7—not bound by one office or function, 8.

Pictland, position of, 58—secular affairs of, controlled by Columba, 65.

Picts, Northern, mission of Columba to the, 60.

Picts, Southern, mission of Ninian to the, 41, 42.

Polycarp, letter of Ignatius to, 28.

Pope, growth of authority of the, 181, 182.

Pope Honorius III., inquires into a dispute concerning the Culdees at St Andrews, 194.

Prayer-Book, the national, superseded by the Directory, 285.

Prelacy, the first foe of the Reformed Church, 263.

Presbyter, the, Dr Hatch on, 20—a recognised order in the Reformed Church, 249.

Presbyterate, the, emergence of the episcopate from, 19—fully developed during the age of the apostles, 22—episcopate not apart from, *ib.*

Presbytery, institution of the, 244—meaning of, 255.

Priest, title of, exchanged for that of bishop, 14.

"Protesters," the, 281, 288.

Psalter, frequent use of the, in the Celtic Church, 137.

"Purging Committee," the, 278.

"Quartodecimans," the, 103.

Reader, the, institution of, in the Church, 251—duties of, *ib.*

Reeves, Bishop, on the jurisdiction of the abbat, 84.

Reformers, the Scottish, work of, 240—revert to the Apostolic conception of the Church, 244—no dogmatic hatred of Episcopacy by the first, 252.

Regulars, parish churches gifted to the, 192.

Index.

"Resolutioners," the, 281.
Ripon, King Alchfrid expels Celtic monks from the monastery at, 101.
Ritual, definitely settled in the reign of David I., 193 — "The Use of Sarum," *ib*.—Puritanic level of, 289—baldness of, in the Scottish Church in the eighteenth century, 309—modern improvement of, 310.
Robertson, the historian, the leader on the side of Moderatism, 303.
Rome, visit of Ninian to, 38—undoubted connection of Ninian with, *ib*.—studies of Ninian at, 39.

Sacerdotalism, effect of, 16 — modern revival of, 17 — growth of, most evident in the eldership, *ib*.
Sacraments, the, changes in the administration of, 31—the Lord's Supper, 32.
"Sang schools," 210—in place of primary schools, 211—extinction of, at the Reformation, *ib*.
"Sarum, the Use of," 193.
Schools, three classes of, in Scotland, 210—primary intention of "Sang schools," *ib*.—"Grammar schools," *ib*.—"Monastic schools," *ib*.—features common to, *ib*.—method of management of, 211—at Roxburgh, *ib*.—at Aberdeen, *ib*.
Scollogs, the, 131 — lands leased by, at St Andrews, Appendix I., 315—Church duties required from, *ib*.
Scone, national religious conference at, 121.
Scotland, aim of the Reformation in, 234.
Seculars, the, 131.
Sedan, Scots Professors at the university of, 281.
Serf, S., mission of, 43—interesting personality of, *ib*.
Servanus. See Serf.
Shairp, Principal, quoted on Kentigern, 49-51.

Skelton, Mr, on Maitland of Lethington, 232.
Smyrna, letter of Ignatius to the Church at, 28.
Soscelaighte, the, 127.
Spottiswoode, the quasi-episcopate of, 270.
St Andrews, seat of primacy of the Columban Church, 120—state of, in Queen Margaret's day, 160—erected into a metropolitan see, 181 — priory of canons founded at, 190.
"Stone of Destiny," the, 65.
Stowe Missal, the, referred to, 145.
Superintendency, necessity of the office of, 311.
Superintendent, mode of appointing the, 257.
Superintendents, appointment of, in the Reformed Church, 253.
Synagogue, the term used by S. James to designate the Christian assembly, 18.
Synedrion, the, 21.
Synod, institution of the, 244.

Tabennæ, the society of Pachomius at, 74.
Teinds, origin of, 191—system of, spontaneously adopted in the Scottish Church, 192 —wrongly regarded as imposts, 203.
Tertullian, remark by, on the introduction of Christianity into Britain, 35.
Timothy, exhortation of S. Paul to, on a preacher's duty, 9—first letter of S. Paul to, 19—how appointed to his office, *ib*.
Titus, instructions of S. Paul to, on the duties of a bishop, 9.
Tonsure, that of Iona different from the Roman, 85.
Tours, Ninian at, 39.
"Tulchan" bishops, abolition of, 264.
Turgot, quoted on the learning of Queen Margaret, 172—appointed Bishop of St Andrews, 178—consecrated at York, 180.

Union, effects of the, between England and Scotland, 304.

United States, Churches in, lack the note of nationality, 3.

Valentia, first authentic proofs of a native Christianity in, 37—Ninian's mission in, 41, 42.

"Veto Law," the Patronage, of 1834, 302.

Vincent, S., the great teacher of asceticism, 76.

Westminster Assembly, the, motive of, 277—service books authorised at, 282.

'Westminster Directory,' the, not sought in Scotland, 284—accepted by the General Assembly, 285.

Whitby, conference at, between representatives of the Anglo-Saxon and Columban Churches, 103-108.

Whithern, work of Ninian at, 40.

Wilfrid, S., enters the monastery at Lindisfarne, 101—visits Rome, *ib.* — installed tutor of King Oswy, *ib.*—in conflict with the Celtic Church, 102—leads debate at Whitby on behalf of the Roman Church, 106—speech of, at Whitby, 107, 108—later career of, 110—foremost claims of, as a moulder of the Anglo-Saxon Church, *ib.*

Winzet, Ninian, condemnation of the priesthood by, 207.

Wishart, George, martyrdom of, 224.

Wycliffite doctrine in Scotland, 223.

Zwingli, intimate relation of Church and State under, 249.

THE END.

PRINTED BY WILLIAM BLACKWOOD AND SONS.

www.ingramcontent.com/pod-product-compliance
Lightning Source LLC
Chambersburg PA
CBHW031850220426
43663CB00006B/562